economic forces, specifically tourism, provoked a public outcry to end the practice.

As dueling and lynching waned, murder and manslaughter escalated. Moore finds that, although South Carolinians may have armed themselves for racially motivated reasons, they were more likely to use their weapons on wives, husbands, lovers, and random strangers of like skin color rather than on people of other races. Examples range from sensational murder cases of the era, such as the killing of Charleston *Post and Courier* editor Francis Dawson, to boisterous shoot-outs and bizarre crimes involving children, food, and game play. Moore also underscores the differences in acquittal rates for whites and blacks and the impact of inexpensive, easily obtained firearms on the overall crime rate.

A compendium of deadly crimes and the social trends that surrounded them, *Carnival of Blood* invites further inquiry into South Carolina's violent transition from the nineteenth to the twentieth century.

A historian and writer, JOHN HAMMOND MOORE has held teaching positions at Winthrop University in Rock Hill, South Carolina; Georgia State University in Atlanta; and Macquarie University in Sydney, Australia. His numerous publications include *Columbia and Richland County: A South Carolina Community, 1740–1990* and *A Plantation Mistress on the Eve of the Civil War: The Diary of Keziah Goodwyn Hopkins Brevard, 1860–1861,* both available from the University of South Carolina Press. Moore lives in Columbia, South Carolina.

Gift of the Estate
of
Colonel John A. May

CARNIVAL
OF BLOOD

CARNIVAL OF BLOOD

DUELING, LYNCHING, AND MURDER IN SOUTH CAROLINA 1880-1920

JOHN HAMMOND MOORE

University of South Carolina Press

© 2006 University of South Carolina

Published in Columbia, South Carolina,
by the University of South Carolina Press

Manufactured in the United States of America

15 14 13 12 11 10 09 08 07 06   10 9 8 7 6 5 4 3 2 1

Library of Congress Cataloging-in-Publication Data

Moore, John Hammond.
  Carnival of blood : dueling, lynching, and murder in South Carolina, 1880–1920 /
John Hammond Moore.
    p. cm.
  Includes bibliographical references and index.
  ISBN-13: 978-1-57003-620-0 (cloth : alk. paper)
  ISBN-10: 1-57003-620-9 (cloth : alk. paper)
  1. Lynching—South Carolina—History—19th century. 2. Lynching—South
Carolina—History—20th century. 3. Homicide—South Carolina—History—19th
century. 4. Homicide—South Carolina—History—20th century. 5. Dueling—South
Carolina—History—19th century. 6. Dueling—South Carolina—History—20th
century. I. Title.
  HV6465.S6M66 2006
  364.15209757'09034—dc22

                                                                    2005029341

This book was printed on Glatfelter Perfection Antique Recycled paper.

CONTENTS

ILLUSTRATIONS

Figures

Maps

Tables

ACKNOWLEDGMENTS

Staff members at various institutions and a number of individuals were especially helpful. These include Charleston Library Society, Duke University, the Old Edgefield District Archives, the South Carolina Department of Archives and History, the South Carolina Historical Society, and the South Caroliniana Library. Individuals providing valuable assistance include Fred Holder, Seneca; B. M. Ellison, Jr., Lancaster; Claude Crocker and B. F. Harvey, Clinton; Paul Begley, Michael Dickson, Herb Hartsook, Helen Milliken, John S. Rainey, Harvey S. Teal, and Rita Wallace, all of Columbia; Bryant Simon and Richard Wellman, Athens, Ga.; Fox Butterfield, Hingham, Mass.; Bruce Eelman, Niskayuna, N.Y.; Jim Megginson, Jackson, Miss.; Steve West, Takoma Park, Md.; Tom Price, West Shokan, N.Y.; John R. Oldfield, Southampton, England; and two Maine librarians, Betty Fraser, Houlton, and Marilyn Clark, Presque Isle.

The state of South Carolina

CARNIVAL OF BLOOD

INTRODUCTION

The business of killing human beings in South Carolina in the period from 1880 to 1920 is marked by three distinct trends: the demise of dueling, the rise and fall of lynching, and a galloping murder rate fostered by a proliferation of pistols and shotguns. These developments are by no means limited to this state, although dueling and lynching tend to be southern phenomena during those decades. The former affected only a handful of honor-bound hotheads, while the latter was largely the work (at least in South Carolina) of whites living in rural or backwoods enclaves.[1] Even though newsmen often cited well-known communities such as Charleston and Columbia in their datelines, most lynchings took place far from the eyes of community leaders, clergy, friends, relatives, and anyone else who might have interfered. After all, a mob or swift-moving posse is bound to attract attention in an urban setting.

Lynching was, of course, an integral part of a rampant Jim Crow mood and, in the view of some observers, a form of social control that frequently enjoyed the approval of men seeking and holding public office. Yet, for the most part, at least in South Carolina, lynching seems to have been random rural violence lacking both pattern and plan—sudden outbursts of frustration, anger, and fear. If calculated to intimidate and frighten certain individuals into submission, such frenzies seldom achieved their goal. Nearly all of those lynched in South Carolina during these forty years were black, although a few whites also fell victim to mob violence, and the precipitating incident—as was true nationwide—frequently was murder or rumors of murder, not sexual assault as was generally assumed. Racial hostility and ineffective law enforcement certainly were contributing factors, but some causes of lynching lay deeper, among them a jury system that was no longer working and a people who had lost faith in their courts —a situation not unlike that often found in newly settled, frontier regions.

In cases of homicide, as a rule whites in South Carolina killed whites and blacks killed blacks, and such deaths often resulted from domestic disagreements aggravated by liquor and/or sexual tension. Interracial shootings, if they occurred, sometimes were spawned by friction between employer and employee or landlord and tenant, as well as disputes between lawmen and those suspected of crime. Few South Carolina murders of those years exude any air of mystery, subtlety, or intrigue. They were simply "bang-bang" acts of passion. If the murderer was black, he fled; if white, he went straight to the sheriff, gun in hand, and claimed self-defense.

Until the turn of the century, any white of secure social standing could count on acquittal. Blacks, less certain of the outcome, tried to hide from the law, which, contrary to public opinion, did investigate and prosecute black crime; penitentiary rolls prove this to be so. True, an upscale white might have to sit through one or two mistrials and see that a few jurors were properly compensated, all of which did little to instill public confidence in the judicial process. Nor did the many roadblocks lawyers threw into the path of the prosecution assure people that justice would prevail. As Governor Ben Tillman observed in his first annual message to the General Assembly in November 1891, this multiplicity of delays had exhausted the patience of the people: "Continuances are granted upon the slightest pretext. Appeals are taken upon no pretext at all sometimes, and crime, when backed by money, appears to override or break through the meshes of the law with such impunity, that it is no wonder our citizens have at times forgotten themselves and taken the law into their own hands."[2] Tillman, it should be remembered, first tried to enforce laws against lynching; but when the General Assembly refused to grant him power to remove sheriffs who failed to protect prisoners, he reversed field and began to exploit the race issue.

Legal shenanigans, jury incompetence, and political infighting aside, fewer guns and some form of gun control would have saved many lives. And more attention to the Second Amendment to the Constitution citing "a well-regulated Militia" as the reason for permitting citizens "to keep and bear Arms" might have helped too. If nothing else, concern for the intent of those words could have made the much-talked-of First Amendment (free speech, free press, peaceable assembly) much more secure.

In the absence of such, millions with no ties to a bona fide militia unit or any interest in "the security of a free State" (a phrase also found in the Second Amendment) now use weapons with such abandon that the "free State" itself often is less secure. This is the precise wording of that amendment: "A well-regulated Militia, being necessary to the security of a free State, the right of the people to keep and bear Arms shall not be infringed." It is difficult to see how this translates into a "constitutional right" to use lethal weapons whenever and wherever an owner wishes to do so.[3]

South Carolina lawmakers of the late nineteenth and early twentieth centuries tried to limit the use of concealed weapons (that is, pistols); however, sheriffs, constables, policemen, and the public at large failed to support such measures. Guns were sold openly without restrictions throughout the state, even though an 1890 law presumably limited such sales to licensed dealers. During the decade that followed, one could, for example, obtain a top-of-the-line pistol for about twelve dollars or order a cheap but effective seven-shot, 22-caliber "special" from Montgomery Ward for fifty cents, plus five cents postage. A similar, death-dealing wonder was sold by Sears Roebuck for fifteen cents more (ten cents postage). On rare occasions one could even get a *free* pistol merely by buying a box of cartridges—a promotion much like those wonderful prizes that once came with Cracker Jack boxes. For several months in the spring of 1878, readers of the *Laurensville Herald* were offered a seven-shot revolver with every supply of bullets purchased from J. Brown & Son of Pittsburgh.[4]

The custom of going forth armed is attested to by the frequency with which guns were fired with devastating effect in stores, law offices, and courtrooms; at social gatherings; and even during Sunday school and prayer meetings. As late as World War I some young men had their suit coats tailored with "revolver" pockets, and South Carolina's attorney general testified in 1913 that a loaded pistol was in his auto because his mother and an uncle had taken a drive into the wilds of Lexington County across the Congaree River from Columbia, the state capital.

The reasons for so many guns can be summed up rather quickly. In the eighteenth century a frontier existence seemed to make them necessary to ward off Indians, kill game for food, and shoot predators that threatened livestock, among other reasons. The Civil War taught an entire generation of males to shoot; Samuel Colt and then Messrs. Smith and Wesson made pistols cheap, reasonably accurate, and easy to carry and conceal; and farm boys took their weaponry along with the rest of their belongings as they moved to town. In addition, after 1865 white southerners believed they needed guns to protect themselves from former slaves, who for the most part were not armed for another decade or so. By the 1890s, however, somewhat better off financially and emulating white behavior, they too had pistols and rifles. (To some degree, in sprawling northern centers such as Chicago, Pittsburgh, and New York, a strange, immigrant population provided a similar rationale for stocking up on arms and ammunition.)

BAD PRACTICE—Nearly every male urchin in and around this city, from eight years old and upward, black, white, and colored, includes some sort of pistol among his assets. Go where you will, in field and hedge, in all our suburbs, and you will find a group of these liliputian [*sic*] murder-mills comparing weapons and shooting at targets. Boys, boys! put down those pistols. Drop them. There is death, anguish, remorse, in every one of them, even the smallest.

Columbia Daily Register, 15 March 1876

Some South Carolina killings were shoot-outs between angry individuals or groups of angry individuals. Others were simple murders in often-public settings—for example, a hapless, unarmed victim gunned down in a store or on the street. And some were so bizarre (insane?) as to defy ready classification. Through it all, one type of death was well-nigh unique to this state: murder by educated men prominent in the world of commerce and government. This may have been a hangover from dueling, penalties for which increased dramatically in 1881, but it was nonetheless true. Perhaps, as some suspect, with the demise of the code duello, many South Carolinians thought the manly response to ill temper and insult was to shoot at once and while still angry. Fortunately, by the close of this era, this type of homicide—much like lynching—was going out of style.

Yet, in time the dueling ban was seen as a grave mistake. The *State* on 9 January 1898 called the antidueling law "one of the blunders of the century." Dueling was moribund when banned, this daily said, but its code of honor served a useful purpose since men knew they could not assail each other without being held accountable for their words: "If they were insulting, they invited a challenge and a challenge meant they must fight or flunk." The code, the newspaper added, saved a hundred times as many lives as it cost; and with its passing, those trained to resent insult felt denied the redress assured by the code and began to carry pistols. More important, they did not hesitate to use them.

But *why* was little done to curb violence throughout South Carolina during those four decades? The answer is far from simple and elusive. Revisiting briefly various aspects of late nineteenth-century mayhem reveals duels usually were provoked by political differences and alleged slurs on one's reputation, family name, or honor. Bertram Wyatt-Brown's *Southern Honor: Ethics and Behavior in the Old South* (1982) provides a fine analysis of this strange pastime. And dueling disappeared in the New South for the obvious reason that authorities got tough with duelists. Since an antidueling crusade was waged on both sides of the Atlantic simultaneously, the Civil War can take only limited credit for the demise of this sport. Nevertheless it is apparent that (a) some would-be duelists had their fill of smoke, powder, and blood during that struggle and (b) few southern households of postwar years could risk the loss of a breadwinner over some antiquated sense of "honor."

Lynching is a harder nut to crack. Historians, psychologists, and sociologists have wrestled long and hard with the causes of this brutal phenomenon. Some have seen correlation between lynching in the former Confederacy and political ferment, the price of cotton, black-white competition for jobs, poverty, rural life, and seasonal factors, to name a few. But James R. McGovern in 1982 and Edward L. Ayers a decade later greeted these theories with skepticism. McGovern, whose *Anatomy of a Lynching: The Killing of Claude Neal* presents a penetrating review of the subject, concludes none of these hypotheses is "entirely satisfactory." Many individuals, he notes, have lived in poverty and amid frontier conditions without resorting to lynching. The key to a successful lynching, McGovern writes in his introduction, is "community approval, either explicit, in the form of general participation by the local citizenry, or implicit, in the form of acquittal of the killers with or without a trial."[5]

In pages that follow he concedes that through lynching, southern whites as a caste often gained social and political dominance, cheap labor, sexual favors of black women, and prevention of miscegenation between black males and white females—hence few of them cared enough to protest or, perhaps one should say, dared to do so. Ministers, policemen, and business leaders, especially in towns and villages of the post-Reconstruction South, fearing for their jobs, families, community standing, and maybe even their lives, went along with the mob or kept their thoughts to themselves. Lynching was, according to Edward Ayers in *Vengeance & Justice* (1984), "madness, but with a method." Much like those who persecuted the Salem witches, those who lynched believed they were combating "an elusive but terrible foe."[6]

Ayers, in his awesome *Promise of the New South* (1992), covers much of the same ground as McGovern and is critical of attempts to tie lynching to politics. In his opinion, leaders such as Ben Tillman certainly encouraged lynching, and yet this state had relatively few such incidents compared to some other parts of the South. North Carolina, torn by political and racial turmoil in the 1890s, also failed to react as one might expect. For Ayers, the most promising avenue of inquiry is a regional approach to lynching (not summaries of what happened in each state) and analysis of lynch-prone areas possessing three common traits: little or no police protection, few ties to the outside world, and a transient population. Such a setting, in his opinion, fostered fear since old and new residents did not know each other. And when lynching loomed, the target of community wrath had no one to turn to for protection. Under these conditions, lynching became in and of itself a form of law enforcement.[7]

In fact, many South Carolina lynchers sincerely believed they were "correcting" faulty courtroom decisions or doing work they were certain local juries would not do. Their mobs frequently exhibited considerable organization, often taking a poll concerning what course to pursue. Sometimes they voted to whip their victim, not kill him, providing that individual promised to leave the community. This "democratic" process also could reveal internal division. On 3 June 1893 the *State* published a vague account of a nonlynching in the Piedmont town of Woodruff. Public sentiment was for hanging, it said, "but lack of organization and the need of a leader prevented anything being done."

Although neither McGovern nor Ayers says so specifically, one shortcoming of various lynching theories is a tendency to shed more light on *when* such violence occurred or *where* (in which states or in what parts of each state) than *why*. Yet at times during these four decades such incidents were rare in South Carolina and so scattered that any geographical analysis is statistically meaningless. From the end of 1906 through 1911, for example, this state recorded only seven lynchings when eight blacks were put to death in these counties: Edgefield,

Hampton, Florence, Colleton (2), Newberry, Anderson, and Orangeburg—communities in nearly every section of the state.

The regional approach advocated by Ayers—gulf plain, cotton uplands, and mountains—possesses distinct advantages since it ignores capricious state and county borders that tend to distort findings. However, explaining what seems to be irrational behavior in a rational manner will always pose problems. And there is yet another major hurdle. As virtually every scholar who studies crime and violence will likely admit, hard evidence is hard to come by. Law breakers and murderers rarely display much interest in becoming statistics, and both police and court records frequently are compiled in an alarmingly casual manner. In short, long columns of carefully "crunched out" numbers, as impressive as the computerized totals may be, all too often rely on rather tenuous data, and any theory or thesis based on such is inherently suspect.

To digress for a moment—leave the South and focus attention on a place where one might least expect to encounter lynching. On a Saturday night in April 1873 a country store in Maine's Aroostook County (my birthplace and a still-rugged land in the "far north" of a truly northern state) was broken into and burglarized. Three days later one James Cullen was tracked down deep in the woods and arrested. The two deputy sheriffs who apprehended Cullen—Granville Hayden and Bill Hubbard—decided to spend the night in a camp owned by a man named Swanback, who, with the aid of an assistant, was shaving shingles. During the night the prisoner somehow escaped but then returned, beheaded the deputies with an ax, and set fire to the camp, thus burning their bodies. Cullen's scheme to conceal his crime was thwarted, however, by Swanback and his helper, who fled in terror and spread the alarm. Within twenty-four hours Cullen was found hiding in the cellar of his home; however, en route to jail, he was seized by a disguised mob and hanged.[8]

Although this affair occurred more than a thousand miles from South Carolina, some elements stressed by Ayers are present: a rural setting with few ties to the outside world, weak law enforcement, and a newcomer to the neighborhood (Cullen had migrated from Canada a year or so earlier). Politics, race, market forces, and things of that sort play no role in this tragedy. Yet two factors common to many lynchings are there: anger stirred by what a brutal murderer had done and fear that a relative or close friend might suffer a similar fate—thus the overriding impulse to kill in return and make an example of the evildoer as a stern warning to others. Perhaps more emphasis on the deeds, real or imagined, that move a community to lynch and analysis of the communities, as suggested by Ayers and others, will yield dividends.

Of course, in addition to unbridled emotions, any first-class lynching required weaponry; and although the shotgun seems to have starred at such gatherings, it was the pistol that caused the most concern as South Carolina's death toll mounted (1880–1920). It was cheap, easy to use, easy to conceal, and—one might say—the weapon of choice when contemplating a duel or overwhelmed with the urge to kill someone. But why during those decades did so many people feel the need to own, carry, and use small, compact revolvers? Whites (as noted earlier) blamed the end of slavery, the turmoil of Reconstruction, and black "assertiveness" for conditions that, they insisted, made firearms necessary. Blacks, on the other hand, could point to the Ku Klux Klan, "whitecappers," and a hostile justice system. Even if one did not feel threatened, once friends and neighbors acquired pistols and shotguns—for whatever reasons—many individuals felt compelled to follow suit.

Yet, the basic tenet of whites that they needed guns to protect themselves from blacks in the wake of war and Reconstruction is weak and perhaps even false. Scattered comments indicate blacks in great numbers did not have weaponry until somewhat later and certainly not until after whites had armed themselves. Also, this argument runs smack into the often-told tale of loyal "darkies" who remained on the plantation and were solicitous of "massa's" welfare. If whites (and blacks too, for that matter) had said they needed guns to protect property from brigands and thieves of all shapes, sizes, and shades, that claim would have been more plausible. For, with the smashup of the plantation economy, which provided a surveillance system of sorts, there is little question that theft was rampant throughout the state.

Until 1865 each rural landowner maintained whatever peace and order existed within his or her realm. In cities such as Columbia (population eight thousand in 1860), a small police force did much the same, locking up unruly blacks at the request of masters and apprehending those drunk or on the streets after curfew. In July 1865 the United States Army even permitted white men in that city's Fourth Ward to arm themselves and patrol their neighborhood so as to protect property. Thomas D. Russell argued in a 1993 article that sheriffs throughout antebellum South Carolina were concerned mainly with civil litigation, not peacekeeping.[9] It took time for ordinary citizens, the courts, and even sheriffs to adjust to their new, expanded role as enforcers of the law. This was especially true in a confused era when federal troops were at hand.

As for "black assertiveness," this was a natural reaction to Jim Crow and the denial of basic civil rights. Thus one reason for arms (as for lynching) was to keep former slaves "in their place." Yet once both races got guns, they usually turned them not on each other but on wives, husbands, lovers, brothers-in-law, and random strangers. For the most part, as has been emphasized, blacks shot blacks and whites shot whites.

In addition to the pistol, emancipation, the demise of plantation surveillance, and the rise of a Jim Crow mentality, two other forces intruded on the local scene after 1865, namely a great increase in the number of little crossroads settlements and expanding railroad tracks. These two factors contributed markedly to the distribution and availability of strong drink since trains now furnished liquor to scores of new commercial outlets. It was not that people were drinking more that caused concern in the final decades of the nineteenth century, for some sources indicate the reverse was true, but that more people were drinking. And to the dismay of many, those tipsy with grog often were toting loaded weapons and frequently were dark of skin, or perhaps both. Thus liquor and pistols became the initial targets of reform, what the *Charleston News and Courier* (8 May 1880) called "whiskey traffic and pocket murder." Seven months later the General Assembly enacted a concealed-weapons law, although it was so capriciously enforced that it became virtually meaningless.[10]

Talk of concealed weapons, whiskey, and lynching leaves us nibbling at the edges of a far greater issue, and a baffling question indeed: what has made South Carolinians and southerners in general so violent? As noted, some have blamed a frontier existence, slavery, and corn liquor, to which can be added, for example, erratic (wild) Scots-Irish genes, a climate conducive to outdoor sports such as hunting, and frustrations engendered by poverty. None of these theories holds up under close scrutiny, nor do they explain why *all* levels of a society (black, white, rich, poor) are so quick to fight, stab, shoot, and kill or how a touchy sense of HONOR so dear to slave masters somehow has come to be valued just as highly by slave descendants who now lead gangs in the urban ghettos of our largest modern cities.

Arrogance engendered by black servitude is a key element in this tale, although just how it plays out is not entirely clear. An owner certainly held sway over those owned, and there is substantial evidence the strong among the latter duplicated this pattern of dominance among the weak of their own kind. In any case, slavery, with all of its woes, seems to have created a tolerance for physical abuse not found north of the Mason-Dixon Line that lingered long after the institution was abolished.

Perhaps the most persuasive explanation of this phenomenon is found in an article that appeared more than three decades ago: Sheldon Hackney's "Southern Violence," published in the *American Historical Review* (February 1969): 908–25. Since that time some historians and sociologists (but not all) have endorsed the views of a man who served as president of the University of Pennsylvania and subsequently headed the National Endowment for the Humanities.[11] To a marked degree, Hackney stressed the existence in the South of a *siege mentality*—a mind-set developed first to protect the region's peculiar institution against abolitionists and then adapted to oppose the Union army, carpetbaggers, Wall Street, Pittsburgh, the federal government, civil rights agitators, daylight saving time, feminism, Darwinism, socialism, communism, atheism, and any other dreaded "ism" that might bring change, ever so slight, to a carefully constructed realm run by and for the benefit of whites. Hackney concluded his perceptive inquiry with these words: "Being southern, then[,] inevitably involves a feeling of persecution at times and a sense of being a passive, insignificant object of alien and impersonal forces. Such a historical experience has fostered a world view that supports the denial of responsibility and locates threats to the region outside the region and threats to the person outside the self. From the southern past arise the symbiosis of profuse hospitality and intense hostility toward strangers and the paradox that the southern heritage is at the same time one of grace and violence."[12]

Hackney sought the words of W. J. Cash to support his thesis but discovered that the author of *The Mind of the South* failed to formulate a consistent theory concerning violence. Cash talks much about regional proclivities of that sort, true; however, he ends up attributing them to excessive individualism before 1860 and the loss of individualism after that date.[13] Yet, there is another son of the South, Ben Robertson, whose *Red Hills and Cotton* (1942) overflows with an "us versus them" theme. Robertson's personal paradise is "our" valley in the northwest corner of South Carolina peopled by "our" kin, all staunch Baptists and Democrats to boot. To see the face of the enemy, one had only to jump into a wagon and drive to the nearest town. Robertson wrote: "All of us hated bankers and we hated merchants. We hated them because they had robbed us—they should have been shot and we should have shot them, but always they had been so legal in their dirty business that we never felt justified in going after them with a gun. We would have felt better about them if we had killed a few, but we do not as a rule shoot people over property matters; when we shoot we do so because of passion. We shoot on the spur of the moment and do not often meditate a murder. Often it is a good way to shoot—to shoot on the spur of the moment; it clears the air like a thunderstorm."[14]

Since Charleston had more bankers and merchants than any other community in South Carolina when Robertson was growing up, this made it easy to hate the "Holy City," although he concedes this upcountry-lowcountry feud stretched back into the dim recesses of early settlement in both regions. Peering out beyond the frontiers of South Carolina, he and his kin encountered still greater evils—Yankees, impersonal northern corporations, and world economic forces that kept the price of cotton low and that of everything southerners had to buy high.

Robertson has less to say about violence than Cash does, and for him it is hopelessly intertwined with war (especially 1861–65) and patriotism. Also, his violence takes on a natural quality. He notes some of his kinfolk have met sudden ends—shot, scalped, thrown from horses, hanged, killed by automobiles—

but, he adds, theirs was a violent country, they lived in a violent time, and they enjoyed violent lives.[15]

Strangely, those southerners most apt to understand any siege mentality theory (because of personal, direct, almost daily confrontation with a hostile force) play only bit parts in Robertson's "upcountry memory" and Hackney's article. Ben Robertson's blacks are playmates and kindly old servants who work hard and tell funny stories; Hackney's are merely part of his statistical base. One suspects that were those authors writing today, blacks would loom much larger in their works.[16]

There is yet another factor that may have heightened southern violence through the decades, something not mentioned by most of those who have pondered this puzzling phenomenon: the system of local government. In the South the county, which could be a huge expanse of territory stretching many miles, ruled supreme. By contrast, in the Northeast and in areas settled by New England stock, the prime unit of local administration was the township. Although older communities often had irregular boundaries, the traditional township along the frontier was a plot of land only six miles square.

Townships were, of course, grouped into counties, but this basic fragmentation created a patchwork of self-contained entities with social, political, and economic ties not always present below the Mason-Dixon Line. And associations such as these may well have curbed violent behavior somewhat, especially if a town had a constable and a lockup. In short, anyone who wreaked havoc in a township might have to answer quickly to enraged neighbors, friends, and relatives. A county, on the other hand, was a much bigger playground where community pressure, if it existed at all, was both more diffused and somewhat weaker.

Definitive, rock-solid answers to questions posed by a study such as this are hard to come by. However, clues to the how and why of violence in one southern state (1880–1920) can be found in the pages that follow. The first two chapters deal with what probably was our nation's last formal duel, the Cash-Shannon meeting of July 1880, and its strange aftermath, which included political demagoguery, a race riot in which four blacks died, and at least three murders, perhaps more. This bizarre tale is followed by an extensive survey of lynching in South Carolina, concentrating (especially after 1900) on incidents that stirred public ire and tended to arouse calls for reform.

The remainder of the book, except for a general wrap-up at the end, is devoted to murder. Two separate chapters contain examinations of the deaths of two prominent newspaper editors—Francis Warrington Dawson of the *Charleston News and Courier,* shot by a doctor neighbor in 1889, and Narciso Gener Gonzales of Columbia's *State,* shot by the lieutenant governor in 1903. A statistical analysis of homicide cases (1887–1920) is followed by three chapters filled with various stories, short and long, demonstrating where those statistics come from and illustrating trends and styles in mayhem. For the most part, much as is the case with the lynchings highlighted, these are the homicides that garnered headlines, captured the imagination of a curious public, and occasionally led to demands for new legislation to deal with such matters.

These three deadly pursuits—dueling, lynching, and murder—obviously are closely related, all pieces of the same quilt. In fact, they are so intertwined (at least in some parts of the former Confederacy) that discussion of one demands more than a passing nod to the other two. As noted earlier, if dueling had not been outlawed, murder among some elements of South Carolina society might have been less common during these turn-of-the-century decades. To complicate matters further, the line between murder and lynching was often blurred. About a dozen deaths in this state's lynching column (1880–1920) probably would have been filed away as routine homicides had they occurred outside the South.

I offer one final "introductory" thought. Many who delve into the nature of southern violence open with a few pages of closely reasoned argument designed to establish the fact it really exists. Since scores of readers know from experience it does, why go through that exercise yet another time? Also, I think the title does the job well enough.

THE CASH-SHANNON DUEL

Those who have heard of the Cash-Shannon affair think of it as an isolated event in South Carolina's past. Two men had differences of some sort, and even though the year was 1880, they met according to an archaic custom, they shot at each other, and one of them died. As a result, the general opinion is, there was great outcry and dueling, for all practical purposes, ceased in America—which is essentially true. In succeeding decades an overzealous reporter occasionally would characterize a sudden blaze of bullets as a "duel," but these spur-of-the-moment confrontations rarely had seconds, attending physicians, spectators, written agreements, or any real class.[1]

The same can be said of many "shoot-on-sight" encounters of the immediate post–Civil War years. Apparently only one fatal duel occurred in South Carolina in the late 1860s, the death of Edward Roe at the hands of Theodore C. Boag on 19 June 1867 near Charleston's well-known Four Mile House. Boag and both seconds were arrested and indicted for murder; but according to the *Charleston Courier* (27 June), a jury needed only fifteen minutes to clear them of all charges.

In the decade that followed, U.S. newspapers such as the *New York Times* told readers of numerous encounters on the field of honor, many of them waged with swords by European journalists and politicians. Close reading of these stories reveals, however, that some of these clashes were not really duels, others were thwarted by alert authorities, and still others were, in fact, mere rumors of confrontations that may or may not have taken place. Nevertheless one truth is evident: as recreational sport, dueling was in deep trouble on both sides of the Atlantic. To avoid arrest, American duelists usually met in a neighboring state (Europeans, in a nearby country), and these individuals sometimes merely went through the formalities of combat in order to save face and honor. Despite almost weekly tales of outraged Frenchmen confronting each other, deaths were relatively rare on the Continent since, according to rules of swordplay, first blood—even a minor scratch—could end an affray. German university students reduced dueling to a ritual known as *mensur*, a form of combat waged with special knives, not swords; however, participants wore protective clothing to ward off all injury except "decorative" facial cuts.

The more familiar pistol or shotgun duel of the American scene claimed few lives in the 1870s. Although the summary that follows in table 1.1 may be incomplete, it appears that only a handful of men, perhaps ten, died during those years in what can be called honest-to-God duels. (Fatalities are in italics.)[2]

TABLE I.I — **Duels in the 1870s**

19 August 1870	Aiken-*Cohen*, Savannah
9 May 1873	McCarty-*Mordecai*, Richmond
1 July 1873	Rhett-*Cooley*, New Orleans
4 April 1874	Phillips-*Bienvenu*, New Orleans
18 August 1874	*Gray-Richard*, New Orleans
23 December 1874	Lay-*Tardy*, Mobile
15 December 1875	Ratcliffe-*Tilley*, Augusta
12 January 1878	Fishburne-*Harley*, Walterboro
5 February 1878	De La Pena-*Maxan*, Brownsville

All of the deaths in the table occurred in the South, and addresses refer to place of residence, not site of the gunplay. Most Louisiana duels, for example, took place in Mississippi, that is, until that state began to lock up those involved. South Carolinians and Georgians often sought out a famous sandbar in the Savannah River near Augusta, a bit of real estate possessing the merit of uncertain ownership.[3]

Only three South Carolinians made this list: former Charlestonian E. B. Rhett Jr., who killed former judge William H. Cooley when they traded shotgun blasts at a distance of forty yards in 1873; and two strong-willed Walterboro Democrats, Robert J. Fishburne Jr. and Walter S. Harley. The latter pair, married to sisters, matched Colt revolvers at a much closer range near Savannah early in 1878. Their dispute, sparked by a local election campaign, centered on Harley's charge that the Fishburnes were "weak and cheap copies of the Rhett family, without their brains or courage." Harley fired over his adversary's head; Fishburne did not. Harley died two days later.

But there have been only eight or ten duels in South Carolina since the war,—hardly as many as used to occur every year. Men will rarely fight duels when death may mean starvation to their families; and I ought to add that from the same cause pistols are not drawn so quickly as of old, and the tendency is to brandish rather than to shoot, so little can our hot bloods now afford the expense of a legal trial; though it is still true that juries, both white and black—where the slayer and slain are of the same race—exhibit a strong disposition to let men off who have shown courage in committing crime.

Belton O'Neall Townsend, "South Carolina Morals," *Atlantic Monthly* (April 1877): 469

Some years earlier Harley's brother suffered a like fate in Texas, and these deaths reminded area residents of a curse placed on their father by a female slave whose children were sold following some indiscretion. Offspring, she vowed, of one "so merciless as he would surely come to some bad end."[4] Although a Georgia jury investigated the duel, Fishburne, then clerk of the Colleton County court, was not indicted and subsequently was elected to the upper house of the South Carolina legislature, where he served two terms (1878–82).

Two Orangeburg editors, James S. Heyward and Malcolm J. Browning, exchanged shots on that Augusta sandbar on 9 December 1872. After two volleys and no hits, the duelists advanced to within three feet of each other, saluted, and left without uttering a word. The root of this disagreement was an editorial by Heyward noting that Bostonians fired a cannon to celebrate the burning of Columbia by Sherman in 1865. When Boston was devastated by flames, he asked, "Who will shoot now?" Browning, a Radical Republican, took offense; thus the confrontation. Six years later James L. Wilson of Yorkville and George M. Sanders of Sumter tried to get to the same stretch of sand but, turned back by Columbia police, went instead to Pineville, North Carolina, where on 27 November 1878 they shot, hit nothing, and retired.

Outside of the former Confederacy, another center of postwar dueling was New York City. But would-be marksmen of that metropolis, often hotheaded foreign nationals, faced numerous hurdles in a region where antidueling laws were rigidly enforced. At first they went across the river into New Jersey, following in the footsteps of Aaron Burr and Alexander Hamilton. When that state was closed to them, a few boarded trains bound for Canada, but the trip was so long that tempers frequently cooled and differences were patched up without recourse to arms.

Those involved in duels or would-be duels of the 1870s, no matter where they lived, risked arrest, fines, and jail terms. Virginia's Page McCarty apparently is the only duelist convicted of murder during those years and sent to prison; however, because of wounds suffered in the fray, he soon won a pardon from the governor. This incident, by the way, was sparked by a slight to a reigning Virginia belle, Mary Triplett, who ignored the proceedings and married someone else. In a sense, this affair was atypical. Most duels involved not fair damsels but politics or published material reflecting on people's reputations; hence the many editors who met on the "field of honor."[5]

The Cash-Shannon meeting of 5 July 1880 was both like and unlike those of the previous decade. It had all the trappings, but it took place close to the homes of both duelists—not in North Carolina or on that famous sandbar—and the star players, nearly sixty years of age, hardly could feign youth or inexperience for their folly. All of these factors shocked the American public, as did events preceding and following this clash, for it was no isolated incident. Instead, this duel was the centerpiece of ongoing turmoil that lasted for at least six years. What began as face-saving encounters with blank cartridges and more bravado than bloodshed ended with at least nine men dead, South Carolina's reputation for lawless behavior greatly enhanced, and the unity of the state's Democratic Party severely strained. Perhaps more important than the fact it marked the end of dueling (which would have come naturally) are the political implications of Cash-Shannon. For although the duel was *not* political, the ensuing controversy revealed the delicate nature of Democratic Party control. Men quickly took sides, pro-Cash or pro-Shannon, and soon both United States senators from South Carolina were involved. Two years later, when Cash, the winner, decided to seek public office, the outlines of Ben Tillman's campaign for governor in 1890 were present.

This story is, admittedly, a tangled web. Through it all one should keep in mind that these two men, both southern colonels prominent in their respective communities, possessed what a romantic might call "fatal flaws." Cash's burden was an often unbridled, violent temper; Shannon's was questionable decisions that led to financial woes not entirely of his own making. Thus both went forth to defend *honor* as they viewed that elusive concept.

Four individuals play key roles in this tragic tale: E. B. C. Cash, William M. Shannon, William De Pass, and Cash's son, Boggan. Ellerbe Boggan Crawford Cash was born in Wadesboro, North Carolina, in 1823. When his father died two years later, his mother returned to her family home in nearby Chesterfield County, South Carolina. Young Cash was educated at Mt. Zion Institute in Winnsboro and South Carolina College. He studied law in Cheraw but soon gave up legal practice to care for his mother's substantial landholdings. In 1848 he married a cousin, Allan Eunice Ellerbe, of Kershaw County.[6] They had four children, a son and three daughters. Cash served in the South Carolina General Assembly in the early 1850s, saw action at the first battle of Manassas, and gave freely of time and money to the Confederate cause. In 1876 he took an active part in Hampton's Red Shirt campaign. By that date Cash had gained a reputation as a stern individualist, a man who might act and consider consequences later. Some saw him as a freewheeling spirit of the Old South, a plantation master who stood firm for his rights. To others, Cash was a dangerous creature who belonged not only to another era but in another area as well—somewhere west of the Mississippi.[7]

William McCreight Shannon, a product of Camden culture, represents a quite different world, the urban milieu of finance and law, not vast fields of cotton. He was born in 1822, son of a self-made man who became a wealthy merchant-banker. Like Cash, he attended South Carolina College, trained for the law, served in the state legislature, and saw service during the opening months of the Civil War. Although their careers were similar and some said they even resembled one another physically, Cash and Shannon were not well acquainted. They met principally as businessmen in Camden, Cheraw, Darlington, and other communities in eastern South Carolina. They were not in college at the same time, nor were they together in the General Assembly. Cash attended classes at South Carolina College for one year (1843) and was in the lower House for a single term (1853). Shannon received his A.B. degree in 1841 and served in the House in the late 1850s.

According to Mary Boykin Chesnut's famous diary, Shannon challenged fellow lawyer William Z. Leitner to a duel in March 1861. Leitner had apparently struck Shannon during a trial in which the latter was defending a black man. Mary's husband, James Chesnut, and several associates managed to have the dispute settled without recourse to arms. At the time, she praised Shannon as "a good husband, good father, good friend . . . nothing can divert me from thinking of the folly of a man like Wm Shannon getting himself shot with a wife and ten children dependent upon him."[8]

But soon this lady's opinion of Shannon changed. One reason for this was his Civil War role, for the exploits of both Shannon and Cash were relatively undistinguished, although the latter performed well enough at First Manassas. Like many, they were caught up in early enthusiasm for the fight but soon lost interest. Cash returned home in May 1862 because of ill health or failure to win reelection as a colonel. In September of that year he informed Confederate authorities he was fit and eager to return to active service, at the same time answering charges of improperly pressing conscripts into the reserves and boasting he had taken the first full South Carolina regiment to Virginia in 1861. In March 1865 Cash wrote to Governor A. G. Magrath seeking men and supplies for the home guard and permission to seize horses for use against the enemy. He also used the occasion to voice his contempt for lowcountry "patriots."[9]

Shannon resigned his commission in June 1862 to assume the business responsibilities of his father, who died the following year. He also served for a time as state coordinator of slaves sent to work on coastal defenses near Charleston. Mrs. Chesnut wrote that she found Shannon pleasant company, but it is obviously she was distressed by his challenge to Leitner and considered him and his brothers less able than their father. On 10 July 1862 she spoke of "Shannon's treachery," and in February 1865 she noted scornfully that, while other men starved and died, William Shannon had been safe for three long years as a bank president, paying himself three thousand dollars in gold.[10]

Shannon's wife was Henrietta McWillie, daughter of a Kershaw County man who migrated to Mississippi and became that state's chief executive. The Shannons had a large family, thirteen children, all of whom were living in July 1880. At first glance, Colonel William Shannon—bank president, highly respected community leader, a pillar of Camden society—might appear to have been the antithesis of Cash, but that is not quite true. In the 1860s and 1870s several of Shannon's financial dealings earned him a substantial number of enemies. These include construction of a bridge over the Wateree River near Camden and his role as executor of the vast Joseph Cunningham estate.

Cunningham (1772–1850), Mrs. Shannon's grandfather, operated mills, factories, and plantations in both South Carolina and Alabama and is said to have owned eight hundred slaves. Shannon's father was one of the original executors and guardian of various heirs, but those duties gradually devolved to his son. In February 1860 William Shannon and his wife entered into a bond of $87,200 relative to management of these matters. Seven years later some of the heirs sued them for $87,200 and received a judgment of $33,350. Commenting on the term of court when this suit was heard, the *Camden Journal* (7 November 1867) noted, "There were no civil cases involving new principles, but heavy judgments were recovered, many of which will no doubt prove barren on account of the common ruin which has fallen upon our people." As predicted, the Cunningham heirs were unable to collect.

Despondent and disheartened, Shannon penned a gloomy will on 2 February 1876. His wife had a first lien on what little property he possessed, and he could leave his large family nothing "but a blessing from a loving heart." Shannon asked his children to continue to love one another as in the past, adding, "as my dying injunction [I] would urge upon my boys to avoid the rock which wrecked my life—surety debts—indeed debts of all kinds, but especially surety debts." Admittedly, in the harsh days of Reconstruction the role of banker-lawyer often was not a happy one.

William De Pass, the individual whose marginal note on a legal brief precipitated the Cash-Shannon duel, was born in 1836. He was educated in the schools of Camden and later served in them as a teacher. De Pass subsequently left the classroom for a law office and was admitted to the bar shortly before the firing on Fort Sumter. During the war he saw action as a lieutenant and was wounded twice. Just before hostilities ceased, De Pass became a major and almost met W. A. Courtenay on the field of honor. According to the *Charleston Courier* (30 March 1865), only capture by a Yankee force prevented De Pass from exchanging shots with the man who later became mayor of Charleston.

Returning to Camden and his law practice, De Pass served several terms in the state legislature and frequently headed the local Democratic organization. His wife was Freelove P. De Loach of Barnwell County, by whom he had ten children, only five of whom survived to maturity. With Shannon's death, De Pass was the man on the spot, for it was *his* act that initiated the chain of events leading to the fatal encounter.

William Boggan Cash, only son of Colonel Cash, was born in 1855. He was educated at Bingham's School in Mebane, North Carolina, the preparatory school of Washington College in Lexington, Virginia, and at Virginia Military

William Boggan Cash in his Virginia Military Institute uniform. From E. B. C. Cash, *The Cash-Shannon Duel* (Boykin, S.C., 1930). Courtesy of South Caroliniana Library, University of South Carolina, Columbia

Institute, also in Lexington. As a cadet, Boggan joined Sigma Nu fraternity and excelled in military matters, standing at the head of the class of 1876 as "first captain." However, he was less successful in the classroom, ranking thirty-fourth in a class of thirty-five during his final year. Following graduation, this husky, six-foot-four-inch youngster returned to Cash's Depot in Chesterfield County and soon became involved in a series of minor scrapes that caused some to wonder if this was merely the horseplay of spirited youth. His refusal in the spring of 1880 to let the Cash-Shannon controversy cool led to disaster—not only for William Shannon but ultimately for Boggan and his father as well.

The genesis of this affair was a drinking bout involving two Kershaw County residents that ended in a fight. In March 1878 Cash's brother-in-law Robert Ellerbe and blacksmith Conrad Weinges (or Wienges) came to blows, although neither consulted a lawyer until some months later. In December, Weinges sued for five thousand dollars in damages, alleging Ellerbe had assaulted him and "struck him in the face and on the head several violent blows with a Pistol."[11] Weinges said Ellerbe not only fractured his skull but also attempted to shoot him, threw him on the floor, and kicked him while prostrate. The blacksmith claimed he had been unable to work for two months and since the fight had suffered from "a dull pain" in his head. Ellerbe retorted that Weinges had come at him with "an iron rod or poker" and he (Ellerbe) had merely defended himself.

During these same months Boggan Cash participated in two harmless duels unrelated to the Ellerbe-Weinges clash. As the result of an argument over a race-horse named Prussian, Cash and his college friend S. Miller Williams met in North Carolina. They were both huge men and stood only ten paces apart, and yet two volleys went astray. According to Thomas J. Kirkland and Robert M. Kennedy's *Historic Camden,* Jane Williams molded the bullets used by her husband. Perhaps this fact, blanks, or agreement not to harm each other could explain the outcome. Then, in ensuing weeks, relations between Boggan and James Cantey, Williams's second, became tense, leading to another, bloodless, face-saving encounter.

Early in 1879 Robert Ellerbe, who had been farming the family homestead in Kershaw County for two decades, visited the Cash household in Chesterfield County, where his elderly mother was living. While he was there, Colonel Cash, without consulting Mrs. Ellerbe or his wife, persuaded his brother-in-law to pay sums Cash claimed were due them by right of inheritance. According to his calculations, Ellerbe had paid rent only during the last two seasons and thus owed his mother and sister approximately fifteen thousand dollars. Cash and Ellerbe went to Cheraw, consulted a lawyer (who drew up a legal confession of judgment), and then returned home to tell Mrs. Cash and her mother what they had done. That same day (27 January 1879) Mrs. Ellerbe signed all claims against her son over to Mrs. Cash, and on the twenty-eighth the papers were filed at the Chesterfield County Courthouse. Two weeks later a transcript of the judgment against Ellerbe was lodged at the Kershaw County Courthouse in Camden.

In August 1879 Shannon's son Charles was involved in a harmless duel arising from criticism by T. H. "Hal" Clarke of the elder Shannon's handling of funds appropriated for construction of a bridge over the Wateree River. Clarke, editor of the *Camden Journal,* charged "the people's money" had been squandered on "a worthless thing." He berated William Shannon as unworthy of the reputation he "once bore" and attacked the colonel's replies as full of trivia and falsehoods. "With you, Sir," Clarke haughtily proclaimed, "I shall not attempt to reason. You are incapable of it."[12] Colonel Shannon was much distressed by this duel, bloodless though it was, since he insisted the disagreement with editor Clarke was his business, not his son's.

Shortly after the Shannon-Clarke meeting, twenty Camden citizens, including several county officials, asked the circuit court to review the financial records of the disputed bridge. A legislative act of 1872 authorized construction not to cost over $20,000. More than that sum was collected in taxes, but no report had

Cash and Shannon. Shannon heirs were not pleased when these photos appeared on the same page in the second volume of Thomas J. Kirkland and Robert M. Kennedy's *Historic Camden* (Columbia, 1926). Courtesy of South Caroliniana Library, University of South Carolina, Columbia

been issued by those involved with the enterprise, notably Colonel Shannon. A few days later it was announced that the bridge commission had spent $22,300 and was nearly $10,000 in debt. In addition the county had incurred a liability of over $5,000. Although the builders were said to be accomplished workmen, the bridge was judged to be unsafe. The court recommended the county dispose of the structure and relieve itself of this burden. A week later the bridge was closed, and area residents began to consider installation of a free ferry.

At this same court session, Weinges won his suit against Ellerbe and was awarded $2,000 for injuries suffered in their brawl. The court closed on 8 September, and the following day Judge Thomas J. Mackey denied an appeal for a new trial. Forty-eight hours later Colonel Cash told the sheriff of Kershaw County to sell the property of his brother-in-law to satisfy what he insisted was a prior judgment held by Mrs. Cash. That sale, scheduled for 2 November, was halted at the last moment by an injunction drawn up by William De Pass, who was pressing the claims of Weinges.

While reviewing legal papers prepared by De Pass, an associate of William Shannon, Cash saw a marginal note that he interpreted as charging fraud: "The plaintiff further alleges that the said pretended confession of judgment has been made by the said defendant, Robert G. Ellerbe, to his own sister, who is the said

Allan E. Cash, and thus by a family arrangement the said defendant intends to defeat the recovery of the plaintiff."

Later that same month Cash and Shannon exchanged letters concerning this matter, correspondence that ended with this cordial note from Cash: "I feel greatly relieved, for I have had no desire at any time to have a rupture with you." But in February 1880 Weinges's suit to set aside Mrs. Cash's claims on the Ellerbe estate was heard, and during the proceedings Shannon examined Robert Ellerbe under oath. Although Cash was in Camden that day, for some reason he did not attend the entire trial. Talking with Ellerbe later, he concluded that—in view of Shannon's line of questioning and despite previous denials—the fraud charge was still alive. Some ten weeks later (19 April), Mrs. Cash died following a brief illness. According to her husband, to the last she concealed concern over this matter so as to prevent bloodshed; but after her death he learned she had been "sorely annoyed by these charges of infamy against her spotless character." Thus Colonel Cash resolved to "revenge her wrongs," transforming the dispute with Shannon and De Pass into a holy war to clear the name of his dead wife.[13]

In May, Ellerbe, still smarting from the charge of fraud, challenged Shannon to a duel, but the colonel refused to meet him, presumably because he considered Ellerbe socially inferior. Cash and De Pass also exchanged challenges and agreed on at least two meetings; each time, perhaps by prior arrangement, De Pass was arrested before an encounter could take place.

Early in June forty leading citizens formed the Camden and Kershaw County Anti-Duelling [sic] Association (really a revival of a similar society of the 1820s), and a county grand jury considered taking action against Ellerbe and others. However, on 27 June, Colonel Shannon—goaded on by Boggan Cash's "Camden Soliloquies" and fearful his sons might become involved—issued a challenge to Colonel Cash.[14] One week later the two men met on the field of honor near Bishopville before some one hundred spectators. Shannon wore a black alpaca coat, a white vest, and light-colored pants; Cash was dressed in a black frock coat, a white vest, and white pants. Shortly before two o'clock on a warm, overcast afternoon, they bade farewell to friends and relatives and with pistols in hand took their places fifteen paces apart.

What happened next would be re-created countless times in saloons, barbershops, country stores—wherever South Carolinians gathered. This is how Cash, who met with Charleston reporter James C. Hemphill on the afternoon of 6 July 1880 (twenty-four hours later), described the encounter:

> The fight took place about half-past 2 o'clock in the afternoon; Shannon's second having the word; Cash's second choosing the position; distance fifteen yards [sic], stepped by the seconds; weapons regular duelling pistols. It was agreed that the signal for firing should be given by discharge of a pistol

in the air, which was done by Mr. W. E. Johnson, Col. Shannon's second.[15] Col. Shannon fired first, upon the word "one," his ball taking effect about five paces in front of me, and throwing sand in my face.[16] At the time I thought I was shot and fired between the words "two" and "three," there being a distinct pause between my shot and that of Col. Shannon. He staggered and was caught by his friend, Col. J. M. Cantey, and I am informed died in about five minutes. My friend, Mr. W. B. Sanders, inquired of Mr. Johnson if he was satisfied, and as well as I can recollect used these words, "My God, what more could we ask for!" I was taken from the field by my second, Mr. [A. H.] Waring.[17]

The community, state, and nation were stunned. Bernard Baruch, then a Camden youngster, wrote in his memoirs that his father, a friend of Shannon, warned the sheriff of the impending duel and expected him to intervene. Baruch also recalled in a letter written shortly before his death that a posse intent on lynching Cash came to the Baruch home but his father persuaded the men to disband. This tragedy had great impact on Baruch's life, for his mother,

CAMDEN SOLILOQUIES

Now ain't this shameful! DePass is to blame for it all. He said he would stir up old Weinges to sue Ellerbe, and we would make a fat thing of it. Well, he has played the Devil. No money up to date and prospects growing dim, and I have had to take water like a dog. I knew I would not fight, but I did not want others to know it. They say blood will tell, and I believe it is true. My daddy was a Gin Maker and I don't think people ought to expect me to fight, but I have tried to make them believe I would. It is over with me now and I am "Bully Billy" no more. I wish I had never heard of the case, and, Oh God, if I could only recall the letters I wrote to that old Devil, Cash. But I know he has got them and will show them. I made him believe I was game, but gave him no chance to try me. I want nothing to do with the old wretch. They say he kills people and then eats them up, and I believe he meant to eat DePass up, if he could have found him.

It may be I am not such bad blood after all, and I am sometimes afraid that it is my own meanness that makes me weak. I let my darling boy risk his life for me, and then this bridge business is a sore to me. I am afraid the people don't know how honest I am. Then I have cheated widows and orphans and my own sister out of all she had—took her toy clock and put it up to the highest bidder, but after all a fellow must live, and is worse than an infidel if he don't provide for his own family. I shall now join old [John O.] Willson's Anti-Dueling Society, and I think I ought to be first president.

> My daddy was a Gin Maker,
>   And worked cheek by jowl,
> With Ellison, a negro,
>   ('Tis a secret), by my soul.

continued on next page

My daddy was a Gin Maker,
    And worked on old saws,
I am stealing Billy,
    An expounder of the laws.

My daddy was a Gin Maker,
    A damned old fool was he,
I make my money,
    By bridging the Wateree.

My daddy was a Gin Maker,
    Damn such an occupation,
I can live by swindling,
    And on my reputation.

My daddy was a Gin Maker,
    No fighting man was he,
And so long as I have legs to run,
    No man shall shoot at me.

Compliments of W. B. CASH.

The recurring theme ("My daddy was a Gin Maker") refers to the elder Shannon's role as a manufacturer of cotton gins in association with William McCreight of Winnsboro and William Ellison (1790–1861), a remarkable black man who accumulated considerable wealth. See Michael P. Jordan and James L. Roark, *Black Masters: A Free Family of Color in the Old South* (New York, 1984).

long wary of the restless Camden scene and conscious of the fact that her husband once had been challenged, convinced the elder Baruch to move to New York City.

With the exception of the *Greenville Daily News,* which chafed under the political power of the Bourbon "ring" headed by Wade Hampton, the press of South Carolina heaped scorn upon Cash. In fact, throughout May and June various editors told both daily and weekly readers of the Camden troubles and lauded those trying to suppress dueling. With Shannon's death, the verbal assault grew more intense.

Meanwhile, on the afternoon of 6 July (while Hemphill was meeting with Cash near Cheraw) all business came to a halt in Camden and hundreds watched as the body of William Shannon was conducted to its final resting place. Six days later Cash was arraigned before a Cheraw trial justice, charged with murder. South Carolina, it should be noted, passed a relatively strict antidueling law in 1812, but authorities soon lost interest in enforcing it. The 1868 constitution, in turn, contained a provision barring from public office those involved in duels and threatening to impose whatever punishment "the law shall prescribe."

During these weeks Colonel Cash's name remained on front pages as he tangled with U.S. Senator M. C. Butler of Edgefield and a local editor. Angered when Butler praised the *News and Courier's* antidueling campaign, he attacked Butler as a coward, liar, and sordid politico whose support went to the highest bidder. Then, irked by what Richard H. Pegues printed in the *Cheraw Sun,* Cash vowed to take action against him. While in Cheraw to arrange bond for murder, the colonel and his son, both flourishing pistols, sought out Pegues. Cash, throwing off his coat, declared there would be "a fair fight," but bystanders intervened and bloodshed was averted.

Late in July, William De Pass published a rambling, verbose defense of his role in this affair. He admitted writing the marginal note that initiated the trouble but claimed it was omitted from the final draft and referred only to Robert Ellerbe and not to the Cashes. De Pass emphasized he held Mrs. Cash in the highest esteem, never doubting she knew nothing of the entire proceedings. He stoutly maintained it was testimony at the February trial, not his marginal note, that led to the tragic meeting near Bishopville.

However, the most penetrating analysis of the duel is found not in newspapers but in letters Shannon's second, W. E. Johnson, wrote to his brother in Mississippi in July and August 1880.[18] Though obviously biased, Johnson discloses that, in his opinion, Shannon was "a noble, splendid man" who nonetheless had "a great many enemies," a factor that "helped drive him into the fatal duel." There seemed to be no way out of this dilemma. Cash insisted the good name of his dead wife be defended. If Shannon stepped aside or was arrested, then two of his sons (William and Charles) were poised to meet the Cashes. In fact, even as their father lay dead at Du Bois Bridge, they wanted to issue a challenge to Boggan and, according to Johnson, had "seconds, surgeons, and everything complete to follow on."

So Colonel Cash would not compromise; and if Colonel Shannon withdrew, one of his sons might die, which he told Johnson would make him "a disgraced & ruined man." Johnson also disclosed that (a) Shannon was virtually penniless and (b) his sister Mattie had told anyone in Camden who would listen that her brother had cheated her—the same charge cited by Boggan in his "Camden Soliloquies."

Johnson placed much of the blame for what happened on De Pass. He told his brother on 12 July, "Capt. De Pass is really the cause of the whole trouble. He did insert the *marginal note.* And with drew it after he got the benefit of it & had not the manhood to say to Cash that Col[.] Shannon knew nothing of it. He is utterly damned in the estimation of all good people here. He has always been known as a tricky shystery lawyer that would grab & hold on to all the money his client had." Johnson wrote that De Pass also contrived to be arrested en route to his scheduled meetings with Colonel Cash. In fact, on the second occasion the Kershaw County sheriff told De Pass he had sent a warrant for his arrest to Chesterfield, whereupon the captain went there to spend the night and was duly apprehended. "He has I hear," added Johnson, "left for a six weeks tour North. I think he had best not return."

But Johnson saved a bit of his venom for the Boykins and the Chesnuts. Although Dr. Edward Mortimer Boykin lived next door to the Shannons, he never called to offer condolences, and James Chesnut—presumably Shannon's lifelong friend—provided little assistance. General Chesnut was as elegant as ever, wrote Johnson, but got "pretty comfortably drunk *about every* evening." Informed of all the preduel maneuvering, he showed little concern, even though his office was across the street from that of Shannon. Johnson credited Mary Boykin Chesnut with having a hand in her husband's attitude toward this matter, pointing once more to disagreements Shannon had with her nephew and Hal Clarke.

The first attempt to try Cash for murder ended in confusion. In October the state conceded it was unprepared and obtained a postponement. Several weeks later South Carolina's other U.S. senator, Wade Hampton, wrote Cash and asked him to cease his attack on Butler and other political luminaries. Cash agreed to do so, concluding that, in turn, the state would drop all charges against him. Early in 1881, when it became apparent he would be prosecuted, Cash sought out political enemies of men such as Butler and editor Francis Dawson of the *News and Courier* in an effort to get "dirt" on those critical of his exploits. In February, with or without this information, Cash was brought to trial in Darlington. Thirty-eight witnesses, including two women (Mrs. Eugenia Stuckey, a spectator at the duel, and Shannon's widow), were ordered to appear. Despite expectations of a speedy "not guilty" verdict, that did not happen. With jurors knotted eight to four for acquittal and unable to reach a verdict, the judge declared a mistrial and brushed aside charges pending against others involved in the duel.

Nevertheless the *News and Courier* hailed the outcome as a victory. The General Assembly already had tightened antidueling laws, provisions that included an oath all state and county officials had to take, pledging they had never participated in a duel—and they continued to repeat those words until 1954.[19] In addition this influential daily thought (correctly, it turned out) these new regulations, public outcry, and Cash's mistrial marked the end of dueling in South Carolina. For Colonel Cash, the eight-to-four stalemate meant still more notoriety. An enterprising Yankee offered him ten thousand dollars if he would tour the nation, but he declined, possibly because he was busy composing a pamphlet defending his recent activities. However, before Cash's version of the duel was published by the *Greenville Daily News* in mid-1881, the colonel was brought to trial once more and acquitted.[20]

During the next twelve months or so, Colonel Cash argued publicly with no one and kept his name out of the papers. Privately, however, he was laying plans to get even with those who had heaped scorn upon his head. Soon he was corresponding with Edgefield's Martin W. Gary and others disenchanted with political trends in South Carolina. Then in June 1882 Cheraw was swept with excitement as Cash's temper flared once more. On Saturday, the seventeenth, he exchanged blows with storekeeper Theodore F. Malloy when the latter allegedly made offensive remarks concerning Major L. W. R. Blair, the Greenback gubernatorial nominee. Blair, a Camden-area resident and Shannon's second in the abortive duel of 1861, was busy organizing Kershaw County blacks to vote in the fall election. Cash vigorously defended his friend Blair, who subsequently was shot and killed in Camden on 4 July 1882. This tragedy occurred only minutes before he was to appear at a political rally where Colonel Cash was scheduled to speak. (Captain James L. Haile, his assailant, was acquitted of the charge of murder, an assault presumably planned and carried out by local Democratic forces.)

Eventually the differences with Malloy were settled short of bloodshed, although both the colonel and Boggan tried to goad him into a duel. This uproar had barely subsided when E. B. C. Cash announced plans to run for Congress on the anti-Democrat, Greenback-Independent ticket. Why? There are several explanations. Cash clearly was irked by leading Democrats who criticized his exploits, and there is a distinct possibility that he represented a grassroots, pre-Tillman protest against Wade Hampton's Bourbons. In fact, speaking notes found among Cash manuscripts at the South Caroliniana Library contain numerous populistic ideas. Specifically, these are some of the charges he made on the stump:

1. Appointed commissions were doing too much legislative business.
2. State laws were being administered unjustly.
3. The General Assembly was too expensive and it was wasting public funds.
4. Counties, "which are only a curse and excuse to help imbeciles to office," should be eliminated.
5. The Democratic Party had violated all promises made to voters and continued to perpetrate "heinous frauds" at each election.
6. Blacks, persecuted by lynch law, were being driven from South Carolina, and no substitute for their labor could be found. (Cash even adopted a positive attitude toward the black man, praising his faithful labor and citing in minute detail "what the Negro has done for us.")

During the late summer Cash expounded on these themes in various communities throughout his congressional district, among them Florence, Rock Hill, Chester, and Lancaster. Since the press was overwhelmingly hostile toward Cash, it is difficult to gauge his true strength or that of his new political party. According to the *News and Courier,* a Florence speech early in August was "interlarded with a good deal of profanity which hurt its force." A month later a Rock Hill attack on the new registration and election law was cut short by a fight staged by whites. Cash declared (as was true) that the law's intent was "to defeat and defraud the Negroes and poor whites." The *News and Courier* correspondent came away from the rally convinced that Cash was "a firebrand": "He panders to the prejudices of the Negroes by expressing abhorrence of the oppressions he alleges are heaped upon them by the state government and by charging Hampton with violating his pledges to these people. He is opposed to an influx of 'lager beer-drinking Dutchmen and spotted-faced Italians,' but is in favor of bringing the Negroes of Virginia and North Carolina down here and making South Carolina, as he expressed it, 'a black New York.' His presence excited curiosity, but his speech has aroused an intense disgust for the man."[21]

In Lancaster on 27 September, shortly before Cash's candidacy won Republican endorsement, his appearance sparked a full-scale riot. The newspapers blamed Cash, blacks, and whiskey for the trouble. Apparently a fight erupted between a black man and a white Democrat just as the colonel finished speaking. Shots rang out, and the white man was wounded. In the uproar that ensued, four blacks were killed and several other people injured. Early in October an inquest was held; although there was no more violence, each night, amid rumors of blacks drilling in nearby Waxhaw Settlement, Lancaster citizens patrolled their community to protect it from incendiaries.

At Chester on 10 October, according to the *News and Courier,* Colonel Cash spoke "long, loud, and loosely" and elicited not even a "dat's so" from his audience. The day, the paper added, was without incident and brought "neither strength to Republicanism nor weakness to the Democrats."

In November, Fifth District voters went to the polls and, not surprisingly, chose as their congressman John H. Hemphill, a veteran Democrat who had been in the state House of Representatives since 1876. Hemphill (1849–1912), endorsed by the *News and Courier* as "the candidate of the party which is the sole representative in South Carolina of Anglo-Saxon civilization and liberty," would serve in Congress for a decade but was defeated for reelection in 1892. He also was an unsuccessful candidate for the U.S. Senate in 1902.

What is surprising about the Hemphill-Cash race is the margin of victory: Hemphill 9,518, Cash 7,471. This encounter and the First District clash (Charleston and vicinity) were the only close contests in the state that year. The colonel carried Chesterfield County and rolled up impressive totals in Kershaw, Lancaster, and York. The official returns are listed in table 1.2.

TABLE 1.2 — **Fifth district election, 1882**

COUNTY	HEMPHILL	CASH
Chester	2,008	1,300
Chesterfield	992	1,320
Kershaw	1,497	1,435
Lancaster	1,655	1,296

Table 1.2 continued

COUNTY	HEMPHILL	CASH
Spartanburg	345	9
Union	500	159
York	2,521	1,952
Totals	**9,518**	**7,471**

Thus, despite the new "Eight-Box" ballot law that created a white majority at the polls, Hemphill and the Democrats actually had a fight on their hands. Yet so many factors were involved that it is impossible to assess the outcome with much accuracy—the duel, black-white relations, new balloting procedures, Democratic and Republican policies at the state and national levels, and, of course, Cash's dynamic personality. However, it is apparent that *some* of the colonel's appeals were heard. South Carolina voters were restless. Times were hard, and the Democrats did not seem to be doing much for the farmer, white or black, and this was overwhelmingly an agricultural state in the 1880s. Within a few years a one-eyed man from Edgefield would give voice to some of the same words uttered by E. B. C. Cash in 1882.

Following this unsuccessful bid for high office, the colonel again retired from public view. The Cashes made headlines on only one occasion in 1883—in a report of a Columbia row that really was a minor spin-off from the political campaign of the previous year. On the evening of 21 March, Boggan, who had been drinking, was in the lobby of the Central Hotel talking loudly about election fraud and an ongoing investigation into the Chester County vote count. James Herron, an elderly Fairfield County Democrat, took offense, heated words were exchanged, and young Cash struck Herron a hard blow in the face.

Police quickly arrested both men and put them in jail for a few hours. At a hearing in mayor's court the next morning, it became apparent that Herron (who was in town to testify concerning election irregularities in his home county) was not blameless. He, too, had been drinking and, in the mayor's opinion, provoked Boggan. Both were fined twenty dollars, and Cash had to pay another ten dollars for carrying a concealed weapon. His attorney argued that Cash, who somehow had become a deputy United States marshal, was armed in an official capacity, but Boggan conceded that was not true.

For nearly a year after this minor altercation at the state capital, there were no duels, no brawls, no bold headlines. Then, early in 1884, all hell broke loose. This time it was Boggan, not his father, who caused the uproar, although admittedly young Cash never was far from the colonel's side throughout these tempestuous times.

— 2 —

BOGGAN CASH, OUTLAW

On 16 February 1884 Boggan Cash did what many young men still do on Saturdays: he went to town and got drunk. While under the influence of strong drink he tangled with Cheraw's town marshal, a former Yankee named Richards. With the aid of bystanders, Richards subdued Boggan, who eventually slept off his stupor at a local hotel.

Documents filed in the Chesterfield courthouse reveal this incident was not unusual. During 1882–83 this high-spirited young man frequently purchased whiskey and lager at C. A. Brock's store in Cheraw. Also, at the court term of February 1883, Boggan was fined twenty dollars and costs for a fracas that occurred on 4 July 1882. Officials charged that he "did disturb the peace and quiet of the town or a portion of the citizens thereof and did alarm the same by cursing on the public streets." The February 1884 brush with the law seemed at first to be just another of Boggan's weekend sprees, but it soon took a more serious turn.

There are conflicting reports concerning what happened on the Saturday following the fight with Richards. According to the *Charleston News and Courier* (8 March), Cash promised Cheraw's intendant he would not harm Richards, and local residents thought he would keep his word. But Colonel Cash, who had been visiting in Laurens and Columbia, was furious when he learned that Richards, in his opinion, had beaten up his son and swore he would settle matters. Thus, if we follow this scenario, Boggan tangled with Richards once more to prevent his father from becoming involved in what he considered his fight— much the same motive, it is said, that prompted Shannon to challenge Colonel Cash in 1880.

Sperry W. Henley, editor of the *Wadesboro Intelligencer,* published just across the border in North Carolina, tells a somewhat different tale. His sensational, sixty-one-page opus, issued several months later, bears this provocative title: *The Cash Family of South Carolina: A Truthful Account of the Many Crimes Committed by the Carolina Cavalier Outlaws.* In essence, this is a rebuttal of Colonel Cash's pamphlet of 1881. Yet, although Henley provides Shannon's version of events leading up to the duel, he tells the reader much more, often overstating his case and adding bits of unsubstantiated gossip. In fact, one cannot help but question his motives.

Henley writes that Boggan brooded for a week and then returned to Cheraw on the afternoon of 23 February and paid a fine of forty dollars for once more having shattered the peace of that little community. However, he did not, says Henley, leave immediately for home; instead, he strode about the main street, passing W. H. H. Richards several times. At about 4:30 P.M. Boggan entered a saloon where the owner was entertaining customers by reading an account of the Cash-Richards fight that had appeared in the *Wadesboro Intelligencer*. According to this highly colored report, Cash quickly dominated the struggle and might have beaten Richards to death but for the intervention of Peter S. Terry.

> Boggan then turned upon Mr. Terry in a savage manner and advanced upon him menacingly, but Mr. T. was too quick for him. Whipping out a small volume of explosives, commonly denominated Smith & Wesson, he serenely leveled the same at Mr. Cash and calmly warned him not to approach another inch, or he would quickly make him an angel, "with a crown upon his forehead and a harp within his hand."
>
> Cash, appreciating the fact that Mr. Terry meant business, and that he would do just what he promised, muttered an oath and withdrew.
>
> By this time the peaceable, long-forbearing, long-suffering people of Cheraw were thoroughly aroused, and if Boggan Cash had not made himself scarce in those diggings, in all probability he would now be sojourning in that place where it is said there is weeping and gnashing of teeth—where the fire is not quenched and the worm dieth not.
>
> Boggan, dripping with blood, went to a saloon in the vicinity to get a drink of liquor, with which to revive his spirits and restore his valor, but when he felt for his money, he discovered it to be gone. It is said that before the fracas he had a considerable sum on his person, and some have charged that Richards, being a nimble-fingered Yankee, attacked Boggan in the first place with a view of robbery. . . .
>
> Boggan next went to the Timmons Hotel, where he received all necessary attention. After his wounds were dressed he attempted to return home, but loss of blood and the exercise he had just taken rendered him too weak to travel and he passed the night at the hotel. In the morning a friend carried him home in a buggy, where he has since remained in peace, reflecting, it may be, over the vanity of human affairs, and especially upon the folly of going to Cheraw and getting drunk.[1]

It is not difficult to appreciate the effect of these words. A short time later, according to Henley, Boggan received a note from his father. Soon Cash was back on the street once more; and as he passed Brock's Corner where Richards was leaning against a tree (the *News and Courier* said the marshal was seated on a dry-goods box), he suddenly wheeled and commenced firing. The volley, at least three shots from a 38-caliber Smith & Wesson, hit Richards in the chest and seriously wounded James Coward, a bystander. There were some seventy-five people in the immediate vicinity, and witnesses said Cash was about ten feet from Richards when the firing began. Richards died six days later; Coward, paralyzed from the waist down, lingered until 2 June, when "he quietly passed away, with a smile of recognition to his weeping friends, with the light of heaven in his eyes, and a prayer of forgiveness upon his lips."[2]

On Sunday, 24 February, the day after the shooting, the sheriff, accompanied by a deputy, went to the Cash home to arrest Boggan, but the colonel said his son chose to avoid apprehension while public opinion was so inflamed against him. (On 3 March, Colonel Cash wrote to H. W. Finlayson of Cheraw, "My son would not live a week were he sent to jail—the tingle of the so-called Democratic bell of Columbia would be his death knell.")[3] This standoff continued for several days, but the death of Richards meant assault became murder, and on 4 March the *News and Courier* published the first of several critical editorials, concluding with these words: "Cash is at large. Is it right, is it just, that this should be, while any effort on the part of the State authorities to bring him to account for his crime remains untried?"

The following day this Charleston newspaper reported that a Washington, D.C., man had received a letter from Colonel Cash alleging the marshal attacked Boggan, who merely defended himself. Both he and his son, wrote Cash, would rather be shot down than taken from jail and lynched. According to this account, when informed that the Cheraw town council might offer a reward for Boggan's arrest, Cash countered with an offer of one thousand dollars to anyone who would kill a member of the council. Boggan, his father vowed, would not flee from the state, "but will go down with his colors flying."

On the same day that these words appeared, K. C. Timmons, a special deputy sheriff, went to the Cash home in yet another attempt to arrest Boggan but returned to Cheraw empty-handed. Meanwhile, South Carolina's governor offered a five-hundred-dollar reward for the apprehension of the renegade gunman. By this date the affair was attracting the attention of numerous out-of-state newspapers, and even the *Greenville Daily News,* long a friend of the Cash family, said enough was enough: W. B. Cash should be behind bars pending an official inquiry.

According to an editorial in the *Charleston News and Courier* (7 March), conditions in Cheraw were becoming intolerable. That community, it warned,

is held in complete subjection by the two Cashes, father and son. Col. E. B. C. Cash has threatened to burn down the town if any demonstration is made against his son, W. B. Cash, and has notified, it is said, the Intendant of the town that he will kill him "on sight" for giving official information concerning the murder which his son has committed. Cash is promptly informed of every step taken by the authorities, whether in Chesterfield or Columbia. No posse can be obtained in Cheraw to execute the Sheriff's warrant for the arrest of W. B. Cash. The Sheriff is, or pretends to be, seriously unwell and is absent from his post. Col. Cash, be it understood, is one of the Sheriff's bondsmen. The Chief State Constable, who was sent to Cheraw by the Governor on Tuesday to enforce the arrest of W. B. Cash, was unable to accomplish his mission. Meanwhile, W. B. Cash, a red-handed murderer, is at large, and the elder Cash boldly announces that his son shall only be arrested at his own time and in his own way.

The law, stressed the *News and Courier,* was now at trial. This was the Cashes, father and son, versus the people of the state of South Carolina, and justice must prevail. Colonel Cash certainly was an accessory to his son's misdeeds and, as such, should be arrested. "It is sickening," the editor continued, "to read that he is parlayed with and conferred with as though he was a sovereign power, when he is merely a coarse and common criminal. Col. E. B. C. Cash is as guilty in morals as his son. It is an imperative duty to arrest him. And there should be no delay. The people are growing impatient. They look to the Governor to assert and defend the majesty of the law, and they will sustain him, in so doing, to the last extremity."

While state and local authorities pondered these words and weighed what to do next, the Cashes were gaining considerable notoriety. The *News and Courier* (8 March) reported people in eastern South Carolina talked of little else but the exploits of Boggan and his father:

As the train leaves Florence, the thriving town at the junction of the fertile fields of the Pee-Dee section, the talk becomes intensified, and pretty soon the entire company in the coach is engaged in it. The conversation is invariably carried on in a subdued tone of voice, and very much in the style in which a nurse relates a ghost or goblin story to her appalled and frightened child. If an unusually large stranger enters the coach at any of the stations along the line, the talk is hushed altogether and there is a general feeling of uneasiness until it leaks out that the stranger is not a Cash. Those who live within the reach of the nimble pistol and deadly rifle of Cash Castle are fond of relating anecdotes illustrative of the desperate deeds of the Cashes. Most of them preface their stories and incidents with the remark: "I'm a friend of Col. Cash, although I don't uphold him and Bogan [*sic*] in this thing," referring to Mr. Bogan Cash's latest bloody exploit at Cheraw and his subsequent defiance of arrest.

At Cash's Depot, the abiding place of Col. Cash and his son, there is a general throwing up of windows and a craning of necks with anxious inquiries from strangers on the train. "So that is where they live?" "Is either of them there?" "Where's the depot?" etc.

Cash's Depot viewed from the railroad is a dreary enough place. A low, half-damaged platform constitutes the "Depot." About a hundred yards to the south of this is a rickety one-story store known as "Larkin's." The Cash mansion stands on a knoll about 500 yards to the right of the railroad track. It is a substantial two and a half story frame residence with a double piazza, and surrounded by a grove of majestic pines. Few outbuildings are near it, and the usual enclosure or park partially hides the noble proportions of the mansion. The place has a peculiarly dreary look. It is a fine residence set down in the midst of a barren pine forest.

This reporter, who alighted at the depot, was told by a resident that Boggan was living in a new log house in a clearing about nine hundred yards south of the mansion, land sometimes referred to as the colonel's "lower plantation." Whenever anyone appeared, his outlaw son presumably took refuge in one of the stout barns located nearby.

In Cheraw the newsman heard still more about the Cashes—on the streets, in stores, and in his hotel. As a crowd gathered about him in the hotel lobby, one gentleman commented Cash could be taken easily enough, "but there are some men in office who are afraid of him." Another claimed that he knew someone down in Darlington who could arrest Boggan in fifteen minutes flat. But a lad on the outskirts of the crowd thought otherwise: "Well, didn't he go down to Darlington and clean out the town once? I seed him once on a bender in Society Hill. He shot a nigger—not to kill him, you know, only just to scare him a lettle [sic]. The nigger bolted, I tell you, in a hurry. Bogan [sic] was on a 'bender,' and I tell you when he gets on a 'bender' he makes things howl!"

An elderly gentleman observed that the killing of Richards was "cool, deliberate murder." Another said he had heard it was self-defense, while the youngster volunteered the information that Colonel Cash had offered to pay Coward's debts and medical expenses at the rate of one dollar a day. A prominent citizen later told this reporter that there really was no reign of terror in Cheraw but the sheriff seemed incapable of acting against the Cash family; the colonel, he conceded, often was not a pleasant man to deal with. And yet others declared that anyone who went to the Cash home in peace would be received "in the old-fashioned style of the old-fashioned Southern gentleman."

The next day (9 March) the *News and Courier* noted there was nothing new to report on the whereabouts of Boggan Cash, although five gallons of whiskey had been sent down to the depot from Cheraw, "from which it is inferred that there will be the usual Sunday frolic." However, no Sabbath kickup took place, for at 5:00 A.M. state constable R. N. Richbourg and twelve handpicked militiamen armed with Springfield rifles arrived at the depot by special train from Columbia. (Among them was *News and Courier* reporter Narciso Gonzales, who in 1891 would help found the Columbia *State*.) Surrounding the Cash home before sunrise, they easily disarmed the colonel, but Boggan was nowhere to be found.

Richbourg soon activated the Cheraw Guards and returned to Cash's Depot with fifty armed men. Meanwhile, the colonel was formally charged with being an accessory to murder. After it was deemed inadvisable to lodge him in a local jail, he was placed in the custody of two deputies and dispatched by train to Columbia. Their journey was broken, however, by a layover in Florence, where the colonel attracted a large and curious crowd. Still undaunted, according to the *News and Courier* (10 March), at one point he reportedly turned to one of his guards and said, "Yes, sah! You have hunted me down, sah! But just wait until I get out of this trouble, and you won't dare to meet me at ten paces!" In Columbia, Cash boasted that his son would not be taken prisoner for six months. Gonzales, writing from Cheraw, vowed Boggan would be captured in a few days. Both were wrong.

Meanwhile, Cash's son-in-law R. C. Watts[4] set into motion the legal machinery to get the colonel out of jail, and early on the morning of the eleventh (Tuesday) the governor ordered the militia detachment to return to the state capital. Just why is not clear—perhaps because these "citizen" soldiers were eager to return to their jobs or because the undertaking was becoming rather expensive and accomplishing little.

Two days later Colonel Cash, free on twenty-five hundred dollars bond, returned home. Gonzales, writing from Columbia, predicted there would be trouble: "I was told in Cheraw that various persons against whom he had sworn vengeance were preparing, in the event of his discharge, to meet him more than half way. They said they did not intend to wait until Col. Cash could make an advantageous opportunity for gunning them." Gonzales also reported that New York's *National Police Gazette* was seeking a photograph of Boggan. "It is desired at any cost," he said. "There is reason to expect, therefore, that Boggan's lineaments will soon illuminate the rogue's gallery of the criminal journals."

After mid-March the Cash affair faded from view, although the *News and Courier* tried to stir up interest from time to time. On 31 March the paper attacked the colonel's conduct at the first battle of Manassas, and a week later it got into a dispute with the *Columbia Register* (a daily that defended the Cashes) over what reporter Gonzales had or had not done at Cash's Depot. Obviously, these two tales of less than chivalrous conduct were not unrelated.

Then on 19 April the *Register* announced that according to Colonel Cash his son would surrender and stand trial when county court convened. At the same time, in a surprise move, Cash issued an appeal for money to aid the starving poor of Chesterfield County. (This strange turn of events apparently was inspired by a report in the *New York Sun* that scores of South Carolinians living near Port Royal were in dire straits.) Although this tale had no basis in fact, Cash maintained that he had been trying for some weeks to arrange a loan so as to aid the needy of his community but, after "my son shot the policeman," bankers terminated those negotiations.

The *Charleston News and Courier* scoffed at this story and sent a reporter to investigate. He found no want in Chesterfield; in fact, businesspeople of the region were incensed by rumors that might give the area "a bad name" and endanger credit. In their opinion, the colonel was trying to cultivate sympathy among those not sufficiently educated to discern his motive. If he wanted to perform a charitable act, they asked, why did he not do it? Why borrow money?

Concerning Boggan, Cheraw residents had little to say. They seemed to look upon his shooting escapade as "old and uninteresting." Most of them were convinced young Cash was still near the depot and scoffed at the sheriff's report that he had fled to Canada. A few reported seeing him in his father's yard, and others told of messages in Boggan's hand seeking provisions from local merchants.[5]

Yet there were those throughout the state who thought Boggan's troubles were political. According to the *Charleston Mercury* (24 May 1884)—quoted in Bessie Cash Irby's 1930 reprint of her father's 1881 pamphlet, *The Cash-Shannon Duel*—Richards had been hired by the "Bourbon Democracy" to get rid of Boggan Cash. His removal, like that of Blair in 1882, had become "a political necessity." Mrs. Irby wrote that, shortly after the election of that year, her brother's duties as a deputy U.S. marshal took him to Lancaster to investigate vote fraud. While there, several shots were fired into his room in an attempt to kill him. The *Mercury* also explained why Cash refused to surrender to authorities. The "State Organ," it maintained, had so inflamed the populace that lynch gangs easily could be secured. Thus, by this line of reasoning, Boggan's only hope lay in giving himself up to the sheriff while county court was in session—precisely what the colonel said his son planned to do.

On the evening of 7 May a posse of thirty men gathered at Chesterfield County Courthouse for yet another attempt to capture Boggan, but again nothing happened. The sheriff reportedly was drunk when they arrived and remained so throughout this fruitless expedition. In addition a member of the party had evidently warned the Cashes that something was up, and the colonel even informed his dinner guests to expect visitors during the night.[6]

The following week, however, Boggan Cash was summarily gunned down while resisting arrest. This time a much smaller force, eight men led by Deputy Sheriff E. T. King, surrounded Cash's hiding place at 4:00 A.M. on Thursday, 15

"Boggan Cash—DIED WITH HIS BOOTS ON," from *National Police Gazette* (31 May 1884). Courtesy of Thomas Cooper Library, University of South Carolina, Columbia

May. King instructed the group to take Boggan alive, if possible; but as the men were moving into position, Boggan emerged armed with "a double-barrel shotgun, a Winchester rifle, and numerous pistols, which were hanging upon his person." He also had, it was said, about one hundred rounds of ammunition on his body. When ordered to halt, Boggan Cash opened fire, wounding at least one member of the posse; but within seconds he was cut down, riddled with bullets. Meanwhile, a companion named Sam Lee (a strapping, twenty-three-year-old who subsequently claimed he was an employee of the Cashes) tried to come to Boggan's assistance but quickly was put out of action when shot in the leg.[7]

An inquest revealed that Cash, who died instantly, had been shot twenty times. His brother-in-law R. C. Watts attended the inquest and then took the remains to Cash's Depot. Watts subsequently made the strange comment that this was the first time he had ever been to the Cash homestead. The following day about seventy-five people gathered as Boggan was laid to rest in a small family plot. The colonel, who did not go to the grave, watched from the piazza "very quiet and uncommunicative."[8]

Two months later Pawley Douglass, the man who allegedly guided the posse to Boggan's hideout, was shot and seriously wounded while plowing. Some pointed a finger at Colonel Cash, but in a letter to the *Columbia Register,* Cash fixed blame on "those who murdered my son." In his opinion, they feared that Douglass might betray them, although to whom is unclear.

At about the same time Sperry Henley put the finishing touches to his journalistic assault on the Cash family. If a reporter ever pushed all buttons simultaneously, this man did. No sin seems to have been overlooked as Henley relates, in his opinion, how Cash debauched his home and ruined his son. The colonel is accused of killing at least half a dozen blacks during the onset of Reconstruction and, on one occasion, would have hanged five more except for interposition of his brother-in-law Robert Ellerbe, who threatened to kill him if he did not desist. According to Henley, Cash so mistreated his wife that she often fled to her family home in Kershaw County, only to be lured back when her husband seized their children and held them hostage.

Henley writes that, upon graduation from Virginia Military Institute, young Boggan found his mother humiliated daily in her own home by his father's black mistress and demanded Cash change his ways or mother and son would depart. In the face of such defiance, Cash, he says, gave in momentarily but then co-opted his son in an orgy of riotous living.

> All [a]long, Col. Cash was his companion, his friend, his counselor—his evil genius—in whom, as has been stated, Boggan seems to have lost his own identity. Never was his father known to rebuke him for a single excess, and never was he known to pause for a moment in his insane course and counsel his son to a life of virtue and of purity.
>
> On they plunged, father and son, into the depths of the most appalling sins, until we find both guilty of the infernal crime of incest (with their mulatto daughter and sister) and uniting all of their hellish energies in goading to desperation an unoffending gentleman that an excuse might be offered for murdering him—that they might murder him to gratify a malign spirit—all under the pretext of vindicating wounded honor.[9]

This strange, ten-chapter work, which is laced with amateur psychoanalysis of the most primitive sort, concludes with the bold assertion that Colonel Cash marked no less than twenty-five men for death. The attack upon Douglass, Sperry Henley warns his readers, was by no means the end of this trail of bloodshed and mayhem. But he was wrong.

By mid-1884 E. B. C. Cash was sixty-one years of age and a broken man, although some of the old fire still remained. Writing to William Courtenay of Charleston in February 1886, he requested a copy of Voltaire's works criticizing Christianity and bewailed the low state of South Carolina politics, expressing hope that "the 'Reign of Terror,' fraud, rascality, and villainy that now distinguishes our poor, God-abandoned State" soon would cease. In the fall of 1886 Cash again wrote to the former mayor detailing his troubles (including a paralyzed right side) and urging him to come to the depot for a visit.[10]

In December 1887 yet another letter, written not by Cash but by his daughter Bessie, told of increasing infirmities. His health was so poorly, he remarked, "that the preachers have commenced to visit me." E. B. C. Cash died on 10 March 1888, and even the *Charleston News and Courier* spoke rather kindly of the deceased. The obituary—while not forgetting the duel and the political campaign of 1882—stressed his well-known generosity and concluded with these words: "Col. Cash was a man of strong passions and ill-regulated mind, but he had undoubtedly some high and good qualities, and it is pleasanter to dwell upon these at such a time as this than to recall the darker phases of his sad career."[11]

Thus ends the Cash-Shannon saga—except for several intriguing (and puzzling) details. The Wadesboro editor who researched the Cash family so thoroughly was not named Henley after all. His real name was Sperry W. Hearn. Henley was an alias that Hearn used for a decade or so. Sperry Hearn was born about 1855 in Tappahannock, Virginia, the son of James R. Hearn and Martha A. Fisher. His mother was a local girl; his father, a jeweler from New Jersey. After James Hearn died, his widow married yet another jeweler, Samuel W. Mienly (or Meenley).

Hearn's path from Tappahannock to Wadesboro is obscure, but apparently events unfolded somewhat like this. At about twenty years of age, he was hauled into court in Petersburg, Virginia, and charged with selling fake jewelry to country folk. At that time he gave officials the name of Hearn, but subsequently in Baltimore, Atlanta, or somewhere else he changed his name to Henley, a combination of Hearn and Mienly.

As Henley he worked on several newspapers and eventually settled down in North Carolina, where he edited and published the *Wadesboro Intelligencer.* That paper's masthead, somewhat ironically, carried these brave words: "We have turned our backs upon the past; we stand in the present and look to the future; the past is lost to us; the future is ours; let us make it a glorious one." And this little four-page weekly had a stern, forthright editorial policy. "The *Intelligencer,*" Henley boasted, "is Democratic, but not partisan. It bows to no political Baal. It thinks as it pleases and without fear says what it thinks. It advocates the equality of man and the enfranchisement of woman, and labors for the good of the race."

In Wadesboro, Henley took on some earmarks of a solid citizen. His paper prospered. He courted a local girl, Mary E. Drake, whom he eventually married in 1887, three years after Boggan's death. He even became town marshal. Yet despite his badge (or because of it), Henley often was embroiled in controversy. Usually these were minor fracases—such as petty libel suits, which plagued many nineteenth-century editors, and street altercations. In fact, one cannot help but conclude that this young man wrote of the Cashes not in scorn but out of true wonder and admiration. Boggan and his father fought duels and rode and acted like desperadoes of the West, while Henley merely printed a country weekly, got into insignificant scrapes, and occasionally arrested someone. And it was one of these petty incidents that proved to be his undoing.

In September 1885 Henley accosted two citizens as they were talking with R. H. Chowan, editor of the *Anson Times,* a rival Wadesboro weekly. Chowan was furious and, while failing to explain why his friends were singled out for attention, concluded his account of the affair with these ominous words: "We scorn to make any further allusion to the matter in these columns, except to say that the thinking people of Anson [County] are asking who is and whence comes this man who has at times traduced and abused some of the best citizens of this and adjoining counties and who increases his defamation as he misconstrues the silent contempt of his subjects."[12]

Henley sued Chowan for what he wrote and won in mayor's court, but within a week his adversary was in Virginia "on business." In December 1885 Chowan returned to Wadesboro armed with letters from both Petersburg and Tappahannock. (Chowan later said his suspicions first were aroused when he learned that Henley mailed his personal correspondence wrapped in newspapers addressed to a friend, who then forwarded the material to Tappahannock and other areas.)

As he was unmasked, Sperry Hearn spun a fanciful tale of an impending duel and an ill-starred love affair back in Tappahannock. A low-down Union veteran had stolen his girl, and fearing a clash of arms, he fled and took a new name. When Chowan proved this untrue, Hearn next told of having been arrested in Petersburg and, in panic, giving his name as Henley to local authorities. Chowan had letters proving this to be another lie.

The full story of how and why Hearn became Henley probably never will be known. It is obvious, however, that he used his real name for legal purposes throughout his life and from 1886 to 1888 edited the *Intelligencer* under the name of Sperry W. Hearn. It is equally apparent this name change was no mere whim; he clearly was trying to hide some aspect of his past. In July 1888, because of ill health, Hearn sold his weekly to James G. Boylin, who two years earlier had purchased the *Anson Times* from Chowan. Boylin subsequently edited a combined newspaper, the *Messenger and Intelligencer,* for nearly a quarter of a century.

Hearn and his wife moved first to Raleigh, then to Tappahannock, and eventually to Florence, South Carolina, where he worked for a few months as a journalist. In the fall of 1890, as his health declined, Hearn returned to Wadesboro, where he succumbed to a kidney disorder on Christmas Day of 1890. His obituary in Boylin's *Messenger and Intelligencer* (2 January 1891) was noncommital in tone, making no reference to his alias.

As for the two men who initiated this chain of events with a drunken brawl in March 1878, only one of them survived Colonel Cash. Weinges died in May 1882, and in the fall of 1891 his widow renewed her husband's suit against

Robert Ellerbe, seeking the original award of $2,000 plus court costs and accrued interest—a total of $3,798. Christina Weinges was not the only one interested in overdue judgments, for Cash's daughters decided to press their mother's old debts against their uncle. (It is quite possible, of course, that simultaneous revival of both matters was no mere coincidence.) They claimed Ellerbe owed them $6,000. He replied that the debt had been paid in full, but the case did not come to trial; and following Alleine's death in January 1895, Ellerbe named the surviving daughter (Bessie) as his sole heir, apparently choosing to settle accounts with the Cashes in that fashion. Shortly after this, he paid Weinges's daughter, Mrs. Emily A. James—Mrs. Weinges having died in January 1893—the grand sum of $400. The case initiated in 1878 finally was closed.

William C. S. Ellerbe (Robert's older brother) and his wife both died in 1895. On 15 June 1896 their heirs gave Robert Ellerbe full title to the family homestead "where he resides." He died sixteen months later on 26 October 1897. As for other peripheral figures in this tale, William L. De Pass, the man who wrote the marginal note that caused so much trouble, died suddenly in 1881, the year after the duel took place. Shannon's widow died in 1891, and William E. Johnson, Shannon's second, died in 1897. Charles John Shannon, a son who also was involved in duels, died in his eighty-seventh year in 1933.

Duels with real bullets and blanks, threats to duel, street brawls, murders, aliases, race riots, campaign demagoguery, posses, lawsuits, lies, truths, and half-truths —all weave a fascinating tale of life and death in South Carolina over a century ago. At the heart of the story is the meeting of E. B. C. Cash and William M. Shannon at Du Bois Bridge on 5 July 1880. But radiating from that encounter on the field of honor is a web of detail and circumstance that ensnared not only the duelists and their families but United States senators, country editors, and scores of other citizens as well.

There are, admittedly, unanswered questions. As an experienced attorney living in Kershaw County, William Shannon undoubtedly knew more about the status of the family homestead being farmed by Robert Ellerbe than he divulged. Also, he obviously was plagued by fears that one of his sons might meet Boggan or the colonel in a duel, as well as concern over heavy debt and the Wateree Bridge scandal. Was Shannon in such deep trouble in June 1880 that, out of sheer frustration, he dispatched a challenge to E. B. C. Cash? And having been involved in an earlier duel, did he perhaps assume that this disagreement, too, somehow would be resolved short of bloodshed or be stopped at the last minute by local authorities?

As for Colonel Cash, his pamphlet of 1881 and subsequent letters and statements clearly reveal his intemperate nature. Nevertheless, despite a hostile state administration and the controversial meeting with Shannon, he received the support of nearly 45 percent of the voters in his district in a bid for a seat in the United States Congress. In fact, his opponent carried Shannon's county by only 62 votes, 1,497 to 1,435. Although these returns undoubtedly reflect keen dissatisfaction with the state's conservative government, do they also reveal an endorsement of dueling, a rebuff to Dawson's *News and Courier,* and tacit approval of the swashbuckling colonel from Cash's Depot? After 1881, one might ask, to what degree were the Cash family troubles political? Were the Democrats, as Bessie Cash Irby alleges, determined to eliminate this incipient revolt against Bourbon rule?

It is easy to concoct a scheme by which those in power in 1884 could achieve several desirable goals. Merely by enforcing state statutes, they got rid of the embarrassment of Boggan the outlaw, blackened his father's reputation (thus making any additional political foray unlikely), and served notice on others who might be attracted by the ideas of Greenbackers and similar upstart groups. If this scenario has validity, then in a real sense, as the colonel maintained and had engraved on Boggan's tombstone, his son was "murdered."

Then there is Sperry Henley (or Hearn). What was his role in this affair? He states in his pamphlet that he first met young Cash in January 1877 and that a friend was Boggan's roommate at Bingham's, but he gives no clues as to why and how his keen animosity to the Cashes developed or what relationship he may have had with Boggan. He implies, however, that their association amounted to something more than casual conversation.

He tells us he thought Boggan was "exceedingly handsome"—that this young man was the most magnetic personality he ever encountered, an individual he always would remember "with emotions so strangely blended with pleasure, with regret, with indignation, with disdain."[13] This Wadesboro editor, about the same age as Cash, dug deep, very deep indeed. He wrote letters, searched courthouse records, and talked with scores of people who knew the Cashes. What perhaps began as a reporter's quest for a good story clearly grew into a personal vendetta, at least with Colonel Cash if not with his whole family.

But Henley/Hearn, De Pass, Ellerbe, and others are merely bit players in this drama. The fundamental question is who was *right* and who was *wrong* in the disagreement that led to formal gunplay on that sultry July afternoon over one hundred years ago. The answer, as always, depends on how one weighs the evidence. That Cash had a violent temper no one will deny. Yet he was the challenged party, and it was Shannon, not Cash, who had a history of threats to duel and near duels. The actions of Boggan Cash and Charles Shannon certainly did little to ease tensions in the Cheraw-Camden area in June of 1880—nor did those of William De Pass, the man who wrote the marginal note. Colonel Cash, the winner, has told his side of the story, and Henley/Hearn has done much the same for the loser. Thus, in truth, the conclusion to this tale (if it has one) can be written by each reader.

However, a word of warning. All of these events remain very much alive in the minds of some South Carolinians. Almost any mention of Cash or Shannon may stir old wounds. In 1930 Bessie Cash Irby, distressed by Kirkland and Kennedy's two-volume history of Camden, published an expanded version of her father's famous pamphlet. (According to Kennedy heirs, the Shannons also were less than pleased when photographs of Cash and Shannon appeared on the same page in the second volume.) Two years later *Time* printed a comment on Rumanian swordplay that produced a spate of dueling letters, one of which recalled Cash-Shannon. This, in turn, encouraged an editor (probably John Shaw Billings, a man familiar with the Palmetto State) to compose a capsule history of the affair that concluded on this cautionary note: "Around these facts tens of thousands of words of hot South Carolinian dispute have swirled ever since."[14] Three decades after that, historian Daniel Walker Hollis presented a brief account of the duel on a Columbia radio station, only to be informed within minutes by a member of the Cash family that he had erred.

And on a pleasant Sunday afternoon in October 1989, several hundred people gathered in Florence to listen to a discussion of the Cash-Shannon imbroglio. One of the participants, a self-proclaimed Cash descendant, failed to win over a dedicated band of Shannonites, who were there in full force. He had barely finished speaking when they were on their feet waving scrapbooks crammed with yellowed clippings in a determined effort to bolster the cause of their martyred ancestor. It was almost as if the fatal shot had been fired in 1980, not 1880. So choose to believe a side to this debate if you will, but beware of the consequences.

BACKGROUND

The Origins of Lynching

Lynching is, of course, nothing but a special kind of homicide. In its most typical form an irate mob stirred by rape, attempted rape, murder, or mere rumors of such snatches the alleged perpetrator from the hands of the law and kills him. This gruesome exercise has roots in the so-called Regulator movement of the 1760s in the Carolinas and private efforts to thwart Tory activity during the Revolutionary War. To a degree it was carried on throughout the nineteenth century, especially in the rural South, by "whitecappers," bands of men who rode about at night bent on correcting the morals of certain (in their opinion) immoral individuals. Correction, as with the Regulators, usually took the form of whipping, *not* murder, reinforced with orders to shape up or leave for distant parts.

The term "lynching" apparently honors Captain James Lynch (1742–1820), a resident of Southside Virginia especially adept at disciplining Tories in the early 1780s and brother of the man who gave his name to the city of Lynchburg. In a lengthy letter to the *Nation* (4 December 1902), Albert Mathews, a Bostonian, analyzed the origins of the word and, in passing, mentioned that Regulator meetings were being held at Lynch's Creek in eastern South Carolina in 1768. Although Mathews did not say lynching started there, Charleston historian Edward McCrady reacted angrily. The proud patriots who bestowed their noble name on Lynch's Creek would "utterly have condemned" such an unseemly practice; besides, he noted forcefully in a letter to the same weekly (15 January 1903), "regulation" began at least two years earlier in *North* Carolina.

In the decades following the Revolutionary War, "lynch law" became an integral part of American life, notably in rural and frontier regions where both courts and religious life were not well organized. An elderly lawyer, probably a Virginian, in 1839 wrote of his experience with what he called "private justice."[1] At first it was used merely to straighten out drunks who mistreated their wives. Then these whippings spread to thieves and others thought guilty of various offenses. When he defended such activity, saying it took care of certain crimes the law could not reach, a wise old farmer countered then it was time to change the law. Eventually three bullies accosted and whipped an innocent black man, and the lawyer took his case and successfully sued for damages. That, the lawyer noted with some pride, led to the repeal of "lynch law" in his community.

The public realized, in his opinion, that such a practice, "if allowed in *any* case, however apparently flagrant . . . would at length be used where nothing but weakness was on one side, and bad passions on the other." Yet one legal decision was not enough, he emphasized. A court ruling might check "private justice" for a time, but "it is the LAW-GIVER, alone, who can eradicate this disease utterly and forever, from the body politic." And as this gentleman watched the revival of "lynch law" by degrees in the 1820s and 1830s, he recommended simple remedies: more intelligent juries, improvements in the court system, effective penalties for those found guilty and a better means to enforce such penalties, and more schoolmasters. A half century later, as lynching became a national scandal, no reformer suggested a better solution; in fact, most merely echoed these sentiments.

The story of lynching during the two decades leading up to the Civil War truly is a mass of confusion. Only in the late 1840s did Noah Webster include the term in his dictionary: "lynch, *v.t.* To inflict pain, or punish, without the forms of law, as by a mob, or unauthorized persons. [U.S.]"[2] *Frank Leslie's Illustrated Newspaper* (5 July 1856), following a few lines about traditional Tory origins, warned that "lynch law" never should be associated with mobs, riots, and personal affrays: "It was applied exclusively in cases beyond the jurisdiction of organized government, and the operation of either the common or statute laws; or in those instances which occur in new countries where the conviction of rogues and desperadoes is not possible, where courts and laws exist in form but not in fact." In *Leslie's* view, lynching was something in the past, a *western* phenomenon that proved to be "a pioneer of good order, of civil and judicial authority."

Yet only five months later, using the present tense, abolitionist William Lloyd Garrison saw scores of lynchings occurring throughout the South, most of the victims being those who were trying to spread his gospel. On 19 December 1856 he wrote in the *Liberator* that a record of "Lynch Law" cases "reveals the startling fact, that within twenty years, over three hundred white persons have been murdered upon the accusation—in most cases unsupported by legal proof—of carrying among slaveholders arguments addressed expressly to their own intellects and consciences, as to the morality and expediency of slavery."[3] During that same decade, as North-South tensions mounted, the *Liberator* published numerous columns of "Southern Atrocities," tales of murder, rape, arson, slaves burned at the stake for horrendous crimes, and yes, white men hanged for "tampering" with blacks. Most of those said to have been lynched were white, and some clearly were not killed but merely beaten and whipped.

Similar confusion is evident in the press, both local and national. The *Keowee Courier* (2 May 1857) told of a Texas desperado named Bill Johnson who was "lynched to death." Three years later the same weekly said "Judge Lynch" had visited Anderson, where one John Tomlin "went through the unpleasant operation of being slicked in the outer edge of town."[4] And on 29 September 1860 the

Courier reported "Lynch Law" had been invoked by a vigilance committee in Grahamville, where a man from Maine named McClure was whipped by a slave for "tampering" with local blacks. Garrison's *Liberator* (31 December 1860) cited a "Lynch Law" case in North Carolina—two whites and a black arrested for "hurrahing" for abolition and Lincoln. Convicted by a jury, they were immediately whipped and their heads shaved.

On 29 November 1860 the *New York Times* reported two local men had been lynched in Savannah. Although roughly treated, both managed to escape and make their way back to Manhattan; however, another New York native, Savannah grocer John Byler, fared less well and died of his wounds. Nine months earlier *Frank Leslie's Illustrated Newspaper* (3 March 1860) produced a remarkable engraving of the lynching of James C. Bungings at Chappell's Depot near Newberry. The local vigilance committee, according to this weekly, found papers on Bungings linking him to John Brown, who had sent him south "with a view of corrupting the minds of negroes, to make as many converts as possible to the Abolition faith, and to induce as many negroes as possible to decamp for the North." Strangely, no other editor seemed to be aware of this sensational development, and on 6 March 1860 Newberry's *Conservationist* pronounced the whole thing a hoax. *Leslie's* was cautioning readers during these same months to beware of bogus drawings in rival sheets and on 24 November 1860 pledged that its coverage of events in South Carolina was "strictly and entirely neutral."

Since the meaning of the word "lynching" was both vague and imprecise throughout the 1840s and 1850s (referring to death at the hands of a mob, a nonfatal beating, or perhaps even a legal execution), it is impossible to say how many such incidents actually took place during those decades. Any survey of South Carolina newspapers leads one to conclude that (a) most so-called lynchings of that era occurred in frontier regions of the South and West and (b) few local residents, if any, fell victim to either the fatal or nonfatal variety.

Within a few years, however, propelled largely by black-white tensions, the term began to assume its more familiar guise. It no longer meant whipping at the hands of a mob but rather meant torture and death by hanging (or perhaps burning) and usually featured black men accused of committing heinous crimes. Until 1865 monetary value tended to protect slaves from such cruelty; and in antebellum decades a few whites convicted of abusing, killing, or stealing slaves were hanged. South Carolina slaves who committed crimes—if they were not disciplined on the plantation—were arraigned before magistrates and freeholders courts. These incidents usually involved in some fashion a third party, someone other than master and slave. Those found guilty of arson, murder, or other such offenses might face severe whipping and jail terms; if they were sentenced to die, their owners could seek compensation from the state.

Nevertheless, what may have been South Carolina's first "modern" lynching took place in Anderson County in the summer of 1862 while slavery still held sway.[5] The victim was a Georgia runaway accused of incendiary conduct and attempting to mount an insurrection in the village of Williamston. Trial records indicate Alfred, who claimed Abraham Lincoln knew of his crusade, vowed he was a disciple of Jesus Christ, who, he said, soon would appear. Although this young slave cautioned blacks to obey their masters, he promised that once Christ came, there would be no difference between the races. Alfred was lodged in the county jail for a time and then taken for trial to Williamston, where he was seized by local citizens and hanged.[6]

Had Alfred been a South Carolina resident, it seems unlikely that he would have been dispatched in this manner. Eighteen blacks accused of listening to his words were merely whipped, and those involved in other rumored insurrections of the early 1860s in Spartanburg, Union, and Sumter (as well as another Anderson incident) received varying degrees of legal punishment. A few were found innocent, while others were imprisoned and whipped. The most serious of these affairs, which resulted in the execution of three slaves and incarceration of fourteen more, took place in Sumter in 1862.[7]

Nevertheless the community of Union (then known as "Unionville") also can lay claim to a full-fledged, wartime lynching. On 15 March 1865 an armed mob of white men wearing disguises and Confederate garb stormed the jail, seized slave Saxe Joiner, and hanged him. Joiner was owned by Dr. James Hix; and, in the closing weeks of the war, he allegedly sent a note to Mrs. Hix telling her not to worry about approaching federal troops for he had a "safe place" where she could hide.

As Joan Cashin emphasizes in a careful analysis of this affair, that act raises numerous questions. Joiner, who (despite state law) obviously could read and write, may have felt an obligation to protect those he knew well. In any case a second note to Susan Baldwin, an eighteen-year-old girl living with the Hix family, resulted in a trial and conviction (amid very irregular procedures) of a "misdemeanor." This lenient decision split the community into warring camps and, in the chaos of a dying insurrection, led to a lynching, the first ever held in Union County.[8]

The South and lynching became almost synonymous in the years that followed, although to some degree lynching was but one phase of a national crime scene that gained prominence largely because of better record keeping. Statistics are far from reliable; nevertheless it appears that America's homicide rate increased sharply in the final years of the nineteenth century, while executions for violent crimes remained virtually unchanged. According to one source, 1,808 murders were reported throughout the nation in 1885 and 8,482 in 1904, and yet the number of legal executions rose only from 108 to 116 during those two decades.[9]

Walter Clark, a respected member of the North Carolina Supreme Court, gave a more precise analysis in the *American Law Review.* In 1892, he wrote, there were 6,791 homicides, 107 legal executions, and 236 lynchings. Some sources indicate a somewhat larger number of lynchings (255); but in any case Clark noted that for the decade ending in 1892 there were annually, on average, two lynchings for each legal execution. And he stressed this did *not* reflect any spirit of lawlessness, as was often claimed, for those taking part wanted to *enforce* justice: "Whenever society has lost confidence in the promptness and certainty of punishment by the courts, then whenever an offense sufficiently flagrant is committed society will protect itself by lynching."[10]

Clark then proceeded to enunciate the same remedies advocated a half century earlier in the pages of the *Southern Literary Messenger.* This well-known jurist was especially critical of the many roadblocks thrown in the path of the prosecution whenever serious crimes were involved. In addition to countless delays, once in court the defendant was allowed many more peremptory challenges than the state; errors by the judge in his favor could not be corrected, while only one against him might scuttle the entire proceedings; and a verdict had to be unanimous.[11]

Clark conceded such protection was in reaction to a time when prisoners had few rights but felt it was necessary to redress the balance. He agreed that a unanimous verdict and the concept of "reasonable doubt" must be retained. However, in his view, the number of peremptory challenges should be equal, erroneous rulings from the bench handled differently, and no verdict reversed on appeal unless it adversely affected the appealing party. "The purpose in hanging a man is not to reform him," Clark concluded, "but to deter others. To have that effect the punishment must be prompt and certain whenever guilt is clear beyond all reasonable doubt. This principle which is so often ignored by the courts is one which instinctively activates lynching mobs."[12]

Thus one cause of lynching in the South was the same as in the nation's frontier West: belief that the law was too slow and ineffective to boot. Another cause was racial friction, for the end of Reconstruction and the coming of age of a black generation unaccustomed to pre-1865 restraints and any guidance the master-slave relationship may have provided created a well-nigh explosive situation. The *Charleston News and Courier* (12 May 1877) stated editorially that the need for "more law" was widespread and the reasons obvious. For a decade, with little prospect of punishment, a black had been able to burn an employer's house and even kill him. If sent to the new penitentiary in Columbia, the culprit lived better than at home. Law, it said, has "lost its terrors for our criminal class."

In a remarkable series of articles on South Carolina life published in the *Atlantic Monthly* (1877–78), Belton O'Neall Townsend agreed with this assessment but said whites must share blame.[13] Blacks, he wrote, knew they were held wrongfully in slavery and thus struck back by feigning sickness and stealing. One might add that since everything on a plantation was held in common, including slaves, using "massa's" fence rails for firewood and killing his chickens and hogs hardly seemed like theft. In addition, if whites stole their labor, they reasoned such acts were justified—tit for tat. Lying, Townsend emphasized, was the "worst failing" of blacks in 1877: "They are the most bare-faced perjurers ever seen in courts of justice." But again, this should come as no surprise. Over the generations blacks became expert in saying, true or false, whatever they thought a master or mistress wanted to hear. And with more insight than the *News and Courier,* Townsend pointed out why punishment by the courts and even a stretch in the "penny-tenshun" held little terror for freedmen. As slaves, they were whipped and humiliated so frequently without cause "that punishment came to be looked on as no disgrace." Also, he conceded whites of the 1870s seldom were providing good examples for their darker brethren. According to Townsend, drunken brawls abounded among both races, and should the two collide, friends believed they should join in to help their comrades, not to stop the fight.

One would assume, considering the presence of the U.S. Army, that few lynchings occurred in South Carolina during the height of Reconstruction; or, if they did, details quickly were suppressed. This does not mean that federal troops brought peace and order to rural areas (1865–1875), for many sources indicate they did not. However, assembling a mob could attract attention, and recalcitrant whites had not yet embraced public displays as means of social control. Instead, during the immediate postwar years they simply shot, killed, and went on their way. In addition both the local and national press, much like *Leslie's* of the 1850s, tended to view lynching as something that happened "out West," somewhere in cow country beyond the Mississippi. Readers were prepared for a degree of racial turbulence in the former Confederacy, and outbreaks of violence such as those perpetrated by the Ku Klux Klan in the early 1870s usually were portrayed as postwar "troubles," not lynchings. However, any difference between the deaths of ten black prisoners in Union in February 1871 and the deaths of eight more in Barnwell in December 1889 is difficult to discern even though the first was considered "an unfortunate affair" and the second was called "a lynching."

Similar confusion is evident during intervening years as well. On 1 January 1876 Archie Matheson (black) allegedly assaulted Mrs. Angus McDonald, a respectable white woman living near Clio in the eastern section of the state close to the North Carolina line. Within a fortnight Matheson was hunted down, arraigned before an impromptu "jury" composed of mob members, found guilty, and hanged. According to the *Marion Star* (13 January), "His punishment was neither too speedy or severe. Our social shrine must be preserved pure and inviolable though the heavens fall!" Sixteen men, including Angus McDonald, subsequently were arrested and then quietly set free.

At about the same time the *Charleston News and Courier* (12 January 1876) told of a lynching in Fairfield County. Two young blacks—John Alexander and Albert Poag—were placed in jail following the burglary of John D. McCarley's home on 5 January. A few days later a band of disguised men took them from their cell and "administered a flagellation." This clearly was yet another nonfatal affair, although it was called "a lynching" by the press.

The brutal murder of an elderly upcountry couple in May of the same year led to the first such incident to garner major headlines. A week after Mr. and Mrs. John L. Harmon were slain in Winter Seat near the Abbeville-Edgefield line, three hundred men and boys, among them some fifty blacks, suddenly invoked "lynch law." Just as a lengthy coroner's inquest was drawing to a close, spectators threw a bag over the head of the Edgefield County sheriff and, after pushing him aside, marched six young black men into a field, where they were promptly shot. The dead included two preachers who apparently masterminded the burglary and beating that ended in murder. Two black women implicated in the plot were, in Regulator fashion, merely told to leave the neighborhood at once.

According to the *Abbeville Medium* (31 May 1876), "There was no unnecessary excitement. No whiskey was drank, no loud words were spoken[,] and the assemblage was as orderly and quiet as if it had collected for perfectly peaceful purposes." This weekly ticked off the justifications for what had ensued—a brutal murder, confessions by those thought guilty, the prospect of frustrating courtroom delays, and an "unreliable" jail located in a county that had not witnessed a legal execution in years—yet it stressed that no civilized community ever could sanction "lynch law."

The *News and Courier* (25–26 May 1876) agreed, underscoring the horrific nature of the crime involved and the fact that such violent acts must not go unpunished. Columbia's leading daily, the *Register,* struggled for three days to find appropriate words to describe what had happened. At times it deplored and condemned "lynch law," while noting the Edgefield executions were "universally approved." On 28 May a two-column editorial entitled "Judge Lynch and His Code" appeared. After tracing the history of lynching and conceding it might be "a necessity" in newly settled regions, the *Register* fixed blame on the Republican-dominated General Assembly: "Organized robbery is the distinguishing feature of our legislation." The cruel fate of the Harmons, old and helpless, revealed that neither life nor property was safe amid such anarchy. "After all," the *Register* concluded, "Judge Lynch is an able judge and a more humane man and a truer discerner of equity than many who have figured as justices in our reconstructed and semi-barbarous era."

Three years later, in June 1879, John J. Moore (white), who lived near Vernonsville in Spartanburg County, was hanged in the presence of several hundred spectators. Moore—a forty-year-old farmer, storekeeper, and maker of whiskey—was jailed following discovery of the body of a young white girl with her throat slit. Fanny Heaton of Pickens, while searching for relatives, had asked the Moore family for directions. They, in turn, had invited her to eat supper, after which Moore had offered to show her the way to an uncle's home. A preliminary investigation revealed she had been robbed and sexually assaulted, and Moore apparently was to blame.

Correspondence in the papers of Governor Franklin J. Moses Jr. reveals Moore was no stranger to controversy—drummed out of the Confederate army in the opening year of the war for stealing, forced to flee the county under suspicion of poisoning a neighbor, and involved with the KKK yet named as a trial justice by Republican Moses (to the disgust of one party loyalist, who called Moore "a vicious man"). During the night of 16–17 June the sheriff, fearing a lynching, decided to move his prisoner to safer quarters; however, 150 mounted men overpowered four guards and took Moore to the scene of the crime.

In the hours that followed, he was permitted to meet with his family, who, the crowd agreed, should have his body. While a "committee on arrangements" made preparations for a 10:00 A.M. hanging, Moore also talked with reporter A. B. Williams, who told the *News and Courier* (18 June), "The people showed a terrible quietness and cool relentlessness, but there was an entire absence of all excitement or boisterousness. A person one hundred yards from the scene would not have suspected what was transpiring."

Committee members rebuffed random calls for torture, and a Winnsboro man who implored the crowd to let the law take care of Moore was greeted with cries of "Hang him! Hang him! String him up!" To the chagrin of Williams, the committee did just that at 7:00 A.M. Had they waited until 10:00 A.M. as planned, Williams thought two thousand people—of all ages, classes, and colors—would have been there. Nevertheless the lynching was, in his opinion, "the coolest, quietest, and best conducted on record." On the nineteenth the *News and Courier*, while vowing it did not condone "lynch law," gave editorial approval of the proceedings: "There was no concealment in Spartanburg. To their honor the people went about their fearful work with quiet dignity, their faces exposed to the bright light of day. They were not ashamed of their purpose, and have no reason to blush for their act."[14]

The hanging of John Moore—no relation to the author—exhibits some of the earmarks of other lynchings that would occur in South Carolina during the next four decades, years that witnessed the rise and fall of such activity. Unlike Moore, nearly all of the victims were black males; but as with the Edgefield group and Moore, the press usually laid stress on how quiet and orderly South Carolina's lynchings actually were. And so long as such decorum reigned, few raised their voices to protest the outcome when a black man had assaulted a white woman, little doubt existed concerning guilt, and the condemned man was permitted to pray for a few moments before he was put to death. (Ideally, he also should have confessed to the crime.)

Unlike similar outbursts of mob violence in Mississippi, Georgia, and Texas, there is only scattered evidence of torture in this state, and few, if any, South Carolinians were put to death by burning. However, Henry Welsby, who suffered a slow, painful death near Central in 1890, may be an exception. According to the *Pickens Sentinel* (11 December 1890), Welsby "brutally assaulted" a Mrs. Walters. After she identified the black man as her assailant, he was tied to a tree and riddled with bullets. Several hours later Welsby tried to escape and more shots were fired. His apparently lifeless body then was burned. "Those who saw the negro say that his sufferings were commensurate with his crime as the persons who slew him meant they should be. To his repeated cries for water to quench his thirst as he lay in his blood, the only answer was a laugh. Persons who would have given him a drink were warned not to do so. After the job was finished, a funeral pyre of logs was built and his body thrown on it and cremated, only one foot was left for the coroner's jury to decide the cause of his death."

Black tenant farmer Ed Kirkland, who presumably shot and killed a prominent Allendale man in October 1921 during a dispute over rent payments, suffered a similar fate, although—like Welsby—he too may already have been dead when burned. In this instance the sheriff made a valiant but unsuccessful effort to elude a mob said to have numbered over a thousand. When Kirkland tried to flee, he was shot several times by mob leaders and left unconscious in an auto parked on the main street of the village of Appleton, site of the murder. As darkness fell, most of the crowd dispersed; then, apparently by prior agreement, the vehicle was set ablaze.[15]

Prior to discussion of other aspects of lynching in South Carolina (1880–1920) such as number of victims, geographical distribution, and specific incidents that influenced public opinion, it should be noted that "regulation" continued in a sporadic fashion, and on several occasions what began as moral betterment became murder. Regulators or "whitecappers" were especially active in the Laurens-Fairfield area in the mid-1880s, so much so that in the summer of 1885 the *Charleston News and Courier* published several columns entitled "Lawlessness in Laurens."[16] In a strange departure, according to these reports, Colonel J. L. M. Irby stood by and watched while, obeying his orders, a black servant beat up a white man who had offended his master. Irby, drunk at the time, declined to fight the man but covered him with a rifle and a pistol while the servant did. The colonel, who had been cleared of a murder charge a few years earlier, claimed he immediately surrendered to local authorities, but they disputed that statement. Whatever happened, this episode failed to damage Irby's political career, for he represented Laurens County in the state's lower House from 1886 to 1890, became Speaker, and then was elevated to the United States Senate.

During these same weeks a railroad emigration agent was attacked at Waterloo Station in Laurens County, and in September several white people in nearby Fairfield felt the wrath of Regulators. At least ten families were visited because a daughter was living with a black man or the head of the household had a black mistress. Among the latter was Ridgeway's richest merchant, a man named Tom Davis. Said to be worth forty-five thousand dollars, Davis evidently ignored these threats since he reportedly was whipped by "white caps" ninety days later. The root cause of this distress was, according to the *Charleston News and Courier* (10 September 1885), the fact that mulatto offspring were gaining both social status and property. Angry when the courts failed to act, local residents took matters into their own hands. Yet when a grand jury was asked to probe Regulator activity in Fairfield County, members said they could not act because they knew nothing about such things.

Other reports of Regulator-type pressure would surface from time to time, notably at Broxton Bridge in the northwest corner of Colleton County in 1895, in Florence County in 1898, and three years later at Salem in Oconee County. Each of these campaigns to uplift morals led to bloodshed, and those involved were indicted and charged with murder. In the first instance, six white men and a lone black were accused of whipping three blacks—Isom (or Isham) Kearse, his aged mother, and his wife. Kearse, who was suspected of burglarizing a Barnwell County church, subsequently died, as did his mother. After two trials, one of them held in Aiken County, all of the defendants were acquitted.[17]

In mid-November 1898 a gang of neighborhood blacks assaulted Sam Howard, an elderly black man living near Howe's Station in Florence County. Howard, whose crime was living with a common-law wife, defended himself with an iron bar and, when he hit one of his tormentors in the head, was shot and killed. As word spread, the *Charleston News and Courier* (18 November) termed the proceedings "a perfectly regular lynching" and, as such, "comparatively merciful." It emphasized in a lengthy editorial that white mobs had killed a dozen or so blacks in two counties in recent weeks. This included a biracial election-day brawl at Phoenix in Greenwood County that led to the deaths of at least eight blacks and one white, and nothing had been done about it. Why arrest those who killed Howard? Could it be because of the color of their skin that they were in jail? In the opinion of this daily, the men should be released. However, a few days later eleven blacks were charged with murder, and at a trial held the following February six of them received life sentences.[18]

An incident in Oconee was similar but involved only whites and thus ended somewhat differently. In November 1901 six young men decided to tear down the home of Wesley Powell located fourteen miles north of Walhalla because he was "living in sin" with Rachel Thomas. Rachel and one of the attackers died during the melee that ensued. In March 1902 three of the youths were sentenced to six years in the penitentiary for murder. Whereas blacks got life in the Howard case, whites received only six years in this one.[19]

With the onset of a new century, several developments tended to take the steam out of regulation, whitecapping, or whatever one wishes to call it. These include reform movements on the national scene and the beginnings of a rural police force in various South Carolina counties. The former, which had some local impact, preached a message potential Regulators found appealing, and the latter discouraged overt displays of "personal justice." And, as the Howard and Thomas cases demonstrated, juries were willing to convict those whose moral vigor proved fatal to their neighbors, no matter how wayward those neighbors might appear to be.

Also, by that date the attitude of white South Carolinians toward lynching was undergoing a distinct change. Not only did the brutality and widespread condemnation arouse concern, but there were economic considerations as well. In blunt terms, such incidents usually sent a shudder through the local labor force—blacks failing to show up for work for several days, discouraged northern investment, stimulated black flight to other regions, and blunted incipient tourism. Yet, sadly, it would be nearly half a century before the Palmetto State would record its final lynching and close the books on this sordid chapter in its long history.

— 4 —

LYNCHINGS GALORE

Here we come face to face with basic elements found in any news story—who, what, when, where, why—to which one might add in this instance, and with emphasis, *how many*—how many South Carolinians fell victim to lynch law? Various groups and individuals have searched for answers to such questions, among them the *Chicago Tribune,* Tuskegee Institute, the National Association for the Advancement of Colored People (NAACP), pioneer researcher J. Elbert Cutler, writer Frank Shay, two University of South Carolina graduate students (Jack S. Mullins and Susan Page Garris), and most recently Terence R. Finnegan, a graduate of the University of Illinois.[1] In *Judge Lynch: His First Hundred Years,* Shay, who used data compiled by the *Chicago Tribune* and the NAACP, came up with the totals, shown in table 4.1, for various southern states during the period from 1882 to 1937, with Mississippi leading the pack.

TABLE 4.1 — **Southern lynchings, 1882–1937**

Mississippi	581
Georgia	531
Texas	493
Louisiana	391
Alabama	347
Arkansas	284
Florida	282
Tennessee	251
Kentucky	205
South Carolina	180

Recent research into Kentucky's past by George C. Wright, author of *Racial Violence in Kentucky, 1865–1940,* reveals Shay's figure for that state is too low.[2] This does not seem to be the case for South Carolina. Mullins, who studied the years from 1900 to 1914, found only four victims not listed by the NAACP. He and Garris, exploring local sources, made a sincere effort to verify each affair, and both compiled separate lists of "probable" or "unverified" lynchings. On the other hand, summaries published by the *Chicago Tribune* and the NAACP appear to be a bit error prone—sometimes attributing victims to the wrong state, failing to acknowledge false reports, ignoring lynchings even if well documented by South Carolina newspapers, and confusing lynching and murder (certainly easy enough to do).[3] The *News and Courier* cited 33 South Carolina deaths (1882–90), while the *State* said the total for the years 1891 through 1899 was 50. Mullins found 55 victims (1900–1914), and Garris found 24 (1915–47). These figures add up to 162, somewhat less than Shay's tally.

Yet this sort of exercise, by its very nature, is inherently inaccurate and, despite good intentions, cannot produce a truly definitive list of names. Some, in fact, never were known; others, said to have been lynched, apparently were not. The demise of an "unknown" black man under "unknown" circumstances is not an especially revealing bit of information. But during these turn-of-the-century decades such deaths invariably were chalked up to lynching, which may or may not have been the case. We are dealing, after all, with illegal, often secret, emotionally charged proceedings that are being recounted secondhand or thirdhand, and gossip is rather poor fodder for detailed, computerized analysis.

Crowd size is an especially frustrating phenomenon, as anyone who lived through the Vietnam protest era will concede. One commentator (who probably was not present at a lynching) will swell the attendant mass to howling hundreds or even a thousand in hopes of intimidating local blacks, while another, to salve community pride, may reduce the same gathering to something akin to a midweek prayer meeting. Also, since many lynchings were conducted in the dark, almost any estimate is inherently suspect. As for "types" of mobs as analyzed by W. Fitzhugh Brundage and others, forget it. Nevertheless, bearing these various caveats in mind, see the appendix, which contains tables summarizing South Carolina lynchings chronologically and by county, 1880–1947.

In all, there appear to have been 186 victims during these years, 6 more than recorded by Shay for a slightly different period (1882–1937). Fifty-seven of them (31 percent) died in the brutal 1890s, and the last white man to be lynched was railroad roustabout John Morrison in 1904. Also, at least half of the twentieth-century affairs were carried out in considerable secrecy, far from the eyes of potential witnesses, and some deaths never were reported as lynchings. This was especially true after 1920, when, eager to lure tourists and sensitive about the state's public image, South Carolinians were less apt to publicize such events. This, of course, presents an obvious dilemma. If the goal is to set an example and warn others to mend their ways, one wants to broadcast the news as widely as possible.

The death of an unknown black near Lydia Mill village in Laurens County in May 1934 is a good example of a quasi-lynching that passed largely unnoticed. The trouble began when Deputy Sheriff Kelly F. Johns (age fifty-five) poked a black hobo with a stick as he lay sleeping in a graveyard. The black reacted by shooting Johns in the stomach and seizing his gun. Although Johns was not universally admired—he broke up stills and kept the liquor, which some thought a bit unfair—the Lydia community was quick to avenge the assault. The mill shut down, the company store handed out free ammunition, and some three hundred men cornered the assailant in a nearby swamp. One of them fired a fatal shot into the stranger's back as he sat on a stump reloading a pistol, and then each of the ringleaders, in turn, discharged a bullet into the dying man's body so no single individual could be charged with murder. A short time later they told authorities the deceased had been gored by a bull.

The *Clinton Chronicle* (17 May 1934), amid ads for "get acquainted" days, said a cooperative coroner's jury ruled the black, who allegedly exchanged shots with his pursuers, "came to his death at the hands of unknown parties." Of course, this was not a true lynching in the classic sense and never was reported as such, and local residents, well aware of the lynching death of Morris Denby in the same community twelve months earlier, made certain it would not be.[4]

According to most sources, lynching madness reached its peak some four decades earlier in 1892 when mobs in all parts of the nation hanged, shot, burned, and tortured 255 fellow human beings. Why this tragic exercise was so widespread at that juncture is unclear, but one underlying cause may have been gains registered by two generations of former slaves and their offspring. A more independent air, basic education, and new social freedom brought into question the long-held tenet of racial inferiority. As a result of such changes, coupled with harsh times and five-cent cotton, poor whites often felt threatened. In short, some blacks, they feared, might actually be moving up the socio-economic ladder and leaving them behind.

During the next few years the NAACP lynching count vacillated somewhat, but it never exceeded one hundred after 1903 and fell to a low of thirty-eight in 1917. These trends were reflected in South Carolina, although the Phoenix riot swelled the state's death toll to seventeen in 1898, the highest ever. One might ask if those killed in a riot actually were lynched; however, lynching is not an exact science. Some victims never were in the hands of the law, and others were not taken from a sheriff and his deputies; instead, they were shot (as in Lydia), beaten to death in some isolated pine thicket, or gunned down in their cells. Regardless of the methods, the intent was clear enough.

A more intriguing question is why South Carolina's overall total is lower than one might expect, although higher than those of nearby North Carolina and Virginia, each of which counted perhaps ninety to one hundred victims. Unlike most southern states, South Carolina had a black majority throughout these years. Although the state is small geographically, the total population when lynching was most common (1890–1910) was 1.1 to 1.5 million, a figure comparable to those of Arkansas, Louisiana, and Mississippi, twice that of Florida, but less than those of other states in the former Confederacy. So the answer does not lie solely in white-black ratios or mere numbers. But a relatively small land mass with social institutions somewhat better developed than those found in newer regions (Texas, Florida, and Arkansas, for example) provides clues.

Between 1900 and 1914, according to Mullins, fifty-five individuals died in forty-six lynchings, thirty of which took place within forty-five miles of the Savannah River. That waterway is, of course, the border with Georgia where "personal justice" was much more popular. Mullins notes that most occurred in dirt-poor communities where churches and schools were weak and not well organized, and within such communities lynch mobs often appeared in straggling little settlements that never grew into villages and have since vanished.

Virtually every survey of lynching emphasizes that, despite general assumptions, it was murder that usually invoked "lynch law," not alleged or attempted rape.· (This was especially true after 1900.) A special commission found that homicides were responsible for nearly 38 percent of the 3,703 lynchings that took place throughout the nation between 1889 and 1929, while only 23 percent were related to rape.[5] Although dealing with much smaller numbers, Mullins found virtually the same percentages in his 46 South Carolina lynchings; however, if all alleged crimes against white women were considered, the figure rose from 23 to 48 percent.

As Mullins implies, this is one puzzle that cannot be reduced to the timeworn lowcountry-upcountry equation, nor do regional racial patterns provide ready answers. Richland County, roughly 60 percent black, recorded no lynchings; Lexington, just across the Congaree River and with fewer people, fewer blacks, and equal land area, had eight such deaths. Horry in the southeast corner of the state and Oconee in the northwest, each with twenty-three thousand or so inhabitants in 1900 and roughly the same proportion of blacks (26 percent), posted quite different totals. Horry had one lynching, and Oconee had six. Nevertheless the numbers of blacks living in various communities do indicate subtle trends. (See tables A.3 and A.4 in the appendix, covering racial aspects of state and county population, 1880–1920.) Six counties where blacks enjoyed an overwhelming majority, say three to one—Allendale, Beaufort, Berkeley, Fairfield, Jasper, and Sumter— had only five lynchings. But communities where the percentage of blacks was increasing—Barnwell, Clarendon, and Edgefield, for example—experienced obvious turmoil.

In addition to the onset of Jim Crow and difficult economic times, both of which should be kept in mind, two other factors loom large. Mullins already has pointed to the prevalence of lynching in western South Carolina during the period he examined; and, as Brundage's summary of Georgia lynchings reveals, counties within twenty miles of South Carolina had, on average, one lynching per year, 1880–1920. Thus trends in the "Empire State" are significant, as is the creation of nine new counties in the western half of South Carolina during those same decades. The new-county mania—often driven by desire for more control over local affairs, a more "central" courthouse, and better roads—seems to have heightened tensions for two obvious reasons. It frequently *increased* the proportion of blacks within redrawn boundaries or whites thought such was the case, which is equally important. And these changes sometimes brought to power what undoubtedly were inexperienced, ill-trained sheriffs, deputies, and constables—a situation exacerbated by the bitter feuds of the Tillmanites, the Bleasites, and their adversaries. It may be of some relevance that those nine new western counties reported twenty-four lynching victims, while only one of the new counties in the eastern half of the state (Florence) recorded such deaths.

But, to put this matter into perspective, for a moment forget erratic county boundaries and divide the state into merely two parts by drawing a line from Charleston to Spartanburg. The eastern half of the state, with 45.8 percent of the 1900 population, was responsible for only 44 deaths (1880–1947), or 23.6 percent. In the same period, residents of the western sector hanged, shot, beat, and whipped to death 142 unfortunate souls.

During the height of lynching, the decades from 1880 to 1920, there were at least ten double lynchings, and on four occasions black trios that included one female were killed almost simultaneously at Salem (1880), Gaston (1893), Olar (1912), and Fair Play (1914). The first of these affairs occurred in Clarendon County on 5 December 1880 when three black teenagers allegedly killed a pregnant white woman named Kennedy with a hoe and then robbed her household. Three days later Julia Brandt (fifteen years old), Vance Brandt (eighteen), and Joe Barnes (sixteen), who once worked for the Kennedys, were summarily hanged. In this instance, amid a quasi-democratic atmosphere, the mob took a vote concerning what to do; however, according to the *Charleston News and Courier* (11 December 1880), only twenty-three individuals favored turning the trio over to the authorities. The Gaston tragedy resulted from the rape of a local housewife, while the Olar blacks were accused of arson. The deaths at Fair Play came about because of an interracial riot that really was nothing more than a shoot-out. Yet another racial disturbance, an election brawl lasting several days, left at least one white and eight blacks dead at Phoenix in 1898.

Of these grisly operations, the one at Gaston seems to have been the most inept. Reminiscent of "the gang that couldn't shoot straight," one might characterize this crowd as "the mob that didn't know how to lynch." Things actually began to go wrong on Thursday, 27 July 1893, following the weekend rape of a Mrs. Sightler. Several hundred men who had been tracking the suspects for several days suddenly heard that armed blacks were marching on Gaston. This proved untrue, but in the meantime militia units donned uniforms, rushed to the Columbia depot, and made preparations to defend that little community in lower Lexington County.

New counties, 1880–1920

NO.	DATE	COUNTY	ORGANIZED FROM PARTS OF
1	1882	Berkeley	Charleston
2	1888	Florence	Clarendon, Darlington, Marion, Williamsburg
3	1895	Saluda	Edgefield
4	1897	Bamberg	Barnwell
5	1897	Dorchester	Berkeley, Colleton
6	1897	Greenwood	Abbeville, Edgefield
7	1897	Cherokee	Spartanburg, Union, York
8	1902	Lee	Darlington, Kershaw, Sumter
9	1908	Calhoun	Lexington, Orangeburg
10	1910	Dillon	Marion
11	1912	Jasper	Beaufort, Hampton
12	1916	McCormick	Abbeville, Edgefield, Greenwood
13	1919	Allendale	Barnwell, Hampton

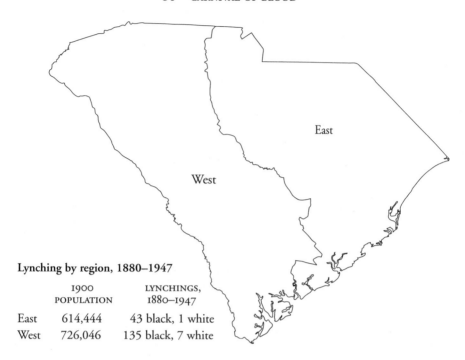

Lynching by region, 1880–1947

	1900 POPULATION	LYNCHINGS, 1880–1947
East	614,444	43 black, 1 white
West	726,046	135 black, 7 white

Forty-eight hours later one of the rapists reportedly had been captured in Irmo, and Columbians clambered aboard a special train bound for the northern end of the county, only to discover this also was a false rumor. Shortly after they returned home in the early hours of Sunday, 30 July, word came that Will Thompson (one of those being sought) was in Gaston. At 3:00 A.M. the weary crowd set out once more, arriving at their destination about daybreak. Thompson was not in evidence because local farmers refused to produce him until they got the one-hundred-dollar reward that was being offered. A public-spirited Columbian quickly supplied sufficient money to solve that problem, although John G. Capers, editor of the *Columbia Journal,* subsequently mounted the depot steps and reminded the throng this was Gaston's lynching, *not* Columbia's.

By sunrise, women and children of the village were beginning to appear, but nothing could be done until Mr. Sightler, the outraged husband of the victim, arrived. Meanwhile, Thompson—a chunky eighteen-year-old—sat on the depot steps with a stout rope around his neck (the other end held securely by mob leaders) and, amid taunts, allegedly confessed his guilt to any who asked. At about 7:15 Archie Sightler rode up and demanded yet another recounting of the horrifying details. By 8:00 A.M. he had heard enough, and some folks wanted to hang and burn Thompson on the spot. However, the Columbians spoke against burning, warning it would "stain" Gaston's good name, while others cautioned,

"They must not do it right here in town with people going to church. . . . they ought to take him out a little way."[6]

So the crowd started down the railroad track, shunning blacks who wanted to join the line of march. About half a mile out of town they found a suitable oak tree, under which Thompson was stripped, whipped, kicked, forced to confess just one more time, and finally prepared for hanging. Only then did the lynchers discover the rope they planned to use was too short. To rectify this oversight, they erected a pile of cross ties, dragged Thompson to the top, looped the rope over a limb, and kicked the platform out from under him. In their haste, however, the leaders forgot to tie Thompson's hands; even though he was barely conscious, with one final gasp he reached over his head and grabbed the rope in a last-ditch attempt to avert strangulation. A volley of shots soon ended this farce, following which the men gave three cheers and set out in search of Thompson's companions. By 1:00 P.M. (after church) Tom Preston had been cornered in his home and hanged, and that evening the Lexington County sheriff released Handy Kaigler to Sightler. On the morning of 31 July three black bodies were hanging from a single limb—"Three on One Tree." Later that same day a local photographer recorded this unusual sight, and the young men were buried nearby in a common grave.[7]

Two other multiple lynchings, both of which took place in the late 1880s, had marked similarities. In November 1886 a white youth named John Lee Goode was killed in western York County when he discovered several blacks stealing cotton from his father's land. An investigation revealed the robbers were members of a black protective society, the Rising Star Lodge, that had embraced crime. Following interrogation of twenty-six members, five of them were taken to Columbia for safekeeping. Several months later they were returned to Yorkville for trial, and early on the morning of 5 April 1887 sixty or so undisguised men broke into the jail, seized the prisoners, and hanged them on a wooded knoll on the Adair's Ferry Road about one mile from town. The account of this affair in the *Yorkville Enquirer* (6, 13 April) is so detailed that one is forced to conclude it was written by an eyewitness. The lynchers were stirred, this gentleman claimed, by the fact that the dead youth's distraught father recently had gone insane. Interestingly, this tragedy led in December of the same year to strict new laws regulating traffic in cottonseed throughout the state.

Two years later, on 28 December 1889, one hundred armed, masked men stormed the Barnwell County jail, seized eight blacks, and took them to a nearby field, where they were shot. Four were being held on homicide charges, and the others were merely being detained as witnesses. The excuse for this massacre— the killing of three local whites in recent weeks in separate incidents—failed to satisfy the *News and Courier;* and when yet another Barnwell black was

Five lynched on Adair's Ferry Road about a mile from York in April 1887. Photograph in private collection

lynched a few days later while en route to jail, the Charleston daily excoriated Barnwell's justice system. This led, as was often the case, to a verbal battle with local editors, who claimed their fair community was being slandered and defamed by "outsiders."

But it was the York County lynching that attracted the most attention. Newspapers throughout the state were especially critical because court was in session at the time and many thought the legal process should have been permitted to run its course. It turned out that one of the victims—a mulatto considered to be "smart, sly, and cunning"—was not actually implicated in young Goode's murder, and the judge fanned the flames when he commented an inquiry into the affair would be "worthless," a statement subsequently modified. The *Abbeville Press and Banner* (20 April 1887) vowed there was an easy solution to this problem: "Arm prisoners with good Winchester rifles, with instructions to shoot the first man who approaches their cell, and we venture to suggest that the cowardly practice of lynching unarmed men who are in custody of the law will cease." Two days later the *News and Courier* agreed this was a desperate measure but conceded any prisoner "threatened with lynching, should be given a chance hereafter to meet the mob on an even footing."

It was left to Greenville solicitor James L. Orr to analyze dispassionately what had happened. In his view, the public seldom demanded punishment for crime, lawmakers too often thought not of citizen needs but of their role as lawyers representing a defendant, and the investigation of any homicide was perfunctory at best. Since it was easy to arrange bail and, if convicted, to launch an appeal or secure a pardon, it was no wonder, he said, that many individuals were ready to hang those accused of heinous acts. He continued, "The people who do the lynchings are not the ones who are responsible for the shortcomings of the law. The responsible parties are the influential citizens of each community, those who govern and control the machinery of government—the legislative, executive, and judicial officers of this State. They have a grave and most urgent duty to perform; for, until the people become satisfied by experience that personal violence will be speedily and unerringly punished, lynching, in outrageous cases, will not only be tolerated, but lynchers will be regarded by the masses as public benefactors rather than public criminals."[8]

Writing a few years later when the lynching fury was at its height, Georgia columnist Bill Arp (Charles Henry Smith), a well-known humorist and lecturer, tended to view matters somewhat differently:

> The law's delay is not the actuating emotion. It is simply the explosion of a gun that has long been loaded. The newspapers speak of lynchings as the act of a howling, yelling, demoniac mob. The newspapers do not know. Editors live in town and feel secure. Their wives can visit and their daughters go to school without apprehension of danger. The police are always within call and neighbors near. But go to the country and get close to the heart of the farmer who has children and he will tell you that the apprehension of some horrible calamity is always with him. That is a shadow that follows him when he leaves home or his children have gone to a neighboring school, not that it makes him miserable, but nevertheless it comes over him in spite of himself. The feeling is common to all country people, especially the poor—the tenants who cannot give protection like the rich. I have heard them talk about it often and I know that fear has kept many a little country girl from school. That dark path through the woods and across the creek and those negroes in the fields or at the mines or wandering up and down the creek with hook and lines. "Who next?" is the thought whenever they read of an outrage, and so when one does occur in their vicinity pentup emotions break loose and they join in pursuit.

Arp went on to say that if anyone "near and dear" to him was the victim of such a crime, "I could see him burned and feel no remorse, but satisfaction rather in the hope that I might intimidate some other brute."[9]

One may view the words of Orr and Arp as pragmatic, pessimistic, or perhaps shocking, but even as they spoke, the attitude of South Carolinians toward "lynch law" was changing. What aroused concern was not only the rising death toll but also the nature of the events. Regardless of skin color, anyone hanged when thought innocent caused outcry, as did the killing of those not involved in sexual matters or put to death for some minor indiscretion such as failure to show proper respect, cursing a white person, mistreating an employer's property, or being caught in a henhouse. Also, the indictment of mob leaders for murder (even if not convicted) and trends outside of South Carolina—burnings and torture in the Deep South and criticism from other parts of the nation—stimulated calls for reform.

Many lynchings are, admittedly, encumbered by unknown details, although this is not to imply those killed were, in such instances, entirely innocent of charges leveled against them. Nevertheless, in the case of the black tenant charged with arson, *why* did he burn down his landlord's barn? White women frequently knew their black assailants, individuals who worked alongside them in their fields or in their homes. Had such associations bred unintended familiarity? For the small gang bent upon stamping out immorality in a neighbor's household, what were the true forces propelling such zeal? Were the members, in fact, trying to exorcise personal devils? And, as strange as it may sound, was lynching a form of democracy run amok? Rank-and-file South Carolinians watched as their leaders defied authority for two decades, first in gray uniforms and then in white sheets. The mob often did much the same when juries and judges failed to honor its wishes. Thus, in the view of many, they were merely hastening, completing, or tidying up the judicial process.

As we have seen, such attitudes were paramount when five blacks were slaughtered near Yorkville in 1887 and eight more killed at Barnwell in 1889. Five years later, at about 2:00 A.M. on the morning of 2 June 1894, another mob stormed the York County jail and hanged Jeff Crawford (black). Crawford had been convicted of murder, and his lawyers were appealing that sentence, but local residents obviously took exception to delay. On 18 October of the following year, four Hampton County blacks were being tried for murder. When three of them were sentenced to be hanged and the fourth man (William Blake Sr.) was given a life sentence, he was seized as he stepped out of the courthouse and strung up on a nearby tree.

Again, it is noteworthy that South Carolina mobs sometimes voted concerning what course to follow. In 1894, according to the *Columbia Register* (7 November), Gus Funches faced an Orangeburg County mob; and after "a jury of justice" was empaneled, he chose two hundred lashes and banishment instead of death. The following year Bill Stokes of Colleton County made the same choice but then hung around Raysor's and tried to get even with those who had whipped him. Both the *State* and the *News and Courier* reported on 26 June 1895 that he had been lynched four days earlier.

August Kohn watched similar drama unfold at Republican Church in Edge-field County on 25 October 1898 during the second session of an inquest into the assassination of a white woman, Alice Atkinson. According to reporter Kohn, some 250 armed men milled about the premises all day, most of them, in his opinion, determined to kill three blacks implicated in the crime. Their reason-ing was direct and simple: "It was too far for them to go to court to see that things went right, and meanwhile it was dangerous not to act for the sake of example."[10] Eventually, with the hearing at an end and despite appeals from the sheriff and several clergymen, the mob prevailed as at least two of the men thought guilty died in a hail of bullets. "It was a sad and most dramatic day," wrote Kohn. "It showed, first, lack of confidence in the execution of the laws, and secondly, a grim determination to set an example to all guilty of assassina-tion, especially of an innocent woman."[11]

Missing from most tales of this sort is the black reaction; but in June 1894 (twenty-four hours after Jeff Crawford was killed in Yorkville), Hardy Gill was put to death in nearby Lancaster. In each case mob leaders resorted to the usual ruse—knocking on the jail door sometime after midnight and loudly proclaim-ing they had a prisoner to deliver to the authorities. Gill's battered body was found three miles outside of town a few hours later. On 4 June local blacks held a mass meeting and issued a stern protest to Governor Tillman. Gill, they empha-sized, always was "subject to fits and half crazy," a proper subject for the asylum. His only crime was, while experiencing a seizure, he struck a white woman who happened to be near him. "Be it understood," they continued, "that we denounce and condemn rapery, home intrusion, or any thing else capable of disgracing society. But when this is done the *law*, and not mobs of lindcers should inter fear. . . . Lawlessness begets lawlessness. An animal will strike in his den." Those guilty of "this horrid crime," they stressed, must be brought to justice.[12]

The deaths of two white men at the hands of mobs in the 1880s were hardly what the *News and Courier* would call "perfectly regular" lynchings. One was a Confederate veteran, and the other was lynched by blacks. On a Saturday evening, 13 September 1885, William Hammond was shot and killed in the yard of an Edgefield County woman, Fannie Prescott Culbreath. Hammond, twenty-four years of age and a former Furman University student, had worked for the Culbreath family for a time; but two years earlier, when Mrs. Culbreath sepa-rated from her husband, Hammond returned to his home a few miles away. At the request of Mrs. Culbreath's son, who had business elsewhere, Hammond agreed to care for the livestock and spend the night. Within a week Fannie's hus-band, Confederate veteran Oliver Towles Culbreath—a "gallant" soldier who apparently had "gone wrong," mistreated his wife, and on several occasions had threatened to kill Hammond—was arrested and charged with the crime. This threat was not strictly personal since Culbreath vowed to strike back at anyone who used his wife's cotton gin and press or associated with her household. (According to the 1880 census, the Culbreaths had four children, two boys and two girls, ages two to thirteen.)

On the evening of the twenty-first, while in the Edgefield law offices of Gary and Evans making arrangements for bail, Culbreath and his attorneys were overwhelmed by about thirty-five masked men. Shoving the lawyers aside, they shot Culbreath and then spirited him out of town, where he was shot again and abandoned. Friends later brought him back to Edgefield, where he died the following day, but not before naming his attackers.

The result was a complex situation, for small-town ties (marriage, friendship, for example) created a communal nightmare. Thirty-three of the lynchers soon were behind bars, and local authorities, taking a hard-nosed approach, for a time refused to release most of them on bail. Among those charged was Culbreath's eighteen-year-old son, Memphis. Trials were postponed on several occasions, and U.S. Senator Matthew C. Butler, chief lawyer for those implicated in the affair, suggested in March 1886 that perhaps all charges should be dropped. Two of the men finally came to trial in August 1887, the defense chose not to offer witnesses, the pair were acquitted, and the case was closed.

Meanwhile, Fannie was waging a court fight for control of her dead husband's estate. His brother, Dr. W. A. Culbreath, insisted she had signed over all rights to him. She said she had not and eventually prevailed. No great sum was involved, but the estate (estimated to be worth perhaps three thousand dollars) included a life insurance policy that she thought should benefit her children, as well as money she reportedly gave Culbreath to leave her in peace. By the time Fannie won in 1893, she was Mrs. Charles W. Hammond, having married an older brother of William (the man her husband shot) in November 1888.[13]

The death of Manse Waldrop in Pickens County during the final days of 1887 posed an acute dilemma for many southerners. "LYNCH LAW REVERSED," the *News and Courier* proclaimed on 3 January 1888 as it told how a group of blacks had hanged Waldrop, a white man. Said to have been a half-witted farm laborer, Waldrop (also known as Manz Gooden) was arrested in Central on 30 December and charged with the death of a thirteen-year-old black girl, Lula Sherman, whom he allegedly raped. The inquest, during which the dead girl's sister identified Waldrop as the guilty party, ended late in the evening; fearing violence, the constables were advised to wait until daylight to take their prisoner to the county seat. However, they immediately set out and soon were met by a band of fifteen to twenty angry blacks, who shot and wounded the prisoner, although not seriously. White neighbors living nearby heard the uproar that ensued and intervened in a half-hearted fashion. The blacks fled for a time but then returned and hanged Waldrop. Five black men, including Lula's father, subsequently were charged with murder, and

R. Gaylor Eaton—a white constable who reportedly was drinking that evening and openly called for a lynching—was indicted as an accessory.

In July an all-white jury was unable to reach a verdict; following the mistrial Eaton was free on bail, while the five blacks remained in jail. At a second trial in March 1889, three of the defendants (including Eaton and Lula's father) were acquitted and the three other men convicted. Two of the latter—Bill Williams and Harrison Heyward—were sentenced to be hanged; the third man, Henry Bolton, was granted a new trial, although charges later were dropped. As a result of extensive protests, on 15 April 1889 Governor J. P. Richardson pardoned both Williams and Heyward.[14] For the most part this outcry centered on the fact that this state never had executed a white man as the result of a lynching, so a black, it was argued, should not be hanged for that crime.

After opening with a strong condemnation of lynching and noting he had done all in his power to prevent "such violations of law and order," Richardson observed that "he did not in the face of the peculiar circumstances surrounding this case, and in consideration of the unfortunate example that has so frequently been set for him by his white neighbors, regard it just, or for the best interests of the State, that the law should be enforced with its utmost stringency upon these erring and mistaken colored men, who had already undergone, through anxiety and imprisonment, prolonged and severe punishment. In addition to numerous letters from citizens, prominent in all walks of life, the petitions for the pardon of these men were probably the strongest ever sent to this office. There were about 5,000 signers, representing every class in the State."[15]

Of the fifty or so lynchings that occurred in the 1890s, several deserve passing comment. The first, a confusing tale of forgery and deceit, took place in Lexington in the spring of 1890. Willie Leaphart (black) was scheduled to hang on 11 April for criminally assaulting a white girl, Rosa Cannon. At the last minute his attorneys submitted evidence to Governor Richardson that won Willie a reprieve so they could seek a new trial. To protect the prisoner, he was transferred to Columbia, which the good people of Lexington interpreted as an insult. A delegation of prominent citizens registered a complaint with Richardson and promised Leaphart would be safe in their jail, to which he was returned and where he was riddled with bullets on the night of 5 May. Some thirty men, many wearing masks, surged into the building and forced the sheriff to surrender keys to the cells. They planned to hang Leaphart, but he resisted so strenuously that they simply shot him where he was. The sheriff and his family were able to identify three ringleaders—F. C. Caughman, Frank Calhoun, and Pierce G. Taylor—who were indicted for murder. (Shortly after Leaphart's death it became apparent that his lawyers had concocted the evidence that won the reprieve.)

In mid-June the lynchers were brought to trial and quickly acquitted, even though Caughman had confessed and bragged publicly of his role in the affair. Their lawyers presented no evidence on behalf of the trio, only asserting that Caughman's statements resulted from strong drink. Women, much in evidence during the proceedings, presented each of the defendants with handsome boutonnieres and publicly berated jurors from outside the jury room when deliberations continued for nearly an hour.[16]

Three years later the death of another black in Denmark under strange circumstances created unprecedented outrage, much of it fueled by the *State* when it sensed an opportunity to embarrass Governor Benjamin Ryan Tillman. In mid-April 1893 a black man reportedly assaulted young Mamie Baxter. For several days the little town seethed with discontent, especially when the original suspect was able to establish an airtight alibi. Meanwhile, one John Peterson came to the governor in Columbia vowing he too was not guilty. Tillman sent Peterson, under guard, back to Denmark (he later said the man wanted to return so as to establish his innocence), where he was killed. The *State* (25 April) proclaimed "AN INNOCENT MAN LYNCHED" and denounced the governor as "an accessory before the fact." Both races held large protest rallies in Columbia, whereupon the citizens of Denmark met and attacked the *State,* accusing it of promoting race war in an effort to revive Reconstruction.

Peterson's guilt or innocence aside, this uproar should be viewed in light of Tillman's stump statement in the summer of 1892: "There is only one crime that warrants lynching, and Governor as I am I would lead a mob to lynch a negro that ravishes a white woman. I do justify lynching for rape, and before Almighty God I am not ashamed of it."[17] Although the *State* often threw these words back at Tillman, its own stand on lynching was virtually the same, at least until after 1900. For example, early in May 1893 when Peterson's death was followed by that of another black at Lane in Williamsburg County, the *State* said the difference was this man clearly was guilty. The paper still proclaimed lynching to be "both wrong and unwise"; such matters should be left to the courts. Yet the editor emphasized, "We have never yet denounced as a crime the lynching of any man clearly shown to be guilty of a nameless outrage."[18]

Ben Tillman may have got a bum rap for his proclamation concerning lynching. Limiting this obscene practice to a *single* crime can be seen in a positive light. It was, after all, an act deplored by both races, and there are indications he had the backing of prominent blacks. At a statewide meeting held in Columbia in May 1893, various leaders attacked lynching, while reminding South Carolinians of amicable race relations during the Civil War years and a promise in 1876 to protect them if they voted for Wade Hampton and the Democrats. Their summary statement also praised Tillman, save for the Peterson case, as "the most aggressive pioneer against lynch law."[19]

Nevertheless lynching increased markedly during Tillman's second administration (1893–94) and continued apace throughout the remainder of the decade. The *State* cited thirteen lynchings with fifteen dead in 1893 and three victims in 1894. The first-year total includes the three Gaston blacks plus others in Bamberg, Ninety Six, Kingstree, Laurens, Lake City, Gaffney, Kitching's Mill, and Reidville, all as the result of sexually related incidents. The Ninety Six man presumably committed a similar crime some years earlier, but nothing was done about it because the woman was of "doubtful character." The Reidville youth's indiscretion, which took place two years before, was complicated by the fact that the girl became infatuated and wanted to run away with him. The *State* was able to dispense with the Kitching's Mill affair in three sentences bearing this headline: "FOR THE USUAL CRIME." In June 1894, as noted earlier, a Yorkville mob, unable to wait, lynched a condemned murderer, and the following day the same fate awaited an insane black in Lancaster.

A Sumter County lynching early in January 1897 has no special significance except for the amount of bloodshed involved. Simon Cooper—a six-foot tall, pleasant-looking, 175-pound black grandson of John Ashemore, a white, antebellum desperado—went on a New Year's rampage that left three whites and two blacks dead. By the time he was taken prisoner, beaten, shot, revived, shot again, and hanged from a sweet gum tree still cursing, both races were happy to see him swing. Yet the black man who fastened the lid of his coffin could not help expressing admiration for a man who was a reasonable enough fellow until he went to Georgia, where he was transformed into a bully and a gambler: "Bad as he was, he died a hero; let him go."[20]

The most notorious lynching of the late 1890s—if one can call it that—was the killing of Lake City's black postmaster and his infant daughter on 22 February 1898. Local whites, angered by the appointment of F. B. Baker, a Florence County native, terrorized the family for several days and then shot up and burned their home. Baker's wife and three other children were injured in the gunfire, two of them seriously. Eleven individuals were indicted for murder, but all charges eventually were dropped following a mistrial in Charleston.

Yet change was in the air. A new state constitution, written in November 1895, provided for removal of any officer (state, county, or municipal) whose negligence contributed to a lynching. Article VI, Section 6, also made a county liable for damages "of not less than two thousand dollars to the legal representatives of the person lynched." The county had the right to recover from lynchers any amount collected under this legislation. Needless to point out, the victim's family faced an uphill battle, but by 1920 at least two counties bowed to court decisions and paid up—Clarendon in 1915 and York in 1919.

Antilynching forces applauded these new statutes but felt they did not go far enough. The true remedy, according to the *State* (15 November 1898), was to

How They Got Calvin Stewart

I was comming along Just above Langley on the Augusta road going to aiken Jail with the Prisner and a Possie of men rose up and ordered me to halt . . . I Said hold up Gentlemen I have him in costady . . . one of them hollard out and said God Dam you and your costady two and the gun fired So close to me till it Singed my Whiskers . . . I Supose there was some 15 or 20 men . . . all mask men . . . I Didnot know any one . . . I Supose the firing was about one half minitt and the Crowd Dispursed . . . this was this morning between the hours of two and three oclock Sept 27 1893 . . . this Negro that was Linched made a confesion to Several parties that he was the man that Kill Charley Carter . . . he also Gave me one Dollar that was taken out of Mr Carters Pocket . . . he also told me that Steamus Dunbar was implicated in the murder . . . that Steamus Rafaled his Pocket . . . he told me this Just about 2 minitts before he was Kiled . . . he told me that I had left the warse man of the 2 behind . . . he also told me that Steamus Dunbar strock him 2 licks after I had knock him Down.

W M Augustine (X his mark)

Augustine, a forty-eight-year-old grocer who lived in Aiken County's Gregg Township, probably was a constable. His words, recorded by coroner Jep C. Couch at the inquest, can be found in the Tillman Papers (Box 62).

---

extend to lynching the same ban that ended dueling. Those involved should not be allowed to vote or hold office: "The gentlemen and the believers in fair fighting have had their hands tied—now let those who believe in free slaughtering be manacled also and similarly." For whatever reasons, South Carolina's leaders never embraced this proposal with much enthusiasm.

For South Carolinians a turning point in this grisly tale—perhaps *the* turning point—came in Dorchester County early in 1904. At about seven o'clock on a Tuesday evening, 12 January, a black man knocked repeatedly at the lowcountry home of Mrs. A. P. Wimberly in Reevesville. When she opened the door he ran away; however, the widow Wimberly told neighbors about the incident. Several of them decided that "General" Lee, a twenty-year-old youth with a "bad" reputation, was the culprit and swore out a warrant. The following day Constable R. E. Mims arrested Lee but was overpowered by some fifty men en route to the jail. On Thursday morning Lee's "terribly mutilated body," ripped by shotgun fire at close range, was found lashed to a tree. The *News and Courier* said he had tried to enter the Wimberly home and was frightened away by screams, but the *State* reporter told a very different story and concluded there really was no provocation for mob action. Mrs. Wimberly (who knew Lee) never saw him near her home and did not intimate he was the caller; nor was she asked to identify him

Governor Duncan Clinch Heyward
(1864–1943), the first chief execu-
tive who tried to suppress lynching.
Courtesy of South Caroliniana
Library, University of South
Carolina, Columbia

before he was killed. Following the usual inquest and the usual verdict, the *State*
(18 January) called bluntly for action. Why, it asked, did not the governor, sheriff, solicitor, or the good people of Dorchester and Reevesville speak out?

Forty-eight hours later Governor Duncan Clinch Heyward did just that, asking the General Assembly to give him the money and power to fight lynching.
Just why the death of "General" Lee triggered this response is unclear. This was
neither the first nor the last truly outrageous example of "lynch law" in South
Carolina, and Heyward had failed to display similar vigor when six lynchings
occurred during 1903, his first year in office.[21] The answer may lie in the national
mood that was gaining strength (progressivism) and a reflection of that movement at the local level, the Law and Order League.

In October 1903, in reaction to lawlessness in general, this association was
formed during State Fair Week at Columbia's YMCA. Four months later field-
worker Reverend Vernon I'Anson was moving about the state organizing chapters in various towns and cities, and in October 1904 members held their first
annual meeting at the Main Street Methodist Church in Columbia. New units
still were appearing five years later, and the group remained active at least until
World War I. Yet for two basic reasons victories were few: interest in reform often
was generated by a specific incident that soon was forgotten; and the league tried

to fight on too many fronts. At the outset the prime targets were pistols and homicide, but members soon turned their attention to liquor, gambling, and other personal devils. Any full-scale inquiry undoubtedly would reveal that the Law and Order League was gobbled up by a much stronger force of that same era, Prohibition.

During the decade and a half following the death of "General" Lee, a handful of lynchings—say nine or ten—garnered special attention. Nine of the victims were black and one was white; half of these affairs did not involve large mobs and might more correctly be classified as murder; and only three were sexual in character. The administration of Governor Cole Blease, who condoned and even encouraged such pursuits, saw a rise from 1911 to 1915 in what he liked to call "a ceremony"; yet the total number of lynchings in those years was virtually the same as under Heyward, who tried to suppress such activity. With the exception of those two administration periods, the annual average fell to about two deaths.[22]

The first of these lynchings occurred in Eutawville in July 1904. As a racially mixed party headed off for a favorite fishing hole, one white playfully pushed another out of a wagon. The latter thought black Keitt Bookhard was to blame and cursed him. Then Bookhard, in turn, threatened to spank his accuser. This led to the arrest of Bookhard, who subsequently was mysteriously abducted from the town lockup and killed. This extremely brutal murder followed by only three months a similar tragedy in Holly Hill and the killing late in June of a prisoner en route from Florence to Columbia for safekeeping.[23] The *State* (22 July) printed two columns of word-by-word testimony heard at the Bookhard inquest (a most unusual departure), and Governor Heyward made every possible effort to convict six men charged with his murder. Despite widespread denunciation, the community refused to cooperate, and the six easily were acquitted in May 1905.

The second affair took place even as the prosecution was collecting evidence concerning Bookhard's death. "It has come! A white man has been lynched and lynched for murder," cried the *State* (3 October 1904). "And it is simply one of the processes in the evolution of mob law." The victim, John Morrison, reportedly had murdered several other men before he shot and killed on the streets of Kershaw a young farmer who refused to loan him ten cents. The governor ordered the militia to the scene, but two hundred or so men stormed the jail just as the train bearing the Kershaw Guards pulled into town. Morrison, a truly bad egg, had few defenders. No one wanted the body, not even his widow, although she did request any money found in his pockets. Solicitor J. K. Henry told Heyward that everyone in the community thought "this the most orderly, quiet, and sober lynching that ever occurred—a real pious lynching, with the preachers in the background, almost audibly saying 'amen.'"[24] Pious or not, arrests and a trial followed but no convictions. In August 1905 the widow, who had declined to accept Morrison's body, sued Lancaster County for fifty thousand dollars. She was not, however, able to collect any money for his death.

Throughout these months the governor continued to press for action whenever a lynching was reported and occasionally removed local officials he thought negligent. Then in the summer of 1906 he came face-to-face with the crime. On 14 August, "Snowball" Davis entered a country store in the Mount Moriah section of Greenwood County. When Jennie Brooks, who was alone, asked what he wanted, "Snowball" replied he wanted her. In the ensuing struggle Jennie was badly cut, but her attacker fled when a customer approached. Word spread, a mob gathered, and the race was on to corner this day laborer, whose brother had been lynched for rape some years earlier. Nevertheless, "Snowball" managed to elude his pursuers for nearly forty-eight hours.

Heyward, realizing Davis probably would be killed if caught and fearing the presence of the militia might hasten his demise, decided to go to Greenwood. Meanwhile, a local newsman named Harry Watson heard that the black man was being taken to the Brooks home to be identified by Jennie. When Watson arrived there, fifty "dreadfully excited men" told him the governor was on his way. Watson thought this unlikely, but a short time later Heyward, whom Watson knew personally, drove up in a small wagon. Watson immediately introduced the governor to various mob leaders and the following day, in a letter to his wife, described what happened next:

> I was about two hundred yards from the actual spot and on this occasion I had an experience which no man in South Carolina has ever had. I saw the law defied, thrown to the four winds and a human life ended by a thousand guns with the Governor of the State, the highest officer of the State, standing by my side, with his hand on my shoulder. These people were respectful to the Governor, listened patiently to him, offered no insult, but went right ahead as if he were any other person, a dry goods clerk or a one[-] horse farmer had the same standing in this affair. There was no drinking, no ribald jests, everything was as orderly as such a thing should be. The psychology of it was to me the most interesting thing I have ever witnessed whenever I could separate myself from the realness of it.
>
> Governor Heyward tried to talk to Mrs. Brooks, the mother, step-mother rather, of the girl, but she was determined that Davis should die[,] then saying she would kill him herself if the crowd did not. He then sent me to Pet Brooks himself to see if it would be worth while to talk to him, but he was beyond reason[,] so Heyward did not go to him. There was a strong sentiment for burning and knowing the temper I pled with all I knew who were leading not to burn, to let the thing be over as quick as possible. I even

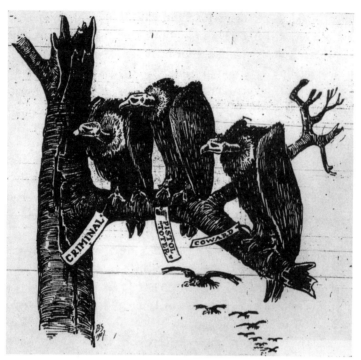

"Birds of a Feather Flock Together—Criminal, Pistol 'Toter,' and Coward," from the *State* (5 July 1907). Courtesy of South Caroliniana Library, University of South Carolina, Columbia

Drawing from front page of the *State* (17 August 1906) inspired by the Bob Davis lynching near Greenwood, which Governor Heyward personally tried to prevent. Courtesy of South Caroliniana Library, University of South Carolina, Columbia

pledged my personal word that I would take Heyward away as soon as he had finished speaking if they would prevent burning. Every one agreed and I tried to get Heyward away at once, tho I did not tell him the agreement until he persisted in going down the road[.] I went again in the crowd and had the assurance that if I kept him off there would be no burning and then I told him. He agreed to stay where he was and when the thing was over we came back to the buggy and I drove him back to town.[25]

Early in 1909 a highly respected black youth named Arthur Davis was beaten to death near the Florence County community of Hymanville with buggy whips and sticks studded with sharp thorns. Solicitor Walter H. Wells said it was murder, not lynching, and eventually three white men (L. S. Bingham, A. H. Fuller, and Dan Hines) were indicted. Wells seemed to have a strong case, and at the outset community sentiment apparently was on his side. Local residents were shocked by such brutality and alarmed when night riders posted signs threatening magistrates, jurors, and witnesses with the same fate as Davis's.

Testimony at the trial, which opened nine months later on 14 October 1909, revealed that Davis, who had worked for Bingham, allegedly mistreated a mule. Bingham had sworn out a warrant for the young man's arrest but then made a strange proposal to his mother. If she would whip her son and promise he would work for a year without pay (that is, slavery), then Bingham would forget the incident. She refused, and Arthur subsequently was dragged from his bed, stripped naked, beaten, and killed.

Some trial witnesses placed Bingham at the scene; others—including a black man originally arrested along with Bingham—altered considerably what they had said at the coroner's inquest. The jury deliberated for over two hours before acquitting all of the defendants. Angered by this outcome, Wells talked openly of perjury and intimidation, claiming he personally had been "shadowed" throughout the three-day trial. Although it is impossible to fathom the forces that caused local opinion to shift, it appears that failure to indict any blacks in connection with the death of Davis (three were arrested in January but not charged) made the jury's task especially difficult. In short, members of the panel were unwilling to convict *only* whites for the death of a black. Also, had a trial been held some months earlier when passions were high, rather than nine months after this murder/lynching, the verdict might have been different.[26]

Five more lynchings stretching from 1911 to 1920 merit attention for diverse reasons. In October 1911 a group of men led by "Citizen Josh" Ashley, barely literate but long a power in Anderson County politics, snatched a seventeen-year-old black youth named Willis Jackson from Greenville police and handed him over to a mob in Honea Path. Jackson, accused of raping a white girl, was summarily hoisted atop a telephone pole, left hanging head-down for several minutes as he begged for mercy, and then blasted with shotgun fire.[27]

This photograph is probably of Joe Brinson and Frank Whisonant, killed in Blacksburg in March 1912. Courtesy of Historical Center of York County

What made this affair unusual was the wild auto chase that preceded the capture of Davis and the presence of Ashley, a member of the state's lower House (except for two years) from 1892 to 1914. Ashley, a "wool-hat" farmer with a shock of red hair, had also figured prominently in an earlier Honea Path lynching in 1905. On that occasion drunken whites bullied an inoffensive black named Allen Pendleton, who fought back and, despite protests from white onlookers, paid the price.

The violent demise of two young men in Blacksburg late in March 1912 raised questions no community wished to confront, among them interracial homosexuality. Sometime during the evening of 27 March, a Wednesday, Frank Whisonant and Joe Brinson (both black) and Jim Childers—a white mill worker who had come to town looking for a job—met in a cemetery for a bit of fun. Childers later claimed he did not drink but was coerced into buying liquor from the pair; however, a letter in the Cole Blease Papers indicates he asked the blacks to procure whiskey for him.[28] In any case, the Childers version of what happened goes something like this: he was compelled to drink at gunpoint, robbed, undressed, and forced to perform what the newspapers called "a most horrible act" (oral sex). It is unclear just how this nocturnal gathering broke up, but the following morning Childers had his associates arraigned in mayor's court and convicted of selling liquor, carrying concealed weapons, robbery, assault, and so on. A short time later they were charged with sodomy and locked up in the city jail.

In the early morning hours of Friday, 29 March, unknown parties quietly took Whisonant and Brinson to a nearby blacksmith's shop and killed them. Technically they were hanged; however, press reports indicate both men died from broken necks under bizarre circumstances—the beams from which they were suspended being too low to cause such serious injuries. Who did it? Blease's friend Noah Webster Hardin, a local attorney, thought he knew: "My idea is that as Childers was a factory operative, the lynching was done by the operatives of the surrounding mills, trying to take care of their own class. I am sorry that it happened, but I had no idea, not even a suspicion that it was going to happen, or, under the circumstances, had I known it, would have had them sent to the County jail. Some of the d——d fools are already saying this is Bleaseism."[29]

Hardin protested a bit too much. The same day that he wrote these words to the governor, the semiweekly *Gaffney Ledger* featured this bold headline: "MAY BE LYNCHING AT BLACKSBURG." It also told readers that word of an "unmentionable crime" had reached the county seat by telephone the previous day; and, since a lynching probably would take place, "Gaffney men were urged to go over." (Gaffney was then a community of about 5,000; Blacksburg, located eight miles to the east, had a population of 1,368 in 1910.) Certainly if Gaffney residents had known a lynching was about to occur, anyone living in Blacksburg would have been equally well informed.

On 2 April 1912 this same newspaper presented more details. As word spread, it said, local blacks became resentful and sullen. So few showed up for work on Friday that some businesses were forced to close. Alarmed by this reaction and fearing a march on the town, community leaders appealed for help: "A riot call was turned in and all neighboring towns were asked to send aid. Train No. 30, which is a through train and does not stop at Gaffney, was flagged here and not less than 75 men, armed to the teeth with shot guns, pistols, knives and weapons of all kinds[,] boarded the train. At Cowpens a similar party had also been recruited and parties went from King's Mountain, N.C., and Gastonia, N.C. By midnight the streets of Blacksburg presented a warlike scene. With base of operations in the city hall, patrols were formed and the town watched from one end to the other by anxious men. Not a negro was seen and the place seemed to be deserted by the negroes." The editor heaped scorn on both the lynchers and white men who caroused with blacks: "The whole thing from beginning to end, was shamefully disgusting and disgraceful." He recommended, though with neither vehemence nor resolute conviction, that the guilty parties should be arrested and prosecuted.

Anthony Crawford. The lynching of this wealthy Abbeville farmer is fully documented in a sensational article by Roy Nash, published in the *Independent* (11 December 1916). Courtesy of Thomas Cooper Library, University of South Carolina, Columbia

Three days later, as Blacksburg continued to blame "outsiders," especially Gaffney residents, this gentleman rose to the defense of his neighbors. The lynchers, he noted, used the rope from the city well to hang the pair, so the perpetrators obviously were local folk, individuals familiar with the town. The jury at the inquest duly found that Whisonant and Brinson came to their deaths "at the hands of unknown parties to us," and Governor Blease requested only a perfunctory report from Cherokee County authorities.

In some respects this was a standard lynching: a lone individual apparently saw a group of men on horseback that night but paid them no heed; no one knew anything about the affair; blacks became angry once they learned of the deaths; and whites were quick to fasten blame on "outsiders." On the other hand, interracial camaraderie that degenerated into homosexual activity added a truly explosive element to the proceedings. It seems quite possible that, in the course of explaining what happened at the cemetery (perhaps to account for his inebriated, seminude state), Childers shifted all blame to Whisonant and Brinson. Then, as lawyer Hardin surmised, fellow mill workers came to his rescue.

The Abbeville lynching of Anthony Crawford in October 1916 resulted from a dispute over the price of cottonseed. Merchant W. D. Barksdale, stung by remarks made by Crawford, a successful, middle-aged farmer, engineered his arrest and then organized a whipping party to teach this "uppity" black man a lesson. Events unfolded somewhat like this.[30] It was Saturday, 21 October, and the county seat was crowded. As Crawford waited for two loads of cotton to be ginned, he approached Barksdale, who offered him eighty-five cents a bushel for seed, five cents less than the prevailing price. Crawford said he had a better offer and vowed he would not sell so damned low, whereupon Barksdale called him a liar. Angered, this well-to-do black replied he was worth as much as the merchant and had earned his money, not married it. This thrust led to more heated words, and Crawford was arrested and fined fifteen dollars for abusive language.[31]

During this lull, Barksdale sought out M. B. Cann, a local bully, and suggested that Crawford be taught a lesson. Cann agreed wholeheartedly, and he and his brothers rounded up a mob that confronted Crawford at the gin. As the men surged forward, Crawford grabbed a four-pound hammer and hit Cann in the head, a blow serious but not fatal. In the melee that ensued, Crawford was knocked unconscious, beaten, and stabbed, although a few whites tried to come to his aid. At this point Sheriff R. M. Burts—recently named to the post, inexperienced, and endowed with neither speed nor intellect—appeared and rescued Crawford, at least temporarily. Burts promised the Canns he would not move the prisoner from the jail until the fate of their brother was known, and he then summoned a doctor to attend to Crawford's wounds. In midafternoon word spread that the sheriff, despite his pledge, planned to sneak the black man out of town on the four o'clock train. The "good old boys," now thoroughly "liquored up," sprang into action and easily gained custody of Crawford since neither Burts nor the jailer offered any resistance. (Burts later said, rather lamely, that he did not anticipate trouble until after dark.) Some sources indicate Crawford was dead before the lynchers, led by the Canns, reached the fairground; but, for good measure, he was hanged from a pine tree and his body riddled with bullets. As a local resident commented to journalist Roy Nash a couple of weeks later, "I reckon the crowd wouldn't have been so bloodthirsty, only it's been three years since they had any fun with the niggers, and it seems as tho they jest have to have a lynching party every so often."[32]

Crawford's prosperity (he held 427 acres of prime cotton land worth twenty-five thousand dollars) and what some whites saw as an insolent, too-proud nature certainly played a role in this story. More important, with the aid of Roy Nash his death received national attention and sparked an exodus of blacks from the Abbeville area, a migration already stimulated to some degree by the lure of war jobs in the North. In the opinion of the *State* (23 October 1916), this lynching was sheer lunacy. Crawford had committed no crime other than being "a rich negro," the boll weevil was within a hundred miles of Abbeville, black labor was badly needed throughout all of South Carolina, and thus lynching was becoming *expensive*. "Shall the mob," the paper asked, "go into partnership with the boll weevil to drive labor from the farms and bankrupt this Southern country?" Those joining such groups, the *State* warned, "may lynch their pocketbooks."

The aftermath of the Crawford lynching, unique indeed, revealed conflict and indecision at the local level. On Monday, 23 October 1916, a mass meeting at the courthouse (the first of three) talked of killing still more Crawfords; however, cooler heads went directly to the dead man's offspring—twelve sons and four daughters—and convinced them to leave the state by 15 November. Yet this did not placate the rough element, which the *Abbeville Press and Banner* intimated were country folk from the northern part of the county. After leaving the meeting they systematically shut down all black businesses and told them to stay closed.

In succeeding weeks the local weekly, although hardly resolute, began to publish editorials from the *State* and the *News and Courier* critical of the lynchers. Early in November another courthouse meeting voted to uphold law and order and root out violence. Several factors help to explain this shift in public opinion. Governor Richard M. Manning, distressed by these events, blasted the local coroner for taking no testimony at the inquest concerning Crawford's death and pledged to use his powers to bring the lynchers to justice. Meanwhile, Will Cann and several of his friends were arrested for whipping blacks; and, perhaps most important of all, blacks were mounting an effective boycott of white business establishments in Abbeville. A third gathering at the courthouse on 13 November once more praised law and order, rescinded the ultimatum expelling the Crawfords, and talked vaguely of inviting federal intervention to deal with local lynchings, if necessary.[33]

A month later eight men were arrested for their role in the Crawford lynching and another eighteen for participating in a riot on the day he died. But the following February a county grand jury refused to indict them. This confusing tale of a community trying to come to grips with mob rule is complicated by obvious internal divisions. Followers of Cole Blease, who had just retired as governor, were not about to cooperate with friends of a progressive reformer such as Manning. Burts (the latter's appointee as sheriff) could count on no assistance from the mayor or chief of police, who thought he should have gotten the job, and so it went. And there were whites who, while not condoning lynching, were irked by Anthony Crawford's self-assured arrogance born of success or, like the editor of the *Press and Banner,* remained convinced that anyone lynched bore some responsibility for whatever violence was involved.

When W. T. Sims, a black preacher, was killed in western York County in August 1917, the *State* called it murder, not lynching, which turned out to be a more accurate assessment. Eventually six whites and five blacks were indicted for his death, which apparently resulted from a financial squabble within Sims's former church and rumors he harbored antiwhite sentiments. Once a York County resident, Sims left to occupy a pulpit in nearby Chester County but then returned for a "protracted" meeting, and trouble ensued. Those involved included merchant Meek McGill (Hickory Grove's postmaster) and Carson Lattimore, a policeman in the same community. In November five of the alleged lynchers—three whites and two blacks—came to trial. Although two of them had signed confessions (they testified they did so without knowing "just what it was"), the jury needed only ten minutes to acquit all five. In this case, however, the widow of Sims sued for damages and at length prevailed.

The final lynching of this era occurred in Laurens on a Saturday evening in April 1920 and was said to have been the first such death in that region in seven years. As patrons were leaving a picture show at the Opera House, a black youth caused a minor stir when he brushed against a white boy. A fight ensued, and Joe Steward (Stewart?), a twenty-five-year-old black teamster who had served in France during World War I, defended the young black. Steward and three whites suffered cuts in a back-alley brawl and subsequently sought medical attention at separate locations. While Steward was being treated, he was arrested for disorderly conduct, and at about 10:00 P.M. he was lodged in jail. A short time later police left the station house unattended, and a small mob (fewer than twenty-five men) entered, broke into Steward's cell, quietly hustled him out to the edge of town, and hanged him from a railroad bridge.

What made this lynching unique was the community reaction. Not only did the *Laurensville Herald* (9, 16 April) call for a thorough investigation, a mass meeting followed at which various ministers, the mayor, and individual citizens added their voices to the outcry. Regrettably, this did not lead to any convictions, but perhaps for the first time forces *on the spot* joined hands against lynching. Until the death of Joe Steward, the pattern was all too familiar: outside groups and the press in other regions criticized while local folks equivocated or even defended the deed.

One fact, often overlooked, is apparent throughout the years from 1880 to 1920. Any South Carolinian who joined a lynch mob risked the discomfort of jail, a trial, and a possible trip to the state penitentiary. Only the blacks who killed Manse Waldrop (1887) and Sam Howard (1898) and the white youths who murdered Rachel Thomas (1901) were convicted; nonetheless, many individuals of both races got into much more trouble than they had contemplated when passions led them to kill another human being.

Yet another truth should be obvious as well. The attitude of the general public was changing. Until 1900 most South Carolina editors were willing to condone lynching for the "unspeakable" crime and quick to condemn outrages committed outside of (but not in) their own communities. After that date these

"Not Guilty"

LYNCH-LAW MENTALITY

Herblock cartoon in the *Washington Post* (23 May 1947) inspired by the Willie Earle lynching verdict in Greenville. Courtesy of South Caroliniana Library, University of South Carolina, Columbia

barriers began to fall, lynchings anywhere and for whatever reasons were deplored, and the names of those present began to appear in print. Even non-lynchings began to assume some significance. In August 1913, for example, the sheriff of Spartanburg County vigorously defended a black drifter named Will Fair who was accused of raping a white woman. When a mob stormed the jail yard, three men were shot (none of them seriously), and W. J. White warned, "Gentlemen, I hate to do it, but, so help me God, I am going to kill the first man that enters that gate."[34] White and his deputies prevailed, and a month later a jury found Fair "not guilty." This unusual verdict came about because (a) the judge, stressing trial costs, applied pressure to six jurors who wanted to opt for a mistrial and (b) the alleged victim was known to be subject to delusions.

A key factor overshadowing and influencing developments such as these was a general exodus of blacks. This presumably eased racial tension somewhat and (as the *State* pointed out) could make the labor of those who remained both more valuable and more costly. According to some sources, the estimated net migration of blacks from South Carolina was 72,000 during the first decade of this century, 74,500 in the years from 1910 to 1920, and a whopping 204,300 during the 1920s, which adds up to 350,800.[35]

Addressing Columbia's Kosmos Club in 1930, former newsman August Kohn cited some of these trends as explanation for the decline of lynching. Kohn, who was present at several well-known affairs, said those in attendance were "generally speaking, substantial, hard-working white men—generally from the farms. Men who really thought they were doing the right thing at the time for the protection of their homes and families." He agreed that a black exodus increased the value of farm labor and, at the same time, made white employers more patient. In addition Kohn pointed to condemnation by the press, "present-day" education enjoyed by both races, better understanding of crimes that led to lynching, and a tendency of blacks to abjure "offensive politics." Nevertheless he viewed the lynchings that he witnessed during the turn-of-the-century decades as "inevitable."[36]

Only the famed Lowman lynching of 1926 marred a clean slate from 1924 to 1930. In that shocking turn of events, three members of one family being tried for assault and murder suddenly were seized and put to death. Kohn stressed both the horror of that Aiken tragedy and the absence of such deaths in the state. Then the NAACP recorded six South Carolina lynchings in the early 1930s, one in 1941, another in 1946, and a final death (Willie Earle) near Greenville in 1947. Four years later South Carolina lawmakers created a strange animal known as a "second-degree" lynching.[37] A "first-degree" lynching, as before, was a homicide and was to be dealt with accordingly, but this new refinement in mayhem referred to violence by a mob (two or more individuals acting illegally) upon the body of another person that did not cause death. In February 1992, when two Sumter policemen were attacked by unidentified blacks, hundreds of Midlands residents were startled to learn that a "lynching" had taken place. It has been a long road indeed from Regulators and whitecapping to a time when those who have been "lynched" can appear in a court of law and point an accusing finger at the "mob" that attacked them.

5

THE CHARLESTON TRIANGLE

Editor, Governess, Doctor

Although dueling ceased in South Carolina in 1880 and lynching was on the wane forty years later, the same cannot be said of murder. Ironically, one of the most celebrated homicide victims of those decades was a man who crusaded vigorously (and successfully) against the code duello and advocated registration of handguns and prohibition of concealed weapons. Francis Warrington Dawson actually was knighted by the Catholic Church for his outspoken stand against dueling, but his war on weapons had little effect and his views on lynching are far from clear. In death he was portrayed in heroic, saintlike terms, as a resolute fighter for justice, and yet his *News and Courier* of the 1880s certainly did not speak loudly against lynching (even advocating it at times)—although, admittedly, that evil was not so widespread in that decade as it became in subsequent years.

Unlike most South Carolina homicides, this tale features a pretty young face and a strong hint of sex. In fact, Dr. Thomas Ballard McDow made no secret of his intentions to bed Hélène Marie Burdayron, the twenty-two-year-old governess of his famous neighbor. On the other hand, Dawson, editor of the *Charleston News and Courier,* was cast in death as an upright, proper Victorian, lord and master of his household, the complete gentleman dedicated to protecting the virtue of those living under his roof. Nevertheless his tragic demise at the hands of McDow caused some to question the true nature of Dawson's chivalry. Was he interested primarily in this young lady's well-being or did he perhaps harbor thoughts not too different from those of the man who murdered him? "There are uncharitable ones," the *New York World* observed during the trial that followed, "who can see naught in Capt. Dawson's championship of the girl save that which should not have been."[1]

Whatever his intentions, Dawson certainly could boast of a romantic past. Born Austin John Reeks in London in 1840, he was the eldest son in a proud Catholic family.[2] Both his father and grandfather were educated in France, and it was assumed that young Reeks would follow in their footsteps. But ill-advised investment wiped out the family fortune in the 1840s, and only an unforeseen development revived these plans when his mother's sister, Mrs. William A. Dawson, received a handsome compensation after her officer husband was killed in the Sepoy Mutiny (1857). With her blessing, Reeks embarked in the company of a tutor on a "gentleman's tour" of the Continent; however, while there, he learned of his aunt's sudden death and diversion of the funds to other heirs.

Francis W. Dawson, from *Frank Leslie's Illustrated Newspaper* (16 October 1880). Courtesy of Thomas Cooper Library, University of South Carolina, Columbia

Facing an uncertain future, this eighteen-year-old youth considered a musical career (he had a fine tenor voice) and also wrote a few plays. Then, in 1861, enamored with the Confederate cause, Reeks announced plans to go to America and fight for the South. His father protested he might be captured on the high seas and hanged as a pirate. These differences led to heated argument and a decision by Reeks to change his name. The result was a fanciful creation that honored his would-be benefactor (Captain William Dawson), his patron saint (Francis of Assisi), and relatives by the name of Warren (transformed into "Warrington").

Early in 1862 Francis Warrington Dawson enlisted in the Confederate navy and sailed from Southampton aboard the steamer *Nashville*. Although he soon won a promotion, Dawson found nautical life boring, and in June of that same year he joined General A. P. Hill's forces in Virginia. Rising from private to captain, he saw considerable action, was wounded, and was held briefly as a prisoner. For this young man, the Virginia campaigns (1862–65) were all one could hope for, except victory. He won glory on the battlefield, and his good looks and aristocratic bearing made him a familiar figure in Richmond drawing rooms.

With peace Dawson remained in the former capital of the Confederacy, working on several newspapers and helping operate an express company. Then in November 1866 he joined the staff of Charleston's struggling old *Mercury*. The following year this young newsman teamed up with Bartholomew R. Riordan, a Virginia acquaintance, to buy the ailing *Charleston News*. Also in 1867 he married a local girl, Virginia Fourgeaud, who died of consumption five years later. Six months after her death, in April 1873, Dawson and Riordan bought the *Charleston Courier* for a mere seventy-one hundred dollars to form the *News and Courier*. And in January 1874 Dawson took as his bride a petite, Louisiana-born lady, Sarah Morgan. They would produce three children: Ethel (born November 1874), Francis Warrington Jr. (September 1878), and Philip (who died in 1882 at the age of six months).

By the 1880s Dawson was unquestionably a commanding figure in the daily life of his adopted state. He was deeply involved in Democratic Party politics but held no elective office, preferring instead to be a power broker in his role as county, state, and national committeeman. Dawson gained this preeminence and (of vital importance) access to patronage by virtue of his editorial mantle and an ability to wheel and deal, not with the most powerful men in the state, but with those thought to be on the way up. As such he was cozy with Republican Daniel Henry Chamberlain in the early 1870s and Ben Tillman in the mid-1880s. He consistently displayed proper deference for the Bourbon old guard led by Wade Hampton, although he sensed that the general disliked him.[3] Maneuvering of this sort did not foster universal esteem, but it did give Francis Warrington Dawson ties to various little courthouse cliques scattered throughout South Carolina, so many of them that E. Culpepper Clark entitled a chapter in his life of Dawson "Lord of the Rings."

However, in the late 1880s cracks began to appear in this carefully contrived realm. As Ben Tillman's agrarian campaign was picking up steam across the state, Dawson's local enemies in February 1888 launched a rival daily, the *World*. For the first time in two decades, because of financial reverses, Dawson had to cut back on services to readers, rather than expand them. Early in 1889 he visited New York City in a vain effort to negotiate a loan. While there, he suffered yet another rebuff when he tried to purchase a life insurance policy. The strain of work and lack of exercise had taken their toll on his two-hundred-pound frame, and he was able to secure only limited coverage. Thus, as Dawson, still an imposing, carefully tailored figure, approached his forty-ninth birthday (which he would not celebrate), his world was less placid than usual. He was beset by financial and health concerns, short-tempered with associates at the *News and Courier*, and uncomprehending when several employees quit to join the *World*. And then there was the matter of the governess.

News and Courier staff in 1886. First row (left to right): Roswell T. Logan, John L. Weber, James Armstrong, Carlyle McKinley, Matthew F. Tighe; (back row) R. M. Solomons, John A. Moroso, R. A. Smith, Francis W. Dawson, J. C. Hemphill, Yates Snowden, D. L. Selke. Courtesy of South Caroliniana Library, University of South Carolina, Columbia

Hélène Marie, a native of Geneva who usually went by the name Marie, joined his household in 1887, having accompanied Mrs. Dawson from Europe, where the children attended school for nearly two years. She certainly was attractive, attentive to the needs of Ethel and Francis Jr., and had given no cause for concern—until recently. Early in March 1889 Dawson received an anonymous tip that Marie had been seen in "disreputable" company. Since he was unaware that she had any acquaintances other than his family, he asked the police to investigate the matter.[4] On Tuesday, 12 March, Chief of Police Joseph Golden came to Dawson's office at the *News and Courier* and informed him that a detective had followed Marie on Monday as she rode about town on a streetcar with Dr. Thomas Ballard McDow.

Dr. McDow, who lived but a few doors from the Dawsons' Bull Street home, was a slight, neat-appearing gentleman. Born in Camden in 1853, he belonged to a Lancaster County family that produced more than its share of physicians in the late nineteenth century. His father, Dr. Robert S. McDow, moved to Tennessee sometime after his son's birth, and young Thomas graduated with first honors from that state's Cumberland University in 1874. After teaching school for a year, McDow came to upper South Carolina and subsequently enrolled in South Carolina Medical College in Charleston.

In March 1879 he was the star of a "brilliant commencement celebration" at the Academy of Music and valedictorian of a class that included twenty-three physicians and two pharmacists. McDow urged his friends, as they went forth into the world, to think independently and ever keep as their watchword "honest, patient, and fearless inquiry." His address, which concluded with various classic allusions and admonition to honor one's alma mater, was, according to the *News and Courier* (5 March), delivered with "easy and graceful style" and "applauded enthusiastically throughout." This triumph won young McDow a temporary appointment to the staff of the city hospital. At the conclusion of his tenure he opened an office in his home at 9 Pitt Street, later moving to 59 Beaufain Street and then to 75 Rutledge Avenue. Only two houses separated this residence from that of Dawson (43 Bull Street), located near the southwest corner of Bull and Rutledge; in fact, they virtually shared a common backyard.[5]

There, much like his editor neighbor, Thomas McDow lived a comfortable Victorian existence. His household included his wife, a five-year-old daughter, at least two servants, and, at times, his father-in-law. Mrs. McDow, the former Katherine Louise Ahrens, was born in New Jersey in 1859. Known as Kate, she was the daughter of a wealthy retired grocer, C. D. Ahrens. They were married at about the time McDow graduated from medical school and were parents of two other children who died in infancy.

After 12 March 1889 McDow would be assaulted with rumor and innuendo, especially in the columns of the *News and Courier.* Unnamed sources reported he had trouble gaining admission to the South Carolina Medical Society, that Ahrens opposed his daughter's marriage, that he was an abortionist and a drug addict, and that he had been involved in a shooting incident in Tennessee, among other accusations. The only such tale with substance, as trial testimony revealed, was that of a less than perfect union. McDow apparently married Kate Ahrens for her money and conceded this fact during his brief infatuation with Marie. The young governess, not swayed by this revelation, replied his certainly was not the only less than ideal marriage in the city of Charleston. As for the medical society, McDow was elected to membership in February 1889 but, for obvious reasons, did not attend the annual meeting two months later, nor was his name listed among those joining the group at that time.

The doctor first became aware of Marie when called to minister to a sick child belonging to the Dawsons' cook. According to a pretrial statement made by Marie, she was told that McDow asked about her and remarked in a joking manner, "If he had occasion to choose another wife he would like to have me as such." This ill-fated relationship was launched in earnest on 1 February 1889, when McDow began chatting with Marie on a street near where they lived.

During succeeding weeks they met almost daily, McDow talking incessantly about his unhappy home life, divorce, and plans to run away with Marie to France. The starry-eyed doctor visited the Dawson home at least three times while the editor and his family were away, and the pair exchanged one or two insignificant gifts. All available evidence indicates McDow was smitten by Marie's undeniable charms and that she—twenty-two, bored, and perhaps lonely for companionship—was flattered by this sudden attention. We will never know how serious this budding affair really was. Maybe McDow never intended to leave his wife, and perhaps Marie was unwilling to consider marriage even if he did. But in the eyes of a third party this was indeed a grave turn of events.

When Chief of Police Golden met with Dawson, he gave him two reports supplied by detective John P. Gunn. Dawson read them carefully and then said he would attend to the matter on his way home to dinner. Something in the editor's demeanor evidently disturbed Golden, for he stated at the inquest following the murder that he cautioned Dawson not to do anything rash and immediately assigned a special policeman to the area near McDow's home. Under oath he said S. G. Gordon was detailed to the Rutledge Avenue neighborhood because of complaints concerning a black flasher, a story many found difficult to accept since such unseemly activity was unknown in that section of the city.

Dawson left the offices of the *News and Courier* at about 3:30 on the afternoon of 12 March, boarded a streetcar that ran down Broad Street and up Rutledge, and chatted with several friends en route to his home. But instead of going there directly, after alighting at the corner of Bull and Rutledge, he approached the McDow residence, a handsome, three-story structure with long piazzas overlooking a large garden. He rang the doorbell and was greeted by Dr. Thomas B. McDow, whose office was on the first floor adjacent to the street.[6]

We have, of course, only the doctor's version of what occurred after Dawson entered his home. When McDow appeared at police headquarters some three hours later, he at first refused to talk to reporters but finally stated with disarming frankness, "Here it is in a nutshell: Capt[.] Dawson entered my office, used abusive language, and knocked me down with a cane. I got up and he was about to strike me again when I shot him."[7] As McDow said, "in a nutshell" that appears to have been what happened. The doctor freely admitted that he shot and killed the editor. Less clear are the circumstances surrounding their quarrel and the activities of Chief of Police Golden and Patrolman Gordon on that fateful afternoon. It should be noted that, on the way to the police station, McDow was permitted to stop at the home of former governor A. G. Magrath and secure his legal services.

Amid an outpouring of official grief and rumors of an abortive attempt to round up a lynch mob, an inquest was held on 14 March at the coroner's office in Charleston's Fireproof Building. As expected, the *News and Courier* kept up its drumbeat of bias—the prisoner had "the look of a hunted man," there were rumors that a mulatto in McDow's employ had been harassing and insulting young white women in the neighborhood, and so on. The testimony, much of which would be repeated at the June trial, revealed that several people were aware of unusual sounds emanating from the office of Dr. McDow that day. They included a passerby, a groundnut (peanut) vendor, and a coachman, as well as those residing at 75 Rutledge Avenue.

George W. Harper, seated on the box of his carriage across the street from the McDow home, watched as Dawson entered. Within moments he heard loud talk, pistol fire, groans, and someone say, "You would take my life and now I have taken yours!" The basement windows then were closed, just as the peanut lady tried to peer in. This old woman—she never was located, nor was the man who was walking past—then rushed across the street toward Harper crying, "Great God, somebody is murdered in there!"

About five minutes later McDow appeared briefly on the second-floor piazza and looked hurriedly up and down the street. Then Harper saw Moses Johnson (the butler-coachman) hitch up a carriage and drive off with Mrs. McDow and daughter Gladys. At about the same time, Harper's party emerged and got into his carriage. As he passed Patrolman Gordon, Harper told him there was "some murdering going on down there." Gordon, he recalled, went *directly* to 75 Rutledge Avenue. The policeman knocked, and McDow opened the door and assured him nothing was amiss. Gordon also talked to the cook (Emma Drayton) at the gate. When asked if there was trouble, she replied it was none of her business. For good measure Emma vowed she knew nothing about a pistol shot.[8]

Still uneasy, Gordon summoned Chief Golden, and McDow once more came to the door and told the chief his household was in good order. While the two lawmen were discussing the situation, McDow emerged and passed them on his way to a shop at the northwest corner of Bull and Rutledge. They noted he looked a bit rumpled and his coat was dusty, but the chief remarked to Gordon that the ruckus, if there was one, might be "a family affair." Nevertheless, within the next hour or so he contacted the *News and Courier* and Dawson's home. Alarmed when he could not locate the editor, he went to the mayor to get an order to search McDow's office. However, before he could do so, the doctor was on his way to the station house.

Since McDow would plead not guilty for reasons of self-defense and thus did not testify at the inquest, some aspects of the murder remained unclear until the trial three months later. The *News and Courier* stated that McDow tried to bury Dawson's body under a basement stairway, which was true, but a report that the editor lingered for up to three-quarters of an hour after the fatal volley was not. Mrs. McDow and her daughter, it turned out, went to the Waverly House on Broad Street, where her father had taken rooms in December 1888. The day after the inquest, McDow's father arrived from Lancaster, visited his son, and then called on C. D. Ahrens and his daughter-in-law. McDow, the *News and Courier* noted, was not eating prison fare; instead, his meals were being prepared by Mr. August Bequest's saloon and restaurant at 226 King Street. In addition his quarters were carpeted and a table, chair, writing materials, and books had been placed at his disposal, as well as a trunk full of clothes. To keep out the curious, only close friends were being admitted. Servant Moses Johnson, on the other hand, thought to have been involved in the murder, was being treated as a common prisoner.

After mid-March, sensational as it was, the affair tended to become old news. Nevertheless people were beginning to take sides. Some saw McDow as "the little man," which he was physically, battling powerful interests embodied by editor Dawson, who, after all, invaded the doctor's home. Others wondered how McDow, seemingly a quiet, respectable citizen living virtually next door to Dawson in an upperclass neighborhood, became "disreputable" almost overnight. Still others recalled the rather exotic past of the deceased—his Catholic faith, foreign birth, change of name, and association with Republicans during the dark days of Reconstruction. But the journalistic fraternity and most establishment figures quickly came to the defense of their martyred friend. Atlanta's Henry Grady, for one, heaped scorn upon McDow. If the doctor actually was caned, where were the bruises and why did he wait three hours to report the crime?

Nevertheless, on the eve of his trial for murder, Thomas McDow scored one minor triumph: reelection as surgeon of Charleston's Lafayette Artillery (founded in 1812). When the *World* casually announced this fact on 21 June, several South Carolina newspapers, including the *Greenville News,* cried fraud. This could not be true. But a few days later the *World* defended the report and produced a signed statement from one of the group's officers. The secretary said McDow held a commission from the governor and had served in that capacity for three years, and members saw no reason "to go back on him."

The trial, which took place during the last week of June (Monday, the twenty-fourth, through Saturday, the twenty ninth), attracted considerable attention, even drawing out-of-town reporters from as far away as New York City. The presiding judge was J. B. Kershaw, with William St. Julien Jervey, solicitor of the First Circuit, and the firm of Smith and Mitchell (H. A. M. Smith and Julian Mitchell) representing the state and A. J. Magrath and Asher D. Cohen defending McDow. The male jury, assembled following numerous challenges, consisted of seven blacks and five whites. According to the *World,* all of the spectators—at least on opening day—also were male.

The first major witnesses (the state said at the outset it planned to call thirty-two individuals) were Dr. Middleton Michel, who performed the autopsy, and coroner John P. DeVeaux. With the aid of an embalmed human torso, Michel tried to demonstrate the course of the bullet. But he failed to find an exit wound because of the tendency of pistol balls, he claimed, to wander or be deflected after entry, a statement that later would assume much importance. Michel did, however, furnish enough testimony to spark sharp debate over whether Dawson was shot in the back, side, or front. The coroner told how the body was found in McDow's office and described in detail the doctor's bungled attempt to bury it in a closet a few feet away.

The second day featured a moment of high drama with the appearance of Marie Burdayron as a witness for the state. Stepping into the witness box at noon, she was dressed in a neat black gown with white lace at the sleeves. She also wore a small hat trimmed with black ribbons that framed an oval face and lustrous dark eyes. After a brief examination by H. A. M. Smith, she matched wits for two hours with Magrath, a cagey old devil, and emerged unscathed. Even the *News and Courier* (26 June) conceded this young lady "displayed a wonderful degree of coolness and attractive simplicity in giving her testimony." In sum, Marie was no tittering, love-struck teenager. Caught up in an adult situation, she performed accordingly.

On one occasion, while struggling with a question, she blurted out, "You think it easy to explain one's self in a strange language. You speak French?"

"No, mademoiselle," Magrath replied gallantly, "if I attempted that I am afraid you would twist me around your finger."

When the former governor asked if McDow ever kissed her, she conceded he had.

"How many times?"

"Two times—two times too much."

"Only twice?"

"Yes, only two times. You want some more?"

During extensive cross-examination, Magrath established that McDow had given her a gold watch with her initials on it and bits of romantic poetry. Also, she testified that while viewing family photos, he seized a likeness of her and refused to return it. Magrath probed each of these matters without much success. Then he turned to a provocative book that Marie had loaned to her admirer, *'Twixt Love and Law* by Annie Jenness Miller. A hot number in 1889, it told the tale of a single woman in love with a married man. Magrath asked if she did not realize the similarity to her own situation. "No," replied Marie, "in the book an unmarried woman loves a married man. It is not the case with me. I love not him."

The pretty governess did not defend her actions; instead, she merely recounted what had happened in a simple, matter-of-fact manner, noting that meetings with McDow often occurred in connection with her duties, taking the children to school or going to pick them up. It appears that the doctor's tale of personal woe perhaps aroused sympathy rather than passion; in any case, few young women without friends in a strange city would have been able to ignore such engaging flattery. Thomas McDow was, after all, well educated and had good manners and proper social graces; but, as Marie constantly stressed in her replies to Magrath, he was "a married man." Yet, the truth was, and the defense underscored this point, her testimony had little if anything to do with the actual crime.

As Marie Burdayron left the witness box, she was escorted through the throng of spectators by Smith. According to the *New York World*, "The crowd parted and started. Men's hearts went with her. There was a narrow way where she was compelled to pass McDow. He moved his chair to let her go by and hung his head, and two thousand pair of eyes were on them both."[9]

Soon after Marie departed, the state rested its case, and the second day of the trial came to a close. The defense opened the following day (Wednesday) with George Washington Harper, the driver who viewed events of 12 March from across the street. Harper—"a sprightly-looking young fellow, very black but elegantly and gorgeously arrayed"—almost stole the show from McDow. His longtail frock coat, lace shirt bosom, rainbow-colored necktie, and collection of gold pins presented a startling vision, but his testimony added little to what he had said at the March inquest.

He was followed by McDow, who for the first time had an opportunity to disclose intimate details of what happened on the day he killed Dawson. He knew who his neighbor was, he said, but never had spoken to him. In what McDow characterized as a "domineering and aggressive manner," Dawson had announced he had just been informed of McDow's "ungentlemanly conduct towards one of my servants. I give you to understand, sir," he continued, "she is under my protection and if you speak to her again I will publish you in the papers." Startled by this unexpected blast, the young doctor had replied he would hold the editor personally responsible for any such action and ordered him to leave. Dawson, he said, had then struck him in the head with a cane and with his left arm, knocking him to a sitting position on a lounge. While there, he received yet another blow to his left side. Fearing for his life, McDow had reached into his pocket for a pistol ("I ordinarily carry it") and fired without aiming, to protect himself from still more blows. This was, McDow insisted, the first time he had ever used the weapon, but he conceded he looked upon it as a necessity in connection with his profession.

McDow was horrified by what had happened, and his initial reaction had been to resuscitate his assailant, but he quickly realized the wound was fatal. The next impulse had been to hide all evidence of the encounter, including the body. (It should be noted that Mrs. McDow had heard the shot and sent the coachman to investigate, and his report had led to her sudden departure in the family carriage.) McDow first threw Dawson's hat and cane into a backyard privy, where they were later found, and then dragged the body to a nearby closet. His plan, which required removal of some earth, was to hide the remains under rough floorboards. However, the excavation had proved too small for such a large frame, and McDow had concluded this scheme would not work. But when he tried to remove Dawson, wedged as he was between two joists, he encountered problems. This had led to the trip to the corner store for candles to provide light in the dark closet.

During this brief outing, which occurred shortly after four o'clock, he had met his neighbor Edward Lafitte, who lived in the house just north of 75 Rutledge, as well as Patrolman Gordon and Chief Golden. All of them later commented on McDow's dusty coat and crushed hat. While out, McDow rang the bell at 43 Bull Street hoping Marie would answer and perhaps agree to break the news to her mistress. But Isaac Heyward, the Dawsons' butler-coachman, opened the door, said Marie had taken the children to dancing class and, despite McDow's pleas, refused to tell him where it was being held. Returning home, the doctor had dragged Dawson's body back into his office and, after walking about the empty house for a time and resting a bit, concluded he must surrender to the police.

The prosecution failed to weaken this story, although the accused was forced to tell once more how he was attacked, made an effort to defend himself, tried to bury Dawson's body, and then took it back to his office and cleaned it up as much as possible before going to the police station. Judge Kershaw brushed aside any mention of McDow's problems with the state medical society and a rumored shooting in Tennessee. Even if the doctor had previously killed someone, so what? "I do not see," said his honor, "that the fact that he had difficulty elsewhere, or that he killed a man elsewhere, would go to discredit him. On the contrary, it might elevate him depending upon the circumstances that surrounded him at the time."[10]

McDow was followed to the stand by Dr. John Forrest, whose task was to describe the defendant's head injuries (as of 13 March when he examined him) and counter Dr. Michel's testimony concerning the course of the bullet. The import of this matter was, of course, whether Dawson had been shot in the back as the prosecution claimed.[11]

The first witness on Thursday was yet another physician, who was watched intently by McDow and McDow's father, eighteen-year-old brother, and father-in-law. Dr. R. A. Kinlock, professor of clinical surgery at the medical college and a man with forty years' experience, was summoned by the state to counter opinions expressed by Forrest. Under cross-examination Kinlock conceded Michel, during the autopsy, should have traced the bullet to its final resting place and suggested that his views concerning the deflection of such projectiles within a human body might be dated. Sensing an opening, Cohen recalled Michel and, after a bland exchange, said in a casual manner, "Well, doctor, would you have any respect for the opinion of a man who stated that a ball could not be deflected from a straight course by anything but a hard, bony substance?" Spectators, remembering Kinlock's testimony, buzzed with excitement, so much so that the question had to be repeated. Michel, who was absent when Kinlock testified, forged ahead: "I would say that such a man had no knowledge of physiology, anatomy, surgery, or medical science." The rest of his words were lost in a roar of laughter as Cohen took his seat, certain he had punctured the testimony of a crucial spokesman for the prosecution.

Another witness potentially damaging to McDow's cause appeared briefly between Kinlock and Michel. Detective John Hogan, who rode with the defendant from the police station to the jail on the evening of 12 March, quoted him as saying, "I know where to shoot to kill. I learned that in my profession. I shot to kill, and would shoot again any man who attempted to cane me." However, this bold assertion, which seemed somewhat contrived, came late in the proceedings and soon was overwhelmed by the drama and laughter that ensued. Most observers already had concluded that Thomas McDow was in a confused mental state on the evening of 12 March, and understandably so.

On Thursday afternoon Jervey began his summation of the testimony, followed on Friday by Cohen and Magrath for the defense. A fourth attorney, Major Julian Mitchell, spoke for the prosecution on Saturday morning, and shortly after noon the jury, which had been sequestered for two nights, received the case of *South Carolina v. McDow.*

By far the most effective arguments were posed by Asher Cohen, and it is possible to sketch, through his words, what probably happened that March day in 1889. Chief of Police Golden, disturbed by the agitated state of Dawson after he received the reports concerning Marie's activities, stationed a policeman near McDow's home. Golden thus anticipated trouble and went to the scene when summoned by Patrolman Gordon. Yet, certain Dawson would prevail in any confrontation with a smaller adversary, he was unable to grasp the fact that things might turn out differently, even when he encountered McDow in a disheveled condition. The state, Cohen stressed, refused to call Golden to the stand even though he testified at the coroner's inquest in March. Why?

Another major point was the prosecution's handling of dapper George Washington Harper. The driver heard and saw much that afternoon, was obviously a key witness, and yet he appeared for the defense, not the state, which declined to call him. And once he appeared, the prosecution did little to shake his story. Cohen asked rhetorically if Dawson thought Marie's conduct offensive why he did not simply discharge her? And if he actually was protecting her, *why* would he consider publishing her indiscretions before the whole world?

Most telling of all were the words used by Cohen to describe the manner in which Francis Warrington Dawson chose to shelter his pretty young governess from harm: "The protection that was extended to her was the protection that the wolf extends to the lamb. That is a matter that never should have been brought into this court." But Cohen undoubtedly was delighted that it had been, for this was the vision twelve men carried with them as they gathered behind closed doors.

Twenty minutes into their deliberations the jurors took a vote and agreed unanimously to acquit McDow. At the time and in decades since, many have interpreted this as a racially motivated decision, pointing specifically to an editorial Dawson wrote shortly before his death. However, this credits some of these jurors with much longer memories than they probably possessed and fails to account for the views of the five white men on the panel.

Soon after deciding McDow's fate, the twelve jurors refused an offer of lunch and stayed closeted only because Judge Kershaw was nowhere to be found. Shortly before three o'clock he returned, and the verdict was announced to the resounding cheers of about a thousand curious spectators. Kershaw tried to quell this outburst and threatened to arrest those responsible but, as is common practice in such situations, did not do so.

The first person to congratulate McDow was his father-in-law, followed by his father, his brother, his attorneys, and scores of friends. Outside the courthouse the doctor was greeted with rebel yells and more cheering by both blacks and whites as he climbed into a carriage and headed for home.

That evening an *Augusta Chronicle* reporter who called at 75 Rutledge Avenue found the house filled with well-wishers—relatives, friends, and patients. Mc-Dow's little daughter played about the room as the newsman tried to get her father to discuss the verdict. No, at Asher Cohen's direction he would not do so. Yes, he planned to stay in Charleston, for he had a good practice and obviously many friends. "It seems a sarcasm of fate," this reporter observed, "that the man who did all to abolish the code duello, the man who caused the law against carrying concealed weapons, should be shot by a man who says he was in the habit of carrying a pistol ever since he entered the profession."[12]

As this newsman was discovering, this tale of a triangular relationship was no morality play and refused to end the way it should. In months and years that followed, Dawson's widow became increasingly bitter, lashing out at the pretensions and hypocrisy of southern life and berating her husband's partner for taking advantage of her helpless condition. She even denounced him to stockholders, sought the aid of other South Carolina editors in her war with the *News and Courier,* and became so outspoken that her attorney, H. A. M. Smith, warned her to desist or he would withdraw his services. However, after daughter Ethel married in 1898 and began a comfortable suburban existence in northern New

Jersey, Sarah moved to Paris to live with her journalist son and there resumed her own writing career in a limited fashion. There she died in May 1909.

Two boxes of materials from Smith's law firm, now at the South Carolina Historical Society in Charleston and known as the Mitchell-Smith Papers, provide intimate details of the 1889 tragedy and the last two decades of Sarah's life. It is patently clear that, in the weeks following the murder, the widow Dawson overwhelmed Smith with both information and advice about how to proceed. In a brief note written on black-bordered stationery and dated simply "Tuesday night," she described how McDow had been seen signaling to Hélène—as she was called within the Dawson household. Hélène, she reported, "was not prepared for this demonstration, and was, and is, badly frightened by this audacity. Ethel has just been in to tell me that some one is whistling at her from his balcony. I went out, walking slowly in a white wrapper, and saw a man's form distinctly. I regret to add that he whistled the same warning note to me. It is now nine, the first act was just after sun-set. Perhaps old Ahrens could be informed, and so avert the tragedy which is drawing near."

This message raises numerous questions. McDow, who, it might be noted, allegedly whistled at *all* of the white women in the household, not just Marie, could not have done so after the evening of 11 March, the night before the murder. He was securely behind bars after that date. Sarah warned Smith of "the tragedy which is drawing near," ominous words indeed. Yet this note is written on black-bordered stationery that presumably was not used until *after* Dawson was killed. Even if the "in mourning" paper relates to another family death that occurred earlier, it is most difficult to see why Sarah thought mere whistling would lead to "tragedy." The logical conclusion is that these words were written amid deep grief and understandable confusion *after* Dawson's death.

Intriguing tidbits can be found in other notes written during these weeks. In one (no date) the widow Dawson expressed concern about the activities of Reverend Edward T. Horn, pastor of St. John's Lutheran Church. Horn was, she asserted, at the McDow home on the evening of the murder.[13] The following day, according to this account, he tried to see Dawson's body and expressed interest in securing a death mask. This is the question posed to Smith: should he be interviewed? "Preachers and policemen," she adds, "will stand close watching."

Another note, dated "Sunday," informed the lawyer that he was about to receive a section of a death mask she had obtained. Sarah cautioned it was still damp and must remain so or it would crumble. Harking back to folklore belief that a murder victim's eye records a final vision of his assailant, she implored Smith to look closely at the corner of the eye: "it may give you some impression of the instrument used. I do pray to God some revelation may come."

On yet another occasion she stressed that Hélène's position was not as governess but "precisely that of an honorable French servant." Jervey, she warned, should not let her pose in court as a governess. If she simply discarded her apron and cap, then everyone would understand her true role: "Her bare head, however, will be a safe compromise." In addition the decision of driver Isaac Heyward to leave her employ caused special anguish. Sarah told Smith she was certain he was being bribed to do so in order that some "tool of the enemy" could be placed within her household.

But the most revealing of these pretrial notes, dated 24 May, concerned the chief of police. Sarah wrote that she summoned Golden to tell him of "a gross insult offered to my sister and myself up the road that evening—Wednesday." (This apparently referred to the mysterious neighborhood flasher.)

> Golden *accidentally* told me "a large sum of money—a *good deal*—will be put up to see McDow through." How much more does he know and will he point out the people, or deny the statement? I believe Golden believes he is devoted to our cause. But if pressed, he will hurt us. For he insists that Capt. Dawson struck that man, and says it cannot be denied after the injury to the man's head and the dent in his hat! I asked him if he also believed Captain Dawson had deposited in that horizontal dent the white wash and cobwebs he had just said he noticed there. He is prepared to state that Capt. Dawson was very angry when he read the report, "and that he would be sorry to have to repeat what Capt. Dawson said about the matter." I remarked that there were a number of gentlemen who could testify that he was quite cheerful before he saw McDow. Golden speaks with the kindest feeling, and with the best intentions. But I thought you should know that his zeal might lead him into serious errors.

After mid-1889 Sarah's letters talk incessantly of finances, impending poverty, and mistreatment at the hands of those managing the fortunes of the *News and Courier*. She complained to Smith when her son's tuition bill was sent to her and not to the paper, as well as when asked to pay for an ad she had placed in its columns. Within a year or so a dispute over an old debt so alienated her brother that he would communicate with her only through lawyers, and by 1892 she was unable to hire maids. As her daughter commented to Smith, "The negroes have boycotted us & we cannot get a servant."

The truth is, Francis Warrington Dawson, though experiencing lean times in 1889, was hardly a poor man at the time of his death. He held *News and Courier* shares and bonds with a face value of $63,500, which represented about one-half of his total assets. Two decades later these holdings were virtually intact and thus passed on to the two children. Their mother had, however, sold a summer place on Sullivan's Island and the Bull Street mansion, which Ethel's husband, Herbert Barry, purchased as an investment in 1905. (Following several abortive offers, Sarah commented bitterly that the house never could be sold so long as it was associated with the Dawson name.)

There is yet another item in the Mitchell-Smith Papers that relates not to the Dawson household but to that of Dr. McDow. It is so bizarre, so far-fetched, that the lawyers, unable to fathom this undated, eleven-page report by a local detective, simply filed it away with the rest of Sarah's endless correspondence. About a month before Dawson was killed, McDow presumably asked his younger brother (identified as "Arthur" in this account) to come to Charleston for "important business."[14] Soon after his arrival, "Arthur" stole some of Mrs. McDow's jewels but then returned them to the McDows, who declined to press charges.

According to "Arthur," the "important business" was a scheme to poison Kate McDow and kill her father so that Thomas Ballard McDow could inherit all of their money. But "Arthur," who was supposed to shoot Ahrens in the street and make the affair appear to be a burglary, hid under a bed in the McDow home in hopes of gaining information that might be used to get a larger share of the Ahrens fortune. While there, his brother came in, dallied with a Miss Smith (a close friend of Kate), and promised to marry her once the plan was completed.

This sordid story, it is said, was disclosed to Ahrens, who then told his "astonished" daughter. The entire episode seems to have been yet another attempt by someone to blacken the doctor's reputation, but the tale is so confusing and improbable that even the prosecution could not take it seriously. However, as we shall see shortly, brother "Arthur" did get to use his pistol on at least one occasion.

As for Marie, she was dismissed following a quarrel in April 1890. Seven decades later, writing from Versailles and perhaps inspired by publication of Robert Molloy's novel *An Afternoon in March*, Warrington Dawson told readers of the *News and Courier* (24 August 1958) his version of what happened. The governess became furious, he said, when she discovered that he had described her in his diary as "the French maid." Seizing the book, she tossed it into a fireplace. His mother, hearing the dispute, entered and berated Marie for her conduct. This led to an emotional outburst: she knew about McDow's plan to murder Warrington's father, was party to it, and was glad it happened. White-faced, Sarah Dawson ordered the young lady to pack her things and leave at once. She told her eleven-year-old son to tell no one about this incident, not even his sister. The case was over, she said, the matter closed. Nevertheless Ethel was told. Her teenage diary (which has no entries relative to her father's death) notes on 16 July 1890 that "Hélène" left for home in April of that year: "There was some fuss, and she went while I was at school. I told her good bye though. We never speak of her."[15]

This dramatic confrontation caused young Dawson to recall that he had discovered the maid weeping uncontrollably at about the time his father was being killed, moaning over and over, "Oh, my mistress—my mistress." At that moment he did not know what to make of this strange scene, which made sense only with her admission of guilt thirteen months later. Dawson went on to claim that McDow had been prowling about the premises of their Bull Street home and also was being sought by New York insurance companies in connection with fraudulent claims. Thus his father went to see the doctor, he wrote, to warn him against further trespass and to tell him that, because of the insurance mess, the *News and Courier* no longer would publish his occasional letters on Charleston civic life.

As for Thomas Ballard McDow, he continued to practice medicine at the same location. Contrary to most accounts and despite embarrassing trial testimony, his wife and daughter did not leave him, although they were vacationing in the North Carolina mountains when he died suddenly in July 1904. On a humid Saturday evening the doctor undressed, folded his clothes neatly on a chair, drank from a glass of water on a bedside table, and stretched out to rest. Sometime during the night his heart simply stopped beating, which was not entirely unexpected since he had experienced several seizures in recent months. His body, "much swollen," was not found for several days, and only then because a servant became alarmed when his master failed to appear.

There is, however, a strange footnote to this story. McDow's young brother apparently learned nothing as he sat in that steamy Charleston courtroom in June 1889. In January 1906 Dr. Edgar S. McDow shot and seriously wounded a Lancaster merchant, J. Hazell Witherspoon. It seems that McDow became angry when Witherspoon, citing an unpaid bill, declined to deliver a lamp McDow had ordered. Two months later McDow was convicted of assault and battery and forced to pay a $250 fine.

In November of same year McDow's name again made headlines. On 8 November, John A. Bridges of Heath Springs raked McDow (his brother-in-law) with shotgun fire. According to the *State* (9 November), "Dr. McDow took the train [from Lancaster] to Heath Springs this morning and the shooting was over before the train left the station." Apparently the two men, long at odds, stalked each other on opposite sides of the street. When McDow began to cross toward Bridges, the latter made good use of "a double-barreled breach-loading shotgun, the shells being loaded with No. 4 shot." McDow—hit in both legs and both arms—had a pistol but was unable to use it. Following several operations, he died four days later in a Rock Hill hospital.

At a trial held in Lancaster in March 1907 with many ladies in attendance, including the defendant's wife and daughter, McDow was portrayed as a "dangerous, quarrelsome, overbearing" man of "bad reputation." Bridges, whom McDow allegedly had threatened to kill, was, by contrast, said to be a peaceable, upright citizen. It took a jury only fifteen minutes to acquit John Bridges, somewhat less than the time required to make Thomas McDow a free man in 1889.

6

THE ASSASSINATION OF
N. G. GONZALES

The deaths of Narciso Gener Gonzales and Francis Warrington Dawson are closely linked in the minds of most South Carolinians. Both of these well-known editors of leading newspapers were household names throughout the state when disaster struck. Both were known for their pet crusades, and both had ties to other lands—Gonzales to Cuba and Dawson to England. These international connections gave each a touch of the exotic. Dawson could boast of his strange change of name, Civil War exploits, and the struggle to create a niche for himself in a devastated South. Gonzales was one of six children born to a wandering revolutionary and the youngest daughter of William Elliott, a lowcountry grandee. He lived in Cuba for a time as a child and in the 1870s experienced the rigors of Reconstruction life in South Carolina. But there similarities end. The murder of Dawson was completely unexpected, even by the man who killed him. Gonzales, on the other hand, had been flirting with trouble in one form or another for over two decades. Few were surprised to hear he had been shot, and without asking, most could guess who had done it.

There also were differences in how these two men approached their work each day. Dawson, with one eye on the news and the other on profit-loss sheets, was more of a businessman. Gonzales, whose Elliott aunts somehow managed to give him and his brothers a sound basic education, came to journalism via the telegraph office and an assortment of jobs in Grahamville; Greenville; Columbia; Charleston; Savannah and Valdosta, Georgia; and Washington, D.C. Most of these positions were associated in some way with the *Charleston News and Courier,* and thus for nearly a decade (1880–89) he was working for Dawson. Yet Lewis P. Jones relates in *Stormy Petrel: N. G. Gonzales and His State* that, despite Gonzales's outstanding work as a gatherer of news, the Charleston editor never accepted him as his heir. One reason was this young man's temper, a mix of Cuban fire and lowcountry pride. He was, writes Jones, "constantly involved in controversies and 'scrapes,' and although his indignation was righteous and his cause perhaps right, his language was rarely restrained."[1]

In addition Dawson was wary of his young reporter's restless nature and well-developed ego. Though barely settled in one place, he quickly became bored and wanted to move on, and it was no secret that he yearned to be his own boss. Few questioned the innate ability of N. G. Gonzales or his courage, integrity, and all of those other qualities any reputable newsman should possess, but much too often—and this was something Dawson understood well—instead of merely reporting the news, Gonzales tended to *become* the news. Whenever this young man was in hot water, Dawson cautioned, as tactfully as possible, that his extracurricular activities must not reflect on the good name of the *News and Courier.*

Gonzales's initial assignment for the Charleston daily was as its Columbia correspondent in 1880. The following year he moved to Washington, D.C., for ten months to cover political events, including the trial of presidential assassin Charles Guiteau. While there he roomed next door to Congressman George D. Tillman, father of the man who would kill him twenty-two years later, and also became acquainted with Tillman's roommate, James R. Randall, author of "Maryland! My Maryland" and writer for the *Augusta Chronicle.* This trio met often and constituted a tight little circle of friends until August 1882, when Gonzales was called to Charleston by Dawson, whom he privately referred to as "the Tycoon."

Early in 1883 Dawson left for a European tour, James C. Hemphill (the *News and Courier* man in Columbia) became acting editor, and Gonzales was sent to the state capital to replace him. This seemed to be a temporary arrangement but became permanent when Dawson's partner and chief backer of Gonzales, B. R. Riordan, departed for New York City to enter the cotton business. Miffed by this turn of events, Gonzales flirted with a scheme to found another Charleston daily; however, the decision of the *News and Courier* in 1885 to expand its Columbia operation to a bureau opened new possibilities. Soon Gonzales, aided at times by two brothers (Ambrose and William) and an Elliott uncle, created what can be seen as a training ground for the *State,* which published its first issue on 18 February 1891.

The principal reasons why Gonzales left to establish his own newspaper were the emergence of Ben Tillman, whose policies he abhorred; the *News and Courier's* relatively mild opposition to Tillman; and advantages presented by timely financial backing of the Columbia business community—plus the fact, as noted, he wanted to be his own boss. In light of these developments a twelve-page, "confidential" letter that he wrote to editor Hemphill soon after the death of Dawson takes on special significance.[2]

The letter opens with apprehension over rumors of scandal concerning Dawson's home life and expresses the hope that McDow "swings." But then Gonzales quickly turns to the future and tells Hemphill how to run the *News and Courier.* The paper, he warns, must hold opinions and voice them boldly or it will lose "moral force." It never should be so "lamb-like" as to become inane nor promote exclusively the interests of its owners or discriminate in favor of any special enterprise. "If I had a paper I would," he continues, "under reasonable limitations, let my worst enemy have access to its columns." Gonzales urged that the *News and Courier* "should be, more than ever, a state institution, and every county in South Carolina should feel that it is its active friend." Hemphill, however, chose not to heed this advice, at least not to the extent Gonzales thought he should and especially in regard to Ben Tillman—hence the birth of a new daily newspaper, the *State*.

Throughout these years Narciso Gonzales exhibited a strange fascination with crime, violence, and lawlessness as he both deplored and reveled in such pursuits. His penetrating 1880 analysis of a lynching in the Newberry-Laurens area, for example, grew into four-and-one-half columns attacking, explaining, and then rationalizing what had happened. Above all else he endeavored to convince northerners that the deaths of two black youths for the "usual" offense were *not* political.[3] The following year Gonzales used two columns to justify yet another two-man lynching, this time in Prosperity.[4] He became personally involved in the Boggan Cash saga in 1884 and a year later, in July and August 1885, spearheaded denunciation and press exploitation of "Lawlessness in Laurens."[5]

With the birth of the *State* these personal interests took on new life. In an editorial (30 May 1892) Gonzales attacked the northern press for berating the South for lynching, emphasizing that Pittsburgh alone was recording twenty-seven murders a year. He predicted lynching would decline, yet defended the practice as akin to legal process since it "represents the popular will which makes and enforces law." This bold assertion, it might be noted, preceded by only ten days Ben Tillman's "I would lead a lynching" statement. Then Gonzales's frontal assault on the governor during the John Peterson affair in April 1893 blossomed into mass meetings in both Columbia and Denmark—the former anti-Tillman, the latter anti-Gonzales.

Meanwhile, as Lewis Jones observes, as reporter and editor, Narciso Gonzales became involved in numerous "scrapes." His adversaries of the 1880s included Congressman Robert Smalls, South Carolina's secretary of state James H. Lipscomb, Columbia businessman John Agnew and his two sons, Charles A. Calvo Jr. (editor of the rival *Columbia Register*), and his onetime friend Walter C. Robertson. The result was a series of scuffles, minor fisticuffs, threats to duel, and hundreds of hot words, but little bloodshed. The most serious of these altercations occurred in February 1886 when Calvo, angered by alleged mistreatment of a *Register* reporter, tried to whip Gonzales. Before the sheriff and bystanders could break up the melee, Gonzales beat Calvo in the face with "a Smith & Wesson, double-acting, 38-calibre revolver." All of those involved subsequently were fined; but, in addition to paying a fine for disorderly conduct, Gonzales had to post a five-hundred-dollar bond and swear to keep the peace for a year and a day—the same penalty levied against him in May 1883 following differences with Lipscomb.[6]

In October 1886 members of the *News and Courier*'s Columbia bureau were aroused late at night in their living quarters by an irate relative of Robertson, whom N. G. Gonzales had tried to oust from the exclusive South Carolina Club and denounced as "a covert, habitual, and cowardly slanderer of women." M. C. Robertson said he knew Gonzales was under bond but such words demanded satisfaction. Narciso spurned this invitation to duel, whereupon brother William agreed to take his place and settle the matter at once. However, their uncle ruled out gunfire at that hour, and nothing happened.[7]

In the 1890s differences of various sorts led to heated exchanges with *News and Courier* reporter Matthew F. Tighe; Barnwell lawyer G. W. M. Williams; Charles A. Calvo once more, as well as his successor at the *Register,* George R. Koester; and of course James Hammond Tillman. Tighe intimated in 1891 that the *State* was exhibiting Republican tendencies (blasphemy in the eyes of Gonzales), Williams had Gonzales arrested for criminal libel in 1892, and editors Calvo and Koester merely continued their ongoing war with a rival that was growing stronger day by day.

For good measure, in November 1891 other members of the Gonzales family jumped into the fray. When the General Assembly awarded the state printing contract to the *Register,* Narciso tangled in the lobby of a Columbia hotel with both J. Walter Gray, S.C. House clerk, and S.C. Senate clerk Sampson Pope. Cries of "coward" and "liar" split the air, and scores of the "dominant element" cheered on Pope as he tried, in the words of Narciso, to gouge out his eyes "in plug-ugly fashion." Gray, who flourished a pistol at one point, later was fined twenty-five dollars in mayor's court for carrying a concealed weapon. The following day, distressed by the account of this fracas that appeared in the *Charleston News and Courier,* Ambrose Gonzales attacked Tighe in the State House. The two men rolled on the marble floor in the presence of brother William Gonzales and other onlookers, and Tighe (a much smaller individual) apparently suffered superficial wounds.[8]

Concerning Jim Tillman, no one would be surprised to discover that, if such exist, he harbored "violent" genes. His grandfather and father both committed murder; two of his father's six brothers died as the result of war wounds, and two more lost their lives in domestic quarrels and family feuds. The Tillmans, certainly well-to-do but not members of the Edgefield aristocracy, represent a strange blend of independent spirit, intellectualism, and lawless behavior. Jim's grandfather, fond of gambling and something of a dandy, was a Universalist in a community where few knew what the term meant. George Dionysius Tillman (1826–1902), his father—often described as "brilliant but erratic" and twenty-one years older than Ben, the baby of the family—entered Harvard in 1845 but quit after a few weeks because the college bells disrupted his thoughts. Returning to Edgefield, he studied law, also becoming a planter, and in 1854 this veteran of several noteworthy brawls won a seat in the General Assembly. There he earned lowcountry scorn by advocating more equitable regional representation and an end to secret ballots.

During his reelection campaign two years later, while engaged in a faro game, George Tillman inadvertently shot and killed a bystander. Fearing the outcome of a trial, he fled to California and then joined William Walker's ill-fated invasion of Nicaragua. After nearly two years of wandering, Tillman returned home, hid for a time, and finally surrendered to the sheriff. In March 1858 he was convicted of manslaughter, fined two thousand dollars, and sentenced to twenty-four months in jail. Imprisonment was, however, only minimal, for this inmate enjoyed comfortable quarters and, except for courtroom appearances, continued to practice law. To his credit, Tillman helped support the daughters of the man he killed.[9]

Following service in the Civil War, George Tillman returned briefly to the political scene (1864–65) as a member of the General Assembly and the state constitutional convention. During the Reconstruction decade he farmed, continued to raise a family, and in 1876 plunged into politics with renewed vigor. Defeated for the U.S. House of Representatives that year, he prevailed in 1878 and, for all practical purposes, served there until 1892, when failure to support his brother's reforms brought his career to a close.

James, one of eight children, was born on 27 June 1869 at Clark's Hill in Edgefield County.[10] Classes at Georgetown University ended his formal education in 1889, following which he studied law with his brother-in-law Osmund Woodward Buchanan of Winnsboro and was admitted to the bar in June 1891. By the late 1880s this young man was beginning to abandon the views of his father, whose influence seemed to be waning, in favor of the ascendant power of his younger and more aggressive uncle. And it was this circumstance that led to the first clash with N. G. Gonzales.

In April 1890, as Ben Tillman's gubernatorial bid was taking shape, two anonymous correspondents clashed in the pages of Winnsboro's *Fairfield News and Herald.* "Fair Play" spoke up for the Edgefield reformer; "Fairfield" did not.[11] On 29 April, incensed by what "Fair Play" wrote three days earlier concerning press coverage of a Tillman speech in March, Gonzales demanded to know the identity of the writer. He found especially offensive references to his Cuban heritage and the suggestion that he was sly and cunning. Gonzales conceded that, while he heard the speech in question, he did not actually write an account of it. "Quixotic to defend it? Possibly," he replied in answer to his own query, "but that is the natural instinct of 'a wily Spaniard' of 'treacherous breed.'"

The Winnsboro editors at first declined to disclose that Jim Tillman was "Fair Play"; yet even before Gonzales wrote his letter of 29 April, "Fair Play" had challenged "Fairfield" on 26 April to debate under their true names. Thus Gonzales was elbowing his way into a two man quarrel already in progress; and when his letter was published in the weekly edition of the *Fairfield News and Herald* on 7 May, it was followed by this note dated 2 May: "Please say in tomorrow's issue of the *News and Herald* that I assume full responsibility for the recent communications to your paper signed 'Fair Play.' James H. Tillman." Gonzales subsequently would make much of the fact that Tillman hid on this occasion behind anonymity; yet it is patently clear that (a) Tillman was willing to acknowledge authorship even before Gonzales asked him to do so and (b) Gonzales soon knew who "Fair Play" was.

In weeks that followed, young Tillman helped organize a masked ball held in Winnsboro, was a "marshal" at commencement ceremonies marking the end of the school year at Columbia College for Women, and, together with Buchanan, launched a short-lived campaign weekly known as the *Farmers' Interest.* He continued to study law in Winnsboro at least until the late summer of 1890, perhaps then moving to his family home in Edgefield County. In any case, Tillman was living there in January 1891 when he learned that Gonzales had denied him membership in the South Carolina Club. During State Fair Week, still smarting because of the temporary anonymity of "Fair Play," Gonzales threatened to blackball Tillman if his name was proposed.

The result was more duel rumors but no action. A Tillman ally told Gonzales that Jim wanted to meet him on the traditional Savannah River sandbar. Gonzales declined to accept an oral challenge, knowing full well that a written message might put his adversary behind bars, and on 8 January he published his version of the incident in the *Columbia Record.* This account, reprinted in the *Charleston News and Courier* (10 January), charged that "a man who would make a false and scurrilous attack upon a gentleman and HIDE BEHIND HIS INCOGNITO was not a fit person to become a member of the club." The anti-Gonzales *World* of the same date noted it was easy to be courageous when spectators were at hand to prevent serious bloodshed. Getting up before daybreak to engage in a lonely duel was quite another matter. Also, it asked, who started these rumors? Gonzales objected to any publicity, yet he, not Tillman, was the one creating it. "People who constantly carry chips on their shoulders now-a-days," cautioned this daily, "get little credit from the world at large, and are liable, sooner or later, to run into a snag."

In October 1903, during his trial for murder, Tillman said he went to Augusta in 1891 to await the arrival of Gonzales and subsequently sent him a bill for hotel expenses. The following year he wrote once more, apologizing for the Winnsboro letters and thanking the editor for the *State's* support of his father's unsuccessful bid for reelection to Congress. None of this correspondence was acknowledged by Gonzales, who also, to Tillman's surprise, once spurned the offer of a cigar in a Washington hotel lobby.

During the early 1890s Jim Tillman continued to flirt with a career in journalism, serving as Columbia correspondent for the *Atlanta Constitution* and as the *Columbia Journal*'s man in Washington. After 1894, however, he turned to law full-time, establishing an Edgefield office with George W. Croft of Aiken as partner. Then on 24 April 1895 this bizarre item appeared in the *Edgefield Advertiser*:

CUBA CALLS FOR EDGEFIELD

Capt. Jim Tillman has received an offer from Gen. Gomez and the leaders of the Cuban insurgents that, if he will raise a company of one hundred men in Edgefield County—no other county will do—each member will be paid five dollars a day during the war and, at its close, the survivors will receive pensions and estates on the island of Cuba and the Captain himself will be knighted and made Duke de Moro.

Although Jim Tillman never became a duke, these words, whatever their source, were inspiration for rumors that Tillman actually was associated with Gomez. A few weeks later he was asked to address the graduating class of Columbian Academy in Washington, D.C., where, according to the *Advertiser* (24 May 1895), he had taken first honors ten years earlier. Columbian, the most prestigious preparatory school in the nation's capital for nearly a century (1821–97), then was located at 1339 H Street, N.W. In 1904 its parent institution became George Washington University. Young Tillman, the *Advertiser* boasted, was recognized as "one of the coming orators of South Carolina."

Tillman also was active as a director of the local lyceum and early in June 1896 graciously turned aside suggestions he run for the state senate. A few weeks later, flanked by twenty-four attendants, he took as his bride Mamie Norris, a Columbia College graduate and only daughter of a local bank president. They would have one child, Helen, during a troubled marriage.

As a newsman, Jim Tillman had yet another clash with Narciso Gonzales in April 1893. Like most such incidents, details are unclear, but Gonzales apparently applied for a consular post. When he learned that at least one South Carolina senator might oppose his appointment, he asked that the nomination be withheld until Congress adjourned. Tillman filed a report of these proceedings in the *Columbia Journal*, whereupon Gonzales said whoever had written those words was guilty of "an unqualified falsehood," adding for good measure one could expect nothing but "malignity" from the *Journal*'s Washington correspondent.[12] The question not aired publicly amid such righteous indignation was *why* was N. G. Gonzales, founding editor of the *State*, job hunting? The probable answer is the fact that this new publication was deeply in debt and struggling to stay afloat. Had things been going well, Gonzales would not have sought employment elsewhere.

Throughout the remainder of the decade Tillman garnered more headlines than Gonzales, and early in 1895 he finally got to fight a duel, although it was hardly a confrontation cast in the classic mold. On 14 January attorney S. Mc-Gowan Simkins arranged for Tillman, who owed Barnard B. Evans a small insurance payment, to meet the latter in his Edgefield office. Just as the three men began to talk, Tillman and Evans drew pistols and started firing amid claims by Tillman that he had been insulted. Both were slightly wounded, one of the eight shots exchanged grazing Tillman's chin and another lodging in his opponent's shoulder.

The *Edgefield Advertiser* chose to ignore this affair, although two weeks later it mentioned in passing that Evans, because of the rapid growth of his insurance business, was moving to Columbia. On 6 February, confused as to when and where his son had published "cards" relative to his role in this shoot-out, George D. Tillman penned a brief note to "Dear Narcisse." In it, recalling their Washington days, he commented, "I have always liked you & like you still in spite of your unpleasantness with some of my family."[13]

Three years later the Gonzales brothers, as well as Tillman, were caught up in the Spanish-American War. Narciso actually got to Cuba; Jim Tillman did not, although his obituary in the *New York Times* (2 April 1911) credited him with being a scout for General Maximo Gomez long before hostilities erupted. As second in command of the First Regiment of South Carolina Volunteers, Lieutenant Colonel James Hammond Tillman organized recruits in Columbia in the summer of 1898 and then took them to training camps in Georgia and Florida.

Shortly after returning to South Carolina in October of that same year, he got into trouble when he whipped two black servants ("Cross-Eyed Jim" Smith and Wiley Williams) who "borrowed" his pistols, went hunting, and lost one of the weapons. Local authorities eventually dismissed all charges because the blacks claimed Tillman actually was good to them and often "feasted" them in the kitchens of fashionable Columbia restaurants. Then unexpectedly, when Tillman's superior became ill, he was elevated to colonel and given command of the regiment. This created a temporary dilemma. As lieutenant colonel, Tillman had championed efforts to disband the unit; now he fought (unsuccessfully it turned out) to have it retained in active service. Colonel Tillman then tried to organize a troop of Indian scouts for duty in the Philippines—a proposal ridiculed by Gonzales—and subsequently beat out General Joseph Wheeler to become vice commander of a national organization of Spanish-American War veterans.

In June 1900 James Hammond Tillman—only thirty-one years of age, six feet tall, broad-shouldered, with raven-black hair and considerable charm—launched his bid for the state's second-highest office, lieutenant governor. He faced four rivals on the traditional speaking circuit, among them Cole Blease. At the first stop, Orangeburg on 14 June, Tillman stressed his recent military service and came out in favor of the liquor dispensary and schools for textile operatives. He subsequently defended editors when they were attacked for failure to print the full text of political speeches ("I never saw a reputable reporter who would intentionally misrepresent any man") and advocated closing all black schools. Tillman admitted he never had held office, adding that before the primaries ended, some of those seeking party backing would wish they could say the same. On several occasions he recalled hearing pistols click when his uncle was campaigning for governor in hostile territory, boasted of voting in the 1876 election at the age of seven, and clearly demonstrated an ability to hold his own in wit and debate. When Richland's Colonel John T. Sloan proclaimed that his horse, but not he himself, had been shot during the Civil War, Tillman retorted that Sloan must have been hiding behind the animal.[14]

In the first round of balloting held late in August, Tillman, to the surprise of the *State,* had twice as many votes as his nearest rival, Sloan, 35,389 to 16,697. (Blease was in fifth place with 9,556.) Two weeks later he clinched the Democratic nomination when he swamped Sloan, 53,600 to 34,798, garnering slightly more votes than the successful gubernatorial nominee, Miles B. McSweeney of Hampton, who succeeded to the post upon the death of William H. Ellerbe in June 1899. The *State* (12 September) had this good-natured comment upon Tillman's victory: "Well, we can stand it if the Senate can."

Throughout these weeks Jim Tillman enjoyed several distinct advantages, among them his last name and the fact that his uncle was running unopposed for his U.S. Senate seat.[15] Also in his favor were his youth, dynamic personality, absence of ties to the State House (which often hurt his rivals), and service in the Spanish-American War. Ironically, the *State,* which in the late 1890s told readers much more about Cuba and Spain than they ever wanted to know, may well have boosted Jim Tillman's political stock. In addition Sloan's defeat was an indication that another conflict had eclipsed the Civil War (at least temporarily) in the minds of some voters.

In October 1900 stories circulated concerning the arrest of the nominee in a raid on a gambling den in Augusta and his appearance in court the next morning under an assumed name. Although Tillman furnished the *State* with "proof" this tale was untrue, Gonzales and his associates remained skeptical. Nevertheless, when he assumed the office of lieutenant governor three months later, they called his inaugural remarks "well chosen." These were, however, the last kind words he would receive from that daily.

The *State* reported in March 1901 that Tillman was acquitted of racing in the streets of Edgefield and three months later said he lost over one thousand dollars at a Bamberg cockfight. When he addressed an Odd Fellows barbecue in Batesburg on the Fourth of July, coverage was cut short by this remarkable statement: "Portions of this speech are too nasty to be printed in *The State*—News Ed."[16]

Fast horses, cockfights, and foul language were mere tastes of what was to come. But, before examining the all-out war that led to murder, one obvious fact should be underscored: this was not evenhanded combat. James Hammond Tillman indeed was a rogue, a high-liver, and "one hellava fellow" among both men and women, and (like most politicians) he played fast with the truth at times. Yet even if his version of events possessed merit, he was well-nigh powerless in the face of constant attacks by the *State* and virtually every other daily in South Carolina. No one could have blunted the onslaught he faced in 1901–2, although many of the salvos were, it must be admitted, fashioned from his own deeds. His famous uncle considered Jim to be very bright, among the most talented members of the family, but sometimes unable to control his passions— an apt appraisal indeed.

During the 1902 session of the General Assembly a sudden, precipitous act by Tillman sent shock waves throughout South Carolina and Washington, D.C. The lieutenant governor helped raise funds to buy a sword for a local Rough Rider hero, Major Micah Jenkins, and President Theodore Roosevelt was scheduled to present the commemorative weapon to Jenkins during a visit to the Charleston Exposition. However, following a fistfight on the floor of the U.S. Senate between John L. McLaurin and Ben Tillman, Roosevelt cancelled a dinner invitation to the latter, whereupon James H. Tillman withdrew South Carolina's invitation to the president. The *State* immediately sparked a drive to atone for "this act of boorishness," the sword was purchased, and Roosevelt, after some grumbling, appeared in Charleston as planned.

At about the same time, a decision by Tillman as president of the state senate drove yet another nail into his political coffin, at least in the opinion of Narciso Gonzales. Early in February as a bill was being hotly contested, the lieutenant governor ruled that "a motion to postpone indefinitely" was not subject to debate, citing as his authority Jefferson's manual on parliamentary procedure, which said nothing concerning this matter. Some lawmakers objected, the question was referred to the senate's committee on rules, and the following week members announced such motions could be debated. Tillman accepted this rebuff gracefully enough but noted in passing, "Since making the ruling the chair has taken occasion to inquire of the two highest parliamentarians of this country as to the correctness of the same [his interpretation of Jefferson's manual] and is much gratified to learn that it is sustained by them."[17]

Some six weeks later, on 24 March, blazing headlines on page one of the *State*—JAMES H. TILLMAN PROVED A FALSIFIER—introduced a three-column avalanche of supporting "exhibits." In addition a lengthy editorial attacked Tillman, rumored to be thinking of running for governor, as "unworthy of public trust." Gonzales, as well as Tillman, it turned out, contacted leaders of Congress concerning this parliamentary puzzle. Telegrams published by Gonzales reveal the lieutenant governor asked if, according to Jefferson's manual, such a motion was debatable. Senator William Frye replied that the manual actually was silent on this point (in effect endorsing what Tillman had said) but added that the senate, under its own rules, debated such motions. The Speaker of the House reported his body did the same but made no direct reference to Jefferson's manual. Thus, when Tillman said the chair was "sustained" by these two gentlemen, he had some basis for saying they upheld his original ruling. On the other hand, if the question was current practice, without regard to Jefferson's views, then Gonzales had his case for "falsification."

Although few South Carolinians cared to wallow in the semantics of this personal disagreement, as with "anonymity" in Winnsboro a dozen years earlier, Gonzales was able to brand his adversary as a knave and rascal in the eyes of many readers. When one looks closely at his ten "exhibits," however, it becomes apparent that nearly all of them come from the columns of the *State,* hardly an unbiased source. The next day (25 March) that same daily published an unsigned telegram from Edgefield. Tillman, involved with a court case, apparently told a reporter he was "too busy to pay attention to the diverse libels and slanders being circulated by a few venal newspapers." He said he knew who was responsible, realized full well the purpose of these attacks, and would reply at the proper time.

Before embarking on the campaign in which the lieutenant governor sought to become South Carolina's chief executive, it might be well to compare these two men who had been sniping at each other for over a decade. Narciso Gonzales, age forty-five and thus twelve years older than Jim Tillman, was of staunch build and, in the opinion of his biographer Lewis Jones, quiet, reserved, and dignified. Although aggressive as an editor, he actually was a somewhat timid, even shy introvert whose nearsighted eyes, encased in steel-rimmed glasses, contributed to an air some thought aloof or even arrogant. Gonzales spoke with a gentle voice, liked to play chess, and seemed to prefer work to romance until 1901, when he married Lucy Barron of Manning, a former state librarian. It is impossible to imagine him slapping anyone on the back, getting tipsy, or telling an off-color story.

Turn that description inside out and you have James Hammond Tillman— gregarious, "one of the boys," a good stump speaker, ever ready to lay a wager, and not one to turn down a drink. When he was taken to task by several editors for attending cockfights in Sumter and Calhoun Falls and once more losing money, the *State* (22 June 1901) published a cynical defense entitled "We Plead for a Sporting Statesman." The *Keowee Courier* suggested, it said, that Tillman's poor judgment at such contests may be due "to the fact that on these occasions (and others, too, for that matter) he is in a condition favorable to 'seeing double.'" Whatever Tillman's vision might be, Gonzales conceded Tillman could do as he wished once a legislative session ended, adding that cocking mains were legal in some parts of South Carolina. The state constitution, he pointed out, prohibited gambling by officeholders; but if gambling meant risking something of value, that would not include Tillman's reputation. Also, some might see his actions as a moral question, and yet morality had nothing to do with the matter since those who voted for Tillman in 1900 knew what they were doing. "We have no penchant for cockfighting and still less for the Hon. James H. Tillman," Gonzales concluded, "so the public will understand that our remarks upon both are free from any taint of favoritism."

At least two other factors set these men at odds. Tillman dabbled in a halfhearted fashion with a career in journalism, a field Gonzales embraced with passion and conviction as his life's work. Furthermore, Gonzales viewed his occupation as a near-sacred trust, an attitude virtually unknown in the rough-and-tumble world of turn-of-the-century politics. This overall disparity even may have stirred a bit of jealousy in both parties, although neither would have admitted harboring such thoughts. Gonzales reportedly expressed the wish to be more outgoing than he actually was, but it is not known if Tillman ever yearned, even fleetingly, for a contemplative existence.

The primary fight began at Donalds on 14 June 1902, and forty-eight hours later the *State* greeted Tillman with a three-column editorial rehashing claims of deceit and falsehood as senate president. Tillman's assertion that he had answered such charges was rejected. Nevertheless reports from meetings throughout South Carolina, even those appearing in the *State,* for the next month and on into August reveal the lieutenant governor usually was well received and could count on his share of applause and cheers. There were, it should be noted, five men in the race for governor—Tillman, Duncan Clinch Heyward (who ultimately would prevail), Martin F. Ansel (who would win four years later), Congressman William J. Talbert, and former lieutenant governor Washington H. Timmerman.

For four weeks these rallies were dominated by a largely courteous exchange of views, good-natured banter, and an occasional outpouring of enthusiasm in the home district of a contender. There seemed to be no front-runner, and no one hurled serious charges until the group appeared in Gaffney on 23 July. E. H. DeCamp, publisher of the *Ledger* (as well as a famous cockfighting journal), had written that Tillman was "a gambler, a liar, and a drunkard," and the lieutenant governor chose to read these insults derisively to the audience. He had barely finished when DeCamp jumped up and uttered those accusations in person. Tillman took gambling and liquor in stride but questioned lying, which prompted DeCamp to produce a bill that, he said, the candidate only paid under protest after asserting it had already been settled. In DeCamp's view, that constituted lying. This exchange attracted considerable attention among northern editors, who concluded twentieth-century South Carolina was indeed different from that of the nineteenth century: one could call a man a liar to his face in public and live. More important perhaps, it enlivened a rather listless campaign and provided Gonzales with an opportunity to go on the offensive.[18]

In the weeks that followed, the editor of the *State* constantly stressed there was nothing personal in his attacks. Yet, as Lewis Jones has observed, while the battle with Ben Tillman in the early 1890s was tinged with humor and rarely invaded the sanctity of the home, this onslaught was bitter, humorless, and, despite denials, personal as well. Some staff members, friends, and even brothers of Narciso Gonzales cautioned that Tillman was a dangerous adversary, but the war of words continued. James H. Tillman, called merely "degenerate" on 31 July, sank under the weight of relentless attacks until by 25 August he had been transformed into "the criminal candidate."

Throughout August the *State,* while insisting Tillman was "a beaten man," published over fifteen columns of inflammatory editorial comment to be sure this was true. New charges included misappropriation of fifty dollars contributed to the Edgefield Monument Association, a claim Tillman sought to refute with a telegram from the president of the group. What had been "exhibits" published in connection with the disputed parliamentary ruling now became "documents," and so it went. Tillman, of course, struck back on the hustings, but without much success.

On Saturday, 23 August, the *State's* editorial page featured over three columns of anti-Tillman material, which Gonzales promised would be the last "extended" comment before the election. Somewhat distressed by the reception Tillman had received in Columbia a few days earlier, he assured readers that "all the liquor-fed enthusiasm he has secured here and elsewhere will be insufficient to put him in the second primary. He is a beaten man, and he knows it. He has been running from the real issue—his character—ever since the beginning of the campaign. And was running harder than ever when the campaign closed."

But that was not really the final word. On Monday, 25 August, Gonzales used yet another editorial column to attack Tillman once more and point out that all of the state's dailies except the *News and Courier* opposed his candidacy with considerable vigor. This departing volley proclaimed that Tillman had lied his way to high office and "it was somebody's duty to stand forth and show his falsity and depravity." Neither the state senate nor rival candidates fulfilled their roles, so the press had to act to protect South Carolina from "blackguardism, debauchery, and dishonesty."[19] The *State,* said Gonzales, had proof of his criminality and would have preferred others took the initiative but "after months of reticence" brought forth the facts. The issue, he reiterated, "is not personal nor political; it is the issue of a united press against vice and corruption in office." Facing this same editorial page were four-and-one-half columns of similar sentiments gleaned from various South Carolina newspapers.

On election day (26 August) the *State* reminded voters no one wanted to see Jim Tillman, the man who embezzled money from a fund to honor Confederate dead, in the chair of Rutledge, Pickens, and Hampton. And, since the next governor probably would represent the state at the St. Louis Exposition, could anyone imagine Tillman "on one of his debauches, reeling off his lies by the mile, as our elected sample of a South Carolina officer and gentleman?" But Gonzales reserved some barbs for his old employer, the *Charleston News and Courier.* Vexed by its quiet stand, he accused that daily of choosing the "primrose path of dalliance" by trying to be "all things to all men." In the opinion of Gonzales, the *News and Courier* lacked the courage of many little weeklies and perhaps through neutrality hoped to gain subscriptions among Tillmanites. He was especially incensed by that paper's claim of trying to "occupy a rigidly impartial attitude" and thus provide voters with information needed to make their own choices. "Having lost its hold upon the interior of South Carolina by like policies in the past, it goes now," Gonzales concluded tartly, "to the last extreme in dereliction of public duty and flaunts its easy virtue as an advertisement."

As it turned out, Heyward won handily with about thirty-six thousand votes, double that of his nearest rival; however, Talbert, Ansel, and Tillman were bunched together with sixteen thousand to eighteen thousand votes. Timmerman was far behind with only sixty-five hundred. In the final tally, Talbert pulled ahead to face Heyward in the run-off, and Tillman came in fourth. On the twenty-ninth the *State* could not resist commenting on the *Augusta Chronicle's* observation that Tillman was "a dead cock in the pit." Wrong, said the *State;* he was no gamecock and never was fit for any pit. If found there, his remains must have been thrown in after excessive weeping.[20]

Two days later the *State* published a letter Tillman was circulating to military comrades thanking them for their support and urging them to back anyone in the second primary who was not endorsed by Gonzales. "But for the brutal, false, and malicious newspaper attacks headed by N. G. Gonzales," he wrote, "I believe I would have been elected. Some day the people of South Carolina will find that I am far, very far, from being the man I have been painted." That evening the rival *Daily Record* reported that Tillman offered to resign as lieutenant governor if Gonzales would call him "a liar, a blackguard, and a coward" to his face. The editor of the *State,* Gonzales retorted, had no taste for such: "In his paper he has called Tillman what he was and what, in the public interest, it was necessary to call him; and what he has said about him he has proved." There was little point in repeating what happened in Gaffney, he added; the play was over. True, the curtain had come down, but Gonzales was wrong. It was merely intermission. There was still a bit more to this story.

No one ever will know for certain what stirred Jim Tillman to shoot N. G. Gonzales four months later. As a result of the *State*'s personal vilification some would agree he had reason enough to act. In addition a headline in that daily of 5 September, soon after the embarrassing defeat at the polls, may have caught his attention: "SLANDEROUS EDITOR DESERVEDLY SHOT." The front-page article that followed described how Fred Marriott, publisher of the *San Francisco News Letter* and the *Overland Monthly,* was assaulted by two friends of a lady who, they thought, had been maligned. Or perhaps, as the *Savannah Press* reported, a triumphant glance by Gonzales during a visit to the State House in mid-January 1903 "unnerved" Tillman.

Tillman's descendants, it might be noted, have their own theory. They claim a cartoon depicting an alleged family incident was the root cause. Since drawings of that sort rarely appeared in local papers in 1902, this tale probably is only partly true. However, on 4 August of that year the *State* published an editorial that came close to accusing Jim Tillman of mistreating his wife and daughter. The following day he reacted strongly during a campaign appearance in Bennettsville. Almost in tears, the lieutenant governor vowed that, no matter how bitter the editor of the *State* might be, he should leave "the name of my wife and child alone." Actually, the Tillman family was not mentioned by Gonzales, but the target of his wrath was obvious, and that editorial was followed by yet another heaping scorn upon the candidate by name. The incident that may have troubled Tillman was a rumor that, while drunk and arguing with his wife, he once held their baby daughter over an open well.

In any case, the sixty-fifth General Assembly opened its first session in a normal fashion on Tuesday, 13 January 1903, with Lieutenant Governor James H. Tillman presiding in the senate. That day—and also on Wednesday—the senators convened at noon to discuss routine matters, introduce bills, and elect minor officials, among them, journal clerk Tillman Bunch, a nephew of Jim Tillman. Thursday's deliberations were much the same, except that they ended after only forty minutes.

Less than an hour later the two adversaries, who had ceased speaking to each other, approached a streetcar transfer station at the northeast corner of Gervais and Main streets in front of South Carolina's capitol.[21] Tillman and several fellow lawmakers were heading for the business district, while Gonzales was en route to his Henderson Street home for a mid-day meal. It was a cold day, and the latter walked head down with his hands thrust into the pockets of a tight-fitting overcoat.

Just as Gonzales was about to turn the corner onto Gervais Street, he met Tillman flanked by two senators. There is little agreement as to what happened next, other than the fact that the lieutenant governor fired a single shot from a German Luger into the editor's stomach. Some witnesses said they exchanged a few

Tillman shoots Gonzales. Drawing from 1961 files of the *Charlotte Observer* reproduced in the *State* (12 January 2003). Courtesy of South Caroliniana Library, University of South Carolina, Columbia

words—Tillman saying "Good Morning" and, as he fired, "I received your message"—but others disagreed. Tillman, who would claim self-defense, testified that Gonzales, instead of passing the trio to the right (next to a building) advanced toward him. Believing the editor, who was not armed, was about to shoot, he fired and would maintain he had been fearing just such an encounter for some weeks.

A policeman immediately arrested Tillman, while Gonzales was helped to the offices of the *State* about half a block away on Main Street. Although press reports held out hope of recovery, Gonzales and the doctors attending him were less sanguine. He lingered for several days and succumbed to blood poisoning (peritonitis) on Monday, 19 January. Among those writing to Mrs. Gonzales expressing regret and the hope her husband would recover was Mrs. James Tillman. Forty-eight hours later businesses closed throughout the city and hundreds stood in the rain outside a packed Trinity Episcopal Church to pay tribute to Narciso Gonzales.

Meanwhile, on 15 January (the day of the shooting) the president of the state bar association addressed fellow lawyers meeting in Columbia on the evils of lawlessness, the pocket pistol, and lynching. The following day the General Assembly met in joint session to certify the election of Heyward as governor and John T. Sloan, Tillman's 1900 rival, as lieutenant governor. Later, with the president pro tem seated in Tillman's chair, the senate accepted more bills, including one "to prevent the sale or keeping for sale [of] any toy pistols, or caps or cartridges for same." This measure, which eventually became law, was introduced by Confederate veteran Thaddeus W. Stanland of Dorchester County. It is unclear whether this was intended as a comment on the shooting of Gonzales. As for Tillman, his jail quarters soon were outfitted with new furniture, books, and other comforts, and on the twenty-first a coroner's jury concluded that he indeed had shot N. G. Gonzales.

These developments put the *State* in an awkward position. Since it seemed unwise to use staff-written stories concerning the murder and events associated with it, the two remaining brothers relied on the pen of W. W. Ball (then editor of the *Laurens Advertiser*), the reporting of August Kohn of the *News and Courier,* and a stenographic transcript compiled during the trial by young James F. Byrnes. In keeping with this "hands off" policy, William Gonzales, who served as local correspondent for the *New York World,* declined to submit material to that publication. Two days after the death of Gonzales the *World* mounted a campaign among newspaper editors to collect funds to hire "the best lawyers in the South" to prosecute Tillman. This move, in the opinion of Lewis Jones, backfired since it smacked too much of "Yankee interference."[22]

As the case of the State of South Carolina versus Tillman began to take shape, battle lines were drawn. In February the accused was denied bail, and two months later his lawyers initiated a successful effort to move the trial across the Congaree River to Lexington County, a Ben Tillman stronghold. They also were able to secure as presiding judge a nephew of Martin W. Gary and a man long associated with the Tillmans, Frank B. Gary.[23] Jim Tillman chose his law partner, George W. Croft, to head up a defense team that included brother-in-law Osmund W. Buchanan, Cole L. Blease, and seven other attorneys. Leading the prosecution was Solicitor John William Thurmond, father of J. Strom Thurmond. He was assisted by five lawyers, among them William Elliott Jr., a relative of the Gonzales family. Thurmond, it might be noted, had sought out Jim Tillman to defend him when he was charged with the murder of Willie Harris, a drug salesman, in March 1897. Now their roles were dramatically reversed. As solicitor, Thurmond was trying to convict the man who, only six years before, had saved him from prison and possibly even a trip to the gallows.

The *New York World,* perhaps because of its association with William Gonzales, took great interest in this trial, dispatching reporter Ewan Justice and artist W. H. Loomis to Lexington. Justice, not happy with crowded sleeping conditions (six to a room at Kaminer's Hotel), described Tillman supporters who camped out near the courthouse as "a rough, uncouth lot." Angered by these words, the defendant took the *World* to task, vowing no such group existed; however, the *World* backed up its words with a drawing by Loomis and a report written by August Kohn. The *World* (27 September 1903) also told of a photographer who toured the county visiting prospective jurors. This gentleman, identified by Lewis

Jones as Tillmanite Ben Covar of Edgefield, presumably offered to enlarge family photos, displaying as a sample of his work a picture of Jim Tillman. In each instance he took careful note of reactions produced and thus was able to advise George Croft and his associates concerning jury selection.

The trial opened on 28 September in Lexington and continued until mid-October. Although the proceedings certainly were sensational, the courtroom sometimes was far from full, especially as lawyers fell to wrangling over legal subtleties or when six hours of *State* editorials (thirty columns) were read into the record. Because of the pressure of business and injuries suffered by his wife in a carriage accident, Senator Tillman attended only one day. Nevertheless his influence was felt, and he reportedly paid his nephew's legal fees. Young Tillman's wife and mother usually were present.

The prosecution completed its case on 7 October, having called numerous witnesses in an effort to prove that (a) Gonzales never went forth armed, (b) he and Tillman met on various occasions as friends, and (c) the editorials the latter found offensive often appeared in papers other than the *State*. Croft and the defense team, on the other hand, sought to show their client had reason to fear an attack by Gonzales and shot only to defend himself. When asked specifically about the murder weapon, a German Luger, Tillman said he had obtained it from his brother, an officer in the United States Army. Questions and answers continued:

> What did you buy the pistol for, Col. Tillman?
> To shoot with.
> Shoot whom?
> Shoot whom?
> Yes.
> Shoot anybody who tries to shoot me.[24]

Tillman had somewhat more difficulty explaining crucial words such as "I received your message" and testimony that, on leaving for Columbia in January 1903, he put copies of several Gonzales editorials in his pocket and told his wife he might be stopping at the penitentiary. The reference to the state prison was, he said, merely a joke. During the last legislative session one Columbia hotel was destroyed by fire and another had closed its doors; thus rooms were hard to find.

By the end of the second week all evidence had been heard, and on Monday, 12 October, three days of final argument got under way. At this stage crowds swelled, and on the thirteenth a special train brought both law classes at the University of South Carolina and numerous interested ladies to Lexington from Columbia. Reporter Ewan Justice, although a Texas native, continued to be amazed by scenes passing before his eyes. Fears that trouble might erupt were, he

WIFE OF JAMES H. TILLMAN, ON TRIAL FOR HIS LIFE.

These sketches of the Tillmans by W. H. Loomis appeared in the *New York World* during the trial. Courtesy of Thomas Cooper Library, University of South Carolina, Columbia

TILLMAN TALKING WITH COL. CROFT DURING RECESS, SURROUNDED BY FRIENDS

The Tillman jurors, flanked by Sheriff Caughman (broad white shirt bosom, standing left) and the bailiff at the other end of the back row. Courtesy of South Caroliniana Library, University of South Carolina, Columbia.

wrote, very real: "Practically everyone here connected with either side of the case is armed. Some of the men carry two pistols, while others are content with but one. These guns are of large calibre, and make the witnesses look as if they had an umbrella under their coats."[25]

The jury finally got the case at 1:42 P.M. on the fourteenth and twenty hours later concluded James H. Tillman was not guilty. (The twelve men apparently voted ten to two for acquittal early in their deliberations.) According to Justice, just before the jury returned, a hundred or so Tillman supporters rushed into the courtroom, where crack shots took prearranged positions to ward off a rumored assault by their opponents. No member of the Gonzales family was present, and several of the lawyers who assisted Solicitor Thurmond also were absent. This New York reporter said both sides were relieved that no blood had been shed, although he predicted trial testimony would spawn several feuds.

A free man after ten months behind bars and said to be somewhat thinner, Tillman thanked his lawyers and then greeted friends and well-wishers. Once more he told reporters he "deeply" regretted the death of Gonzales, asserting, "I was forced to do what I did." At the foot of the courthouse steps he was met by his eighty-four-year-old body servant, and a few moments later his mother, equally happy, threw her arms around her son. His wife, more restrained, awaited him at the hotel, where they shook hands and chatted briefly. As Ewan

State headlines as trial ends. Courtesy of South Caroliniana Library, University of South Carolina, Columbia

Justice observed, Mrs. Tillman's greeting was "not demonstrative" and the pair soon parted. Meanwhile, the jury posed for a photograph, something members refused to do during the trial, and the murder weapon was packed for shipment to Augusta, where it was to be prominently displayed.

Most of the press, both national and local, roundly condemned the verdict reached at Lexington, as did many clergymen. The *World* said editorially that it meant the death of a free press in the Palmetto State, for any editor who criticized a public official clearly could be shot and killed without fear of retribution. The outcome of the trial, it said, branded South Carolina as "a barbarous commonwealth, a disgrace to American civilization."[26] The *State,* now able to speak its mind, on 16 October called the entire trial "a farce" and for several days continued to lash out at Tillman's lawyers and the perjured testimony of their witnesses. In time, however, friends of Gonzales turned their attention to a campaign to erect a monument to his memory—a project temporarily shelved during the trial since it might have proved embarrassing—and on 12 December 1905 a tall shaft was dedicated at the corner of Sumter and Senate streets in downtown Columbia.

Most writers, including Francis Butler Simkins, biographer of Ben Tillman, say the ghost of Gonzales pursued Jim Tillman for the remainder of his days; but, as with Dr. Thomas McDow of Charleston, this is difficult to prove and may merely be wishful thinking. Shortly after the verdict, the *Edgefield Advertiser* (21 October 1903) advised the press to cease criticism now that James Tillman was a private citizen but do "full duty" if he ever decided to seek public office again. That same weekly indicated Tillman soon resumed his law practice, helped instruct recruits who joined the Edgefield Rifle Company, and was active in the Improved Order of Red Men. In fact, selection of Tillman to respond to a toast to "The Press" at a Red Men's banquet in Chester in 1907 caused some outcry.

Tillman's mother died in 1906, and two years later his brother-in-law O. W. Buchanan was mysteriously shot and killed while riding in a train near Johnston. At some point during these years Tillman contracted tuberculosis. The first hint of deteriorating health was a notice in the *Edgefield Advertiser* (4 November 1908) that Mrs. James Tillman was called to Clark's Hill "on Sunday last on account of the illness of Col. Tillman." The pages of this weekly also reveal that the Tillmans probably were living apart by that date. Mother and daughter seemed to exist independently as they traveled to Washington, Asheville, and other points, and by 1909 the *Advertiser* was recording the social life of Mrs. Mamie Norris Tillman, not Mrs. James Tillman.

In April 1909 Tillman returned to Edgefield after spending four months at various health resorts in Arizona and California. At about this time, according to rumor, he began living in a tent on his Clark's Hill property, a last-ditch effort to combat the ravages of his malady. Eighteen months later, in the fall of 1910, Tillman moved to a cottage near Asheville, North Carolina, where he died on 1 April 1911 at the age of forty-one. It is unclear whether family members were at his bedside. Some accounts say his nephew Tillman Bunch was on hand; others mention only a doctor and a nurse. He was buried at Clark's Hill five days later in the tiny graveyard of the Bethlehem Baptist Church (established in 1821) surrounded by his parents and Bunch and Buchanan relatives. A large horizontal slab recording Tillman's achievements bears this message: "His heart was as beautiful as his mind; throughout life he was brave, generous, and kind."

The *New York Times* remembered James Tillman as a high-handed parliamentarian who ran roughshod over the state senate and (incorrectly) as a scout for a Cuban general in the 1890s. The *News and Courier* noted Tillman was enveloped in controversy even as he lay dying. A few weeks earlier his sister and he apparently berated Senator Tillman for not aiding his ailing nephew financially, a squabble that was reported in the press. Yet, at the same time Jim Tillman was quick to deny that he was dying in poverty. The truth is, the senator had his own concerns. A daughter was about to be married, his health was so poor that many thought he would not seek reelection in 1912, and a son and daughter-in-law were engaged in a loud and very public battle for custody of their two daughters.

The most interesting aspect of the *News and Courier* obituary of 2 April is, however, reproduction of a "card" that Jim Tillman published in the *Edgefield News* as he was departing for the West in 1908. Leaving good friends was sad, Tillman admitted, but he hoped he would find in California such as he had known in Edgefield, the land of his birth, indicating he may have thought this move permanent. Tillman thanked these individuals for the many kindnesses extended to him through the years and the forbearance "shown my shortcomings." He must go, he said, to the land of sunshine to wander in search of health, bidding good-bye with these lines from Lord Byron's "To Thomas Moore," first published in 1821:

> Here's a sigh to those who love me,
> And a smile to those who hate;
> And, whatever sky's above me,
> Here's a heart for every fate.

Tillman's choice of poet is revealing since he and Byron both lived relatively short lives marked by scandal, adventure, and controversy. The comment of the *State* (2 April) on the passing of Tillman was much briefer—a single sentence with an Asheville dateline at the bottom of column three on page one: "James H. Tillman, at one time lieutenant governor of South Carolina, died here tonight."

7

ANALYZING MURDER

Facts, Figures, Fiction

Following a couple of sensational murder cases, a handful of duels and would-be duels, and lots of lynchings, it might be well to take a closer look at the nature of homicide in South Carolina. Late nineteenth-century statistics, first compiled statewide in 1887, are a bit erratic and often incomplete. However, a few years earlier H. V. Redfield, a correspondent for the *Cincinnati Commercial*, published a pioneer work, *Homicide, North and South* (Philadelphia, 1880). Based on research in local newspapers, especially the *Charleston News and Courier,* and travels in this state, Redfield estimated there were perhaps 128 homicides in South Carolina in 1878, a figure that seems in line with what local officials reported a decade later—98 murder/manslaughter cases in 1887, 123 in 1888, and 128 in 1889.[1]

As his title indicates, Redfield was comparing life (and death) in several southern states with conditions in the upper Midwest and Northeast; and since South Carolina, Kentucky, and Texas were dominated by a single newspaper, he tended to concentrate on those states for the southern side of the story. The great number of homicides in the South was, he conceded, no secret. By his estimates, South Carolina was recording twice as many violent deaths each year as occurred in all of New England, and to him the reasons were obvious—street fights, brawls, and "personal difficulties." Murder was found everywhere, Redfield wrote, but frequent homicide clearly was an earmark of southern civilization.

In contrast to the North, murder in South Carolina was largely a rural phenomenon since most people lived in the countryside far from the restraining presence of constables and police. Many homicides were altercations that turned deadly because of quick recourse to weapons, which seemed more readily available below the Mason-Dixon Line. Without pistols and guns, Redfield observed, the charge often would have been simple assault, if that. The South Carolina press, he noted, was eager to blame blacks, but in his opinion that was unfair and unsubstantiated. In 1877 he counted 113 murders in this state. Sixty-nine of these crimes were committed by whites, who killed 45 fellow whites and 24 blacks. Of 40 blacks charged with murder, only 5 killed whites. (The racial factor in four cases was unclear.) "While the blacks are not a model as a law-abiding race," he wrote, "yet there is a point to which their example could be followed by the whites with advantage."[2]

Redfield's analysis is correct, it may indicate that blacks embraced murder enthusiastically after 1880 as they got guns and began to emulate white vior. In any case, he discovered some aspects of murder in South Carolina continued to be true for the next four decades. Murder frequently was d by domestic disagreements, usually did not cross racial lines unless oyer-employee or landlord-tenant relations were involved, might feature sex nore often liquor, and time after time seemed utterly pointless. He told of dgefield fray—perhaps the famed Booth-Toney shoot-out of 12 August —that included a participant with a known record of murder and assassi- n who was still at large. "If only desperadoes themselves were killed," Red- remarked, "there would be ause for complaint."[3] Also, he was in South Carolina, dent pointed to a mistrial esulted when a member of ury who had been saved g a previous trial by the dant (then a juror) re- d the favor. As this gentle- remarked, "One good turn ves another." r Redfield, the root causes e great number of homi- throughout the South he lasting effects of slavery e is no other way to nt for them") and the pre- e of concealed weapons. concerning pistols were on ooks, he noted, but rarely honored. South Carolina,

The Southern *gentleman* was celebrated for his affable manners to all, rich and poor, black and white, while the fire-eater was sullen and dogged in his salutations; except when "showing off," he would hardly speak to negroes and whites lower in station than himself at all, and he was continually imagining insults and picking quarrels. A disregard for inflicting pain and shedding of blood became lamentably common. All, even boys but just in their teens, were in the habit of wearing a pistol, as the slightest provocation would ordinarily reveal. It became well-nigh impossible to get a jury to convict anyone (especially an aristocrat) of the most evident murder, provided he exhibited daring in committing it, or had given his victim a chance to defend himself.

Belton O'Neall Townsend, "South Carolina Morals," *Atlantic Monthly* (April 1877): 468

ample, passed a law in 1880 against the carrying of concealed items such as ol, dirk, dagger, slung shot, metal knuckles, razors, or other similar deadly ns usually used for the infliction of personal injury."[4] If convicted of carry- ch, an individual could be fined up to two hundred dollars and imprisoned t more than a year. Anyone who used concealed weapons when assaulting m might face additional penalties, including twelve months in the peniten- tiary. In 1897 this law was weakened considerably (a maximum fine of one hundred dollars and only thirty days in jail for carrying concealed weapons), and courts were instructed to lodge separate indictments when those weapons were used while committing serious crimes. Five years later the manufacture, sale, and use of any pistol weighing less than three pounds and measuring less than twenty inches in length was prohibited, and in 1910 it became a misdemeanor (except in theatrical productions) to point a pistol at any individual.

Since the murder rate soared to new heights during these same decades, it is obvious that many jurisdictions paid scant attention to such legal niceties, although some did. After a pistol dropped from the pocket of Attorney General J. L. McLaurin and crashed onto the floor of a Bennettsville courtroom, the *State* (30 September 1892) reported the incident with a jovial headline: "JOHNNY, GET YOUR GUN." Much less amusing was the accidental death of the black chef at the Columbia Elks Club in December 1913 because of the blatant carelessness of yet another attorney general. Thomas H. Peeples allegedly was handing a cocked, loaded pistol to a friend, who had asked to examine the weapon, when it went off. This happened, Peeples claimed, just after he had stepped up to the club bar and asked for a glass of milk. Although exonerated at a coroner's inquest, the attorney general subsequently was indicted by a county grand jury and then acquitted following a brief trial. He claimed the gun was in his car because his mother and an uncle had been driving in Lexington County, indicating that in 1913 many thought it advisable to go armed when venturing into the South Carolina countryside. However, it is unclear just why Peeples took a *cocked,* ready-to-fire pistol into a crowded club bar.

Writing in the 1870s, Redfield thought the solution to such mayhem lay in law enforcement and education. In an especially biting comment, he observed that Massachusetts had one homicide for every $279,000 spent on public schools; in South Carolina the ratio was a homicide for every $2,000. "Obviously, the people of South Carolina are killing one another with too much rapidity. And it is so inexcusable! It does not grow out of attacks on property, or 'strikes,' or communistic riots, or, in fact, anything that could be pled as an excuse. The fearful aggregate is made up of individual cases of man shooting or stabbing his fellow-man, generally over some trivial matter or so-called insult that in well-regulated and firmly governed communities would not lead to anything more serious than simple cases of assault and battery."[5]

A rough count of murders reported in the *Charleston News and Courier* in 1880 and by Columbia's *State* during its initial year (18 February–31 December 1891) suggests the pattern discerned by Redfield prevailed for a decade or so. In each instance members of both races continued to kill each other at about the same pace, although in the early 1890s homicides featuring blacks and little-known whites often were ignored until those indicted came to trial. This was especially true if the incident occurred in a remote region.[6] Also, until that time blacks were less apt to have pistols or shotguns and instead dispatched their adversaries with razors, knives, axes, hoes, bottles, planks, pine knots, or fence rails. After 1890, however, they tended to use guns.

Throughout these four decades (1880–1920) nearly all South Carolina murders were sudden, unplanned acts of passion. An individual, regardless of skin color or sex, became incensed and struck or shot without considering the consequences. If black, the perpetrator often fled to escape detection; if white, he usually went straight to the sheriff, calmly handed over a gun still warm, and in a firm, unshaking voice claimed self-defense. Blacks, more frequently than whites, committed homicides in connection with robbery, although after 1900 white burglaries on a much larger scale (minus murder and manslaughter) were becoming commonplace. These would include safecrackings by so-called yeggs.

Poisoning of victims was relatively rare, but if attempted, "Rough-on-Rats" was a favorite potion. (On 23 September 1891 the *State* poked fun at "Lexington Logic" when a court in that community ruled in this fashion concerning the demise of a black man thought to have been poisoned: "Albert Wesler came to his death from the effect of a disease that he had before he died.")

As one would expect, few homicides of these years exude any air of mystery. An exception was the death of lawyer Thomas Pinckney Jr., shot three times late one evening in February 1899 on Charleston's Pitt Street. The *News and Courier* mourned editorially on 1 March that he was "the heir of an illustrious name, in the very flush of young manhood, gentle, courteous, and brave, without an open enemy in the world." Pinckney, a University of Virginia graduate, and Arthur Barnwell Jr. had been dinner guests of Elizabeth Bardin and Mary Radcliffe at the Bardin home. Shortly after Pinckney left, shots were heard in what may have been a botched holdup. Several witnesses testified they saw blacks fleeing from the vicinity at about the time of the shooting, but a reputable black carpenter produced evidence indicating the assailant was white. Despite an intensive, six-day inquiry, no one ever was indicted for the crime.[7]

Charleston also was the scene in May 1891 of one of this state's last "near" duels, perhaps the only time such a confrontation was sparked by genealogy. The would-be duelists were T. R. Prentiss of Charleston and George R. Carteret, formerly of Philadelphia. Prentiss, according to the *State* (21 May), was "inordinately vain of his ancestors and had a most objectionable way of insisting upon 'talking shop' upon every and all occasions—genealogical trees, of course, constituted his 'stock.'" The two men met and chatted about bloodlines, and Carteret mentioned "a very respectable family," whereupon Prentiss hooted and called them nobodies, "the scum of the earth." A few days later they met again, and the Charlestonian launched an outright attack on the same individuals. At length Carteret said enough was enough. He did not wish to dwell on the matter further, adding, "but in my opinion you are a damned fool!"

"Sir," Prentiss replied haughtily, "in this part of the country we avenge an insult by recourse to the code duello." His companion laughed and said that in the North men used their fists on such occasions and immediately. Prentiss did not rise to the bait, but that evening when Carteret sat down to dine at his club, he found on his plate a formal challenge to duel. He agreed to do so, selecting fists as the weapon to be used. However, word of the affair spread, the police stepped in, and no blood was shed.

Returning to murder per se, the setting differed somewhat according to color. Whites often were killed in stores and law offices; blacks often were killed at social gatherings such as dances, hot suppers, card games, and church services. The brother-in-law relationship was a high-risk one for both races, and as noted, liquor played a larger role than sex did in this mounting death toll. This was markedly true in the hills of the upcountry where residents tangled with federal revenue agents and throughout all of South Carolina once Ben Tillman's dispensary became a hot issue. Nevertheless scores died simply because their vision and judgment were confounded by spirits, and this had nothing whatsoever to do with protecting the family still or making a political statement. The published totals for all of this mayhem, assembled from annual reports issued by various solicitors, are shown in table 7.2. (See p. 130.)

Looking ahead, 161 murders were reported in 1930, 206 in 1940, 183 in 1950, and 132 in 1960. However, this general decline was balanced by an increase in manslaughter cases, which grew from 47 in 1930 to 158 three decades later. Thus it would appear that homicides more than doubled in the early 1900s, though they seem to have been far less common during World War I. A racial breakdown of murder/manslaughter cases actually decided (1900–1920), based on county clerks' reports, also reveals interesting trends (see table 7.1).

TABLE 7.1 — **Conviction by race, 1900–1920**

	Cases		Not Guilty		Guilty		Percentage Guilty	
	WHITE	BLACK	WHITE	BLACK	WHITE	BLACK	WHITE	BLACK
1900	72	143	56	82	16	61	22.2	42.6
1910	82	176	61	56	21	120	25.6	68.1
1920	68	149	47	51	21	98	30.8	65.7

Source: *Reports and Resolutions.*[8]

The conviction rate for murder cases fluctuated throughout these two decades from a low of 29.4 percent in 1905 to about 45 percent in 1909, 1918, and 1919. By 1950 it had risen to 66 percent. This rate stood, it might be noted, at only 13.9 percent in 1887. If one combines murder and manslaughter cases (1900–1920), the rate of convictions is even more striking, rising from a low of

32.5 percent in 1900 to 56 percent in 1918. The figure was 75 percent at mid-century and by 1960 had increased to 78 percent.[9]

Record keeping, it should be emphasized, often was somewhat haphazard. What began as murder might evolve into a lesser charge of manslaughter, a shift not always reported in a uniform fashion. In addition a trio held for murder sometimes was classified as a single case, or data such as race and the outcome of a trial occasionally are missing. For reasons such as these, crime totals issued by various South Carolina officials differ, especially those published before 1920. (The summaries of solicitors appear to be more complete than those compiled by county clerks.)

Although such statistics obviously are inherently suspect, they reveal, not surprisingly, some correlation between homicide and lynching—communities that murdered also lynched. Between 1887 and 1920, thirty-two counties filed at least thirty annual homicide reports with the attorney general.[10] Growing urban centers—Charleston (on average, 16.5 fatalities per year), Greenville (12.9), and Spartanburg (10.5)—led the parade, but Aiken, Barnwell, Laurens, and Orangeburg also posted high scores, each having on average nine or ten murder/manslaughter cases each year. And these same rural communities recorded a substantial number of lynchings. At the other end of the scale, where authorities usually dealt with only three or four homicides per year, lynching was rare or even unknown. This group included, for the most part, heavily black counties, such as Beaufort, Fairfield, and Georgetown, and those with relatively few black residents, such as Chesterfield, Horry, and Pickens.

Contrary to what one might expect, whites had no monopoly on manslaughter; blacks faced that charge perhaps three times as often as whites did. In other words, if the local power structure bent the rules to aid whites, it did so by failure to indict during the investigation of a homicide, not by arraigning the party alleged to have done the deed for a less serious offense. However, despite erratic statistical procedures, trends pointed to here—more murders, more convictions, more indictments for manslaughter—seem valid enough.

Since blacks were in a majority in South Carolina from 1880 to 1920, one would anticipate more black crime than white during that period, a situation complicated, of course, by poverty and limited educational facilities. Even the black schools that existed often came under fire. The *Charleston News and Courier* (28 May 1884) pondered issues posed by the "literary negro," with editor Dawson wondering if education might not foster racial conflict. He observed that crime by educated blacks, especially forgery, was increasing statewide. A few days later the *Abbeville Press and Banner,* convinced that classrooms failed to improve black morals, declared public education "a farce" and launched a full-scale campaign to repeal the school tax. And as late as 1900 Jim Tillman vowed on the stump that all black schools should be closed.

TABLE 7.2 — **Murder and manslaughter cases, 1887–1920**

	MURDER	NOT GUILTY	GUILTY	OTHER*	MANSLAUGHTER	NOT GUILTY	GUILTY	OTHER*
1887	79	54	11	14	19	0	19	0
1888	117	61	36	20	6	0	6	0
1889	120	69	30	21	8	0	8	0
1890				(incomplete returns)				
1891	151	76	46	29	35	2	33	0
1892				(incomplete returns)				
1893				(incomplete returns)				
1894				(incomplete returns)				
1895	210	112	67	31	0	0	0	0
1896	201	110	67	24	10	0	10	0
1897	215	120	64	31	10	0	10	0
1898	248	105	96	47	7	0	7	0
1899	205	83	97	35	6	0	6	0
1900	224	127	71	26	3	0	3	0
1901	194	86	79	29	11	0	11	0
1902	219	102	97	20	4	0	4	0
1903	201	98	83	20	21	2	19	0
1904	175	95	55	25	28	4	24	0
1905	214	130	63	21	58	0	58	0
1906				(incomplete returns)				
1907	280	148	101	31	35	1	34	0

	MURDER	NOT GUILTY	GUILTY	OTHER	MANSLAUGHTER	NOT GUILTY	GUILTY	OTHER
1908	278	137	101	40	41	0	39	0
1909	243	125	109	9	32	0	32	0
1910	231	113	102	16	52	1	51	0
1911	212	122	75	15	80	0	78	2
1912				(incomplete returns)				
1913	217	124	81	12	69	2	67	0
1914	250	153	85	12	102	8	94	0
1915	269	172	90	7	88	1	87	0
1916	175	105	68	2	82	9	71	2
1917	168	110	53	5	52	1	50	1
1918**	107	51	50	6	55	10	42	3
1919	255	129	113	13	43	2	40	1
1920	178	93	73	12	65	5	59	1

*Case dismissed or continued.

**Fourth Circuit summary from county data; solicitor's report not published.

Source: *Reports and Resolutions of the General Assembly of the State of South Carolina* (Columbia, S.C., 1880–1920).

Comparison of crime in South Carolina with contemporary trends in other parts of the nation is difficult since some states were not compiling such data during these turn-of-the-century years. However, the 1940 census summarized the rate of homicides in most states for 1900–1940. In 1920 South Carolina's homicide rate was 15.3 per 100,000 residents (9.4 for whites, 21.0 for nonwhites), compared to a national average of 6.8 (4.8 for whites, 28.5 for nonwhites). Only two states, Florida and Mississippi, reported higher overall totals; no state had a higher white rate, although Florida, Colorado, and Montana came close. However, the District of Columbia and eleven states—including several outside of the traditional South, such as Illinois, Indiana, Ohio, and Pennsylvania—posted higher homicide rates among nonwhites.[11]

Nearly a half century later there were encouraging signs. A federal survey published in 1964 indicated that South Carolina's overall homicide rate had fallen to 10.0, still one of the nation's highest, and nonwhites living in this state were nearly four times more likely than whites to kill another human being (19.5 compared to 4.9). However, three states posted higher white rates (Virginia, Alaska, and Nevada), and at least seventeen states with substantial nonwhite populations had higher nonwhite rates than South Carolina.[12]

These figures for murder/manslaughter cases, convictions, and homicide rates contain only random surprises. Redfield, the *News and Courier,* and various little weeklies told South Carolinians of the 1880s that the state's acquittal rate was much too high, juries were not doing their job, and crime was increasing year by year. Judges warned these factors fostered lynching, might cause a black exodus from the state, and certainly would discourage northern investment. As a result, newspaper editors waxed hot and cold on the subject of murder, lynching, and general mayhem. It sold papers and could be used to denigrate blacks as Jim Crow fever mounted; however, such stories might stymie economic growth. Both major dailies seem to have discovered city boosterism, image-building, civic pride, or whatever one wishes to call it—the *News and Courier* in the 1880s and the *State* in the 1890s—and this was yet another reason for an ambivalent attitude toward crime, for few wanted to wash their dirty linen in public day after day.

Thus a tendency existed to play down in-state homicide if at all possible and highlight crime in other areas. The *News and Courier,* for example, often published a daily crime column on its front page, but these murders, rapes, and lynchings always took place *outside* of South Carolina, often in the North. And, as noted earlier, the *State* in 1891 was reporting only half as many South Carolina murders as the *News and Courier* cited in 1880, although the number of victims was increasing. After 1900 the Progressive mood presented still greater dilemmas for editors and publishers, as did the impact of the boll weevil, World War I, and incipient tourism.

Table 7.1 reveals that blacks who killed (1900–1920) were more than twice as likely as whites to end up in the penitentiary, an indication that sheriffs and their deputies actually kept a sharp eye on the black community. Most whites thought otherwise, perhaps misled by the limited space newspapers usually devoted to serious black crime—minor headlines such as "Two Killed at Negro Frolic," "Local Negro Stabs Wife," "Another Negro Hot Supper and Another Negro Killing," each followed by a sentence or two with few names, if any.

The violent death of a black sometimes was just a brief item in an out-of-town social column. The *State* (18 October 1893) reported four bits of news from Newberry: the killer of a black man who died in a Saturday night card game had disappeared; the Baptists were holding "a protracted meeting"; the county commissioners had awarded a contract for a new courthouse portico; and funeral services were to be held for Mary Butler Pope. There is lingering suspicion that, no matter what table 7.1 may show concerning white- and black-perpetrated homicides, the figures were distorted by a white establishment willing to ignore crimes committed by whites. In fact, the *State* (7 March 1907) conceded justice was not evenhanded: "If so many guilty whites did not escape conviction, the disparity in the race representation at the penitentiary would not, we regret to say, be so great."

Another facet of life in these decades was realization that festive occasions such as Christmas, circus day, or an election meant bloodshed and bullets.[13] During the Yuletide season of 1883 the *News and Courier* told of fatal shootings and stabbings in Allendale, Red Hill, Vaucluse, Greenville, and Columbia. Its description of the Allendale scene was so graphic—five wounded and two killed in two separate brawls—that local citizens held an indignant meeting to protest such coverage. A decade later the *State* marked the holiday season with details of nine violent deaths in various parts of South Carolina, a tally not unlike the highway toll of more recent years. This newcomer to the journalistic scene often headlined a summary of this sort with a catchy phrase such as "A Bloody Christmas" or "Blood and Booze."[14]

The good citizens of Allendale may have had a point, for late nineteenth-century editors and reporters endeavored to supply virtually every known detail whenever a murder occurred—the type of gun used, how and where the bullets tore through the victim's body, even how much insurance he had and with which fraternal order or burial society. When two Barnwell farmers, James Diamond and James Mimms, shot and killed each other in June 1894, the breast of the latter was "perforated" with "about seventy-five No. 5 shot" as he wielded "a Smith and Wesson No. 38 pistol." Mimms, who carried insurance worth two thousand dollars with the Knights of Honor, had been acquitted several years earlier of killing his uncle with a plank. Convicted of adultery in 1893, he appealed successfully to the state supreme court and was awaiting a new trial. Another farmer

Bullets in Beaufort

Frederik Holmes Christensen (1877–1944), who grew up in both Boston and Beaufort, recorded these thoughts soon after returning south at the age of eighteen.

> Monday, Dec. 23 [1895.] After dinner I got down town just too late to see a shooting affair. One of the state constables and a colored man had a quarel which came to blows[;] the constable nocked down the colored man and snaped his pistol twice while the muzle was not more than 3 inches from the mans head but luckly it did not go off and the man got away in the scufle[.] The constable was shot in his arm with his revolver, then he persued the colored man down Bay St and just as the fugitive turned down Carteret St by our store the constable fired six shots at him but though he was only a few feet away the shots did not hit.
>
> Tuesday, Dec. 24. It is funny how the people here take the shooting[.] I mean the white people. In a civilized country every one would be stired up but here no one seems to have any thing to say against the constable. Teddy Vaness, a boy about my age who runs the overhead cash system in our store and who echoes what he heres at home[,] says he thinks it would be a good thing to kill off half a dozen "niggers."
>
> Thursday, Jan[.] 2, 1896. Christmas day in different parts of the county, in shooting affairs one negro woman was killed[,] one man has since died and four others were wounded[,] two of whom are not expected to live. This happened in four different rows at places far apart. Oh this is a fine country where eleven twelfths of the people are regarded by the influential twelfth as no better than apes (I have heard this several times since I have been here) and where every other man carries a pistol and all celebrate Christs birth day in the true style by getting drunk. Mr. Johnson has promised to show me an unanswerable article to prove that "niggers" have no soul. I do not mean that white men took part in these shooting affairs.

Frederik Holmes Christensen Diaries,
South Caroliniana Library,
University of South Carolina, Columbia

---

thoughtfully held the mules of one participant so they would not bolt and run away during the exchange. The cause of the affair apparently was the fact that James Diamond was paying too much attention to Mrs. Mimms.[15]

A young white man killed in Piedmont in July 1895 when he interfered in a black domestic quarrel was dispatched with "a 38 calibre, hammerless Smith and Wesson."[16] Following a ruckus at a black dance in North in November 1896, host Frank Hook asked Jim Jackson to leave. Jim did so and then returned and apologized.

At that time Jackson was leaning against the door and turned to walk out. As he turned, Hook, who was standing inside with a shotgun, fired. Jackson received the entire contents of the gun in the right side, just over the region of the liver. The shot carried away a space of two-and-a-half inches of flesh, severing the eighth and ninth ribs. The right lobe of the liver was severed by pieces of clothing and a piece of suspender four inches long.

Jackson was shot at 12 o'clock last night and lived until 10 o'clock today.[17]

On other occasions readers were told of "bowels spilled out on the ground" and heads "beaten to jelly." When Conway Oliver was killed near Columbia's Shandon Pavilion in March 1895, "both bullets had gone through a long plug of 'Rebel Spy' chewing tobacco and a copy of *The State* which the unfortunate man had in his right breast pocket."[18] B. R. Carroll was shot at such close range on a Blackville street in March 1900 that the wadding from D. P. Johnson's shotgun entered his clothing. For good measure, Johnson finished him off with a pistol shot to the head.[19] That same year a half-breed girl named Cassie Boan was tortured, slashed with knives, and burned to death near Chesterfield by several white thugs. At the trial her scorched clothing, hat, and finger were introduced as evidence.[20] Following a slaying at Warrenville in Aiken County in July 1907, the *State* correspondent wrote, "In the front yard there is a great pool of blood, with particles of the dead man's brains scattered on the ground and spattered on the edge of the porch."[21]

When merchant John J. Hefferman was "shot near the eye and killed instantly" by a black cotton gin operator in a Barnwell saloon-restaurant, the *News and Courier* (1 November 1889) said that the Knights of Pythias would convey the body to Augusta and pay his family three thousand dollars. A year later Captain Frank M. Wannamaker—distinguished lawyer, Democrat, pillar of St. Matthews commercial and social life—died of stab wounds inflicted on the main street of that town by Milledge L. Herlong, a well-to-do farmer and then foreman of the county grand jury. (The two had argued over the policies of the Alliance, which barred attorneys from its ranks.) In this instance no sum was mentioned, but the *News and Courier* (3 October 1890) reported that the deceased, who belonged to three life insurance organizations, would be conducted to his final resting place by the Knights of Honor and the Orangeburg bar.

This tendency to tell all seemed to abate at times, notably in the early 1900s as large communities and then small ones discovered "Progress." However, in May 1919 when Columbia policeman E. M. Lancaster blasted his wife and her lover near the old Congaree River Bridge, little was left to the imagination:

Lancaster used the guns with terrific effect. Lorick was wounded in seven places. One bullet hit the center of the nose and passed through the head lodging in the back of the head beneath the skin. Two bullets holes were just below the neck. Two bullets entered the chest near the front and center of the body and another ball hit the left leg a glancing blow and lodged in the right leg.

Mrs. Lancaster was struck four times in the front of the body between the neck and the waist line. One bullet passed through a portion of the left arm and penetrated the body on the left side. Five bullets inflicted seven wounds.

Mrs. Lancaster died in the car with her body resting on the right door to the front seat with her head facing the right front wheel. Lorick's body leaned to the right and his head and body rested on the woman. The car barely escaped a plunge over the 25 foot embankment. The wheels were blocked to prevent it falling until it could be pulled away. Lorick was driving a Buick machine.[22]

Lancaster did the deed, we are told, with two 38-caliber Smith & Wesson revolvers and also carried a 32-caliber Smith & Wesson in his pocket. Injured in a motorcycle accident some weeks earlier and presumably on crutches, he had been transported to the bridge by James Harman, black driver of a "transfer car" (taxi), who had picked him up at the Hotel Jefferson. Harman, informed that his fare planned to make an arrest, was startled when Lancaster began firing and then rushed out, jumped onto Lorick's running board, and continued to pump bullets into the pair. Equally surprised was Mrs. Lancaster, who barely had time to cry, "My God! There's Gene!"

At the September trial for the murder of Mrs. Lancaster, not Lorick, Harman testified that Lancaster yelled "Here they come!" as he started shooting amid cries that he hoped his dear wife was not dead, whereupon he shot her four more times. As for Lancaster, he claimed he went to the bridge merely to locate his wife (she had told him she was going to the movies); saw the arm of Lorick, a Lexington County farmer, drop to his side; and initially fired to protect himself. After that his memory went blank and his mind was "unsettled" for several days.

Police at the scene soon after the shooting supported Lancaster's version of events; more important, his lawyer, Cole Blease, managed over the objections of the state to have an affidavit of Lancaster's teenage son Alvin admitted into evidence. It described how Lorick and his mother often kissed and got high on eggnog at Christmas and "raised sand." Alvin, who Blease said could not appear in person because he had a tooth pulled a few days earlier, even told of his mother urging him to kill his father. It took the jury only three hours to acquit Lancaster. Two years later, following a mistrial, he was quietly cleared of killing Lorick.

This case has some of the classic elements of South Carolina murders of this era: the establishment (in this instance the police) looking out for its own, the shopworn plea of self-defense, an appeal from a man on crutches whose home had been defiled by a rake and a libertine, plus a blow-by-blow account of the event. All that is missing, perhaps, is booze, or at least something more provocative than Yuletide eggnog. Yet there are new twists too, among them a memory lapse, an "unsettled" mind, and automobiles. The most important of these is, of course, the auto. As the conviction rate rose, white murderers were less inclined to go directly to the sheriff; instead they sped away from the scene in their Fords, Buicks, and Maxwells. Also, with the advent of Prohibition, the automobile played a special role in the transport and delivery of illegal liquor, a commerce that frequently spawned bloodshed and murder.

By 1920 the auto had become an instrument of death nearly as effective as a bullet and was one factor contributing to an upsurge in manslaughter statistics. The first such incident to attract widespread attention in Columbia, perhaps because of prominent figures involved, occurred late on a Saturday evening, 7 October 1917. Dr. James L. Hanahan, a druggist, and K. C. Hardin, superintendent of a local fertilizer plant, who may have been racing, crashed successively into a delivery wagon in the 2400 block of Devine Street, killing a twelve-year-old white boy. Hardin sped away from the scene but left his bumper behind. The druggist had been drinking (as perhaps Hardin had too), and their vehicles, reportedly only twenty feet apart, were traveling at about thirty-five miles an hour in a fifteen-mile-per-hour zone. Three months later Hanahan received a five-year sentence; Hardin got two years. In August 1918 the state supreme court turned down their appeal for new trials.

Although difficult to prove, auto deaths seem to have presented South Carolinians, as well as residents of other states, with special problems. Lawmakers first took heed of the auto in 1906 when they ordered owners to register their vehicles with county clerks and come to a complete stop whenever horses became agitated. Another eleven years passed before auto theft and drunk driving were recognized as crimes, and only in 1920 were operators ordered to stop and render assistance if their vehicles struck people.

Thus the role of the auto in the commission of crime and an increase in manslaughter cases are changes evident in South Carolina after 1900. The latter may have had roots in a reaction to the great number of mistrials evident in the late nineteenth century, namely that juries, under pressure from judges and the public at large, gradually became willing to break stalemates over murder by convicting on the lesser charge of manslaughter. If nothing else, such verdicts comported well with the reform impulse to reduce expensive court proceedings.

One could cite scores of mistrials (1880–1900), but clearly the most notorious case was that of Robert Jones emanating from (where else?) Edgefield County in 1885. During the next few years Jones was tried six times in court appearances that ended in four mistrials, two convictions for manslaughter, and a successful appeal to the state supreme court. The first news of this triple murder reached Edgefield just as that community was trying to come to grips with the Culbreath lynching, which prompted the *News and Courier* (19 November 1885) to give it front-page coverage:

WILL MURDER NEVER CEASE?

The old county of Edgefield seems somehow to be under a dark and bloody ban. While thirty-one of its citizens are in jail awaiting trial for the murder of Culbreath—while the double murder involved in that case is still under investigation—the Courthouse is appalled this morning to get the news of a triple tragedy in which the blood of three of the best citizens is spilled and an old man and his two sons hurried off to eternity by the hand of an assassin. At noon today [the eighteenth] a white man, named Corley, and a negro, named Charlie Brooks, galloped into the town with news of this most horrible crime. The victims are Edward Pressley, a white man, who is over eighty years of age, and his two sons, Charles and Edward, aged about twenty-six and thirty years respectively. The murderer is Robert Jones, also white, who married the granddaughter of Pressley and who lives on the farm with them. The scene of the tragedy is about eight miles from the Courthouse.

This is what seems to have happened. The Pressleys began buying some four hundred acres of land from the state, which they shared with Jones but then quit making payments and merely rented. As financial pressure mounted, they told Jones on 17 September he would have to vacate. The following morning he went to a field where his in-laws were ploughing and, watched from a distance by Charlie Brooks (who appeared as a witness at each trial), shot and stabbed the three Pressleys. According to the coroner, Edward Pressley Jr. was stabbed in the left arm, groin, and heart ("one-third of his heart was split open"); Charles Pressley was shot in the right lung at such close range that wadding was sticking to the wound ("the lung was all shot to pieces"); and their elderly father was shot in the left thigh and groin. At 2:00 P.M. on the eighteenth Jones, "a short, thickset" man, calmly walked into town, deposited his shotgun with the postmaster, went to the jail, and gave himself up—claiming, of course, self-defense.

How did Edgefield react to this news? Despite the original assertion "the Courthouse is appalled," reporter John A. Moroso told *News and Courier* readers on the twentieth that folks seemed neither surprised nor alarmed. "If a man had stood in the public square and read a bulletin stating that the Czar of Russia had decided to visit Bismarck, the impression made upon the crowd would have been about the same as the news of 'Jones's celebrated unrivalled triple murder.'" According to Moroso, the following was a typical conversation along the streets of the town:

Jones? Who's Jones? Oh yes, Bolivar Jones—used to sell beef here. Lives out yander on old man Pressley's place. Pressley hires the land, don't he? Married Pressley's granddaughter. Good people, Pressleys; always quiet, peaceably disposed. Old man must be nigh on 80 years old, and got the palsy, too. Wonder what he killed him for? Family fuss, I reckon. Killed Charley, too? and Ned, too? Well, that's pretty lively anyhow. Good boys, Charley and Ned. Jest as good as they make 'em. Never knowed 'em to insult anybody. Very peaceable; wouldn't fight till you hit 'em; then they was jest like hawnets! Where's John Pressley? No he wasn't the oldest. The oldest boy was killed in the wah. John he fit through the wah, too, and was a brave soldier. Well, must be going. When you coming out to see a fellow? So long!

Moroso concluded his rambling remarks with Judge T. J. Mackey's recollections of an incident in Mexico in the 1840s when he encountered a young South Carolinian busy dodging bullets:

> "You seem to be rather pert to get out of the way of the bullets," said the judge to the man in question.
> "Wall," replied the soldier, "I don't hanker arter bullets as a general thing."
> "Then why in the deuce did you come down here?" inquired the judge.
> "Wall! you see capen," replied the stranger, "I b'long to old Edgefield deestrick and I jes kim here to get away from danger."

In the years that followed, Jones was tried, without much success, first for the murder of the sons and then for that of their father. It was generally agreed that the original jury had been "packed" in favor of Jones, and in March 1887 William E. Gonzales made this comment concerning yet another trial: "Betting is two to one against a verdict of guilty, and about three to one in favor of mistrial."[23] Three years later an angry Edgefield County grand jury complained bitterly of "continuance upon continuance," a courthouse that was "a disgrace," and an inept sheriff who virtually ran a boardinghouse rather than a jail, allowed his son to act as jailer, and permitted Jones (an inmate for four-and-one-half years) to have keys to cells and lock up fellow prisoners. Finally in June 1891 Jones was tried in Lexington County, not Edgefield, and convicted a second time of manslaughter. The verdict elicited this response from the *State* (14 June 1891):

IN RE JONES

A past-midnight special to THE STATE from Lexington County this morning announces that Robert T. Jones, the slayer of three men six years ago, has, after six trials, been convicted of manslaughter.

The verdict is startling to civilization, perhaps, but it is one which might have been anticipated when the character of the jurors favored by the law and the extraordinary prejudice against convicting white men of murder are considered. Here was a man who deliberately murdered three men in one afternoon's gunning, without provocation and without ruth. Tried five times in his own county of Edgefield, he was convicted of manslaughter, and four times the jury disagreed. The conviction of manslaughter was upset by the Supreme Court; and the resources of justice in Edgefield seemingly exhausted, his case was transferred to Lexington County, where his sixth trial has resulted in a verdict which is preposterous.

How long will our people connive at or endure a system of justice which permits such outrages?

How long will the ignorant or venal juryman be supreme in our courts?

How long will South Carolina be content to rest under the disgrace of such verdicts?

The *State* was not the only one unhappy; Jones was too. Ten days later the *Edgefield Chronicle* (24 June) said he was "kicking" because of his conviction. So was all of South Carolina, this editor added, since most people thought Robert Jones should have been found innocent or guilty of murder, not manslaughter. To compound the confusion, Lexington and Edgefield now were wrangling over court costs. The only consolation, observed the *Chronicle,* was that Jones would be fifty-eight when released from the penitentiary, "too old probably to undertake the extermination of the remaining members of the Pressley family or annihilation of any of the State's witnesses who testified against him."

These casual comments reveal obvious truths. In the 1890s some South Carolinians viewed manslaughter as an unsatisfactory, inappropriate, "weasel" decision. A jury, in their view, should rule one way or the other, not somewhere between absolute guilt and innocence. These words indicate, as everyone realized, that witnesses often feared for their lives, especially in a society where gunplay was becoming increasing prominent. Also, throughout this long case and in many others it is apparent that juries were subject to intense local pressure and sometimes found it expedient to opt for a mistrial or vote "not guilty."

Following the Jim Tillman trial, a Spartanburg police captain told the *New York Sun* that it frequently was impossible to find twelve men who would convict anyone since many South Carolinians believed in the taking of human life. "Especially is this the case," he continued, "when the accused belongs to the party in control, and has much to do with the election of judges. Men who are good and true under ordinary circumstances cannot stand the pressure of the church and partisan politics when brought to bear in trials of murder."[24] Translated into simple English, this means that Democrats and Protestants in the Spartanburg area looked out for their own kind no matter what the facts in a case might be.

A Sheriff Speaks His Mind

In January 1889, A. M. Salley, sheriff of Orangeburg County, wrote to his son, Alexander Samuel Salley (1871–1961), a Citadel student, concerning the current court session, letters now in the A. S. Salley Papers at the South Caroliniana Library, Columbia, S.C.

> 18 January — They are trying the Nortons today. I do not look for a conviction this time, think it will be a mistrial. F. D. Mitchell & Shug Hall are on the jury, and I do not believe they would convict if they saw a murder committed, if five dollars was offered to them the other way.
>
> 26 January — Well, Court is over, and all the white men are out—I have never heard of a clearer case in my life than the Branchville case, but it is the hight [*sic*] of folly to try to convict a white man for killing a poor negro. A certain class think it is something to be proud of. It was perfectly disgusting to me to see men running after those selfe [*sic*] declared murderers. They had a perfect ovation, and all went immediately to DeMars and treated the crowd. I do not know where we are drifting to. If this goes on no man's life is safe.

The Nortons, father and son, sentenced to be hanged for killing a white man named Hamlin in 1887, had won a new trial on appeal. Their lawyers claimed the elder Norton shot to protect his son, and the jury—after being out about an hour—returned a "not guilty" verdict. The Branchville case involved the death of Caesar Stevens (black) at the hands of three white men. To Sheriff Salley's chagrin, jurors needed only five minutes to reach a similar conclusion.

Factors such as an established force—be it a race, political party, church, or police department—using its powers to protect members and their families, manslaughter verdicts replacing mistrials, and the appearance of the auto in the annals of crime undoubtedly could be found in most parts of America in the period 1880–1920.[25] Lynching certainly was not confined to South Carolina or even the South, although by the close of that era Dixie had a near monopoly. Nor was the campaign to blame blacks for a mounting crime wave especially innovative. Redfield said local newspapers were, incorrectly, doing so in the 1870s, and in succeeding years as racial views hardened, this broad indictment became an integral part of the Jim Crow thesis nationwide.

A South Carolina black who committed a serious offense in the 1880s might be characterized merely as "a troublemaker." A mulatto hanged in Spartanburg in August 1886 for killing a white woman was said to have been "a quiet waiter" who got mixed up with the wrong crowd.[26] Even those lynched sometimes were described by reporters as muscular or neat appearing, but by the turn of the century any black thought to have assaulted a white woman was a savage, depraved

animal guilty of "the gorilla crime." It should be noted, perhaps, that throughout these years it was possible for a black to kill a white person in South Carolina and not face immediate retribution at the hands of an angry mob. For much
of this period the state was largely a collection of small rural enclaves, and what
happened next depended on how each community viewed those involved. If the
black had a good reputation and the white did not, the matter might even be settled at a coroner's inquest.[27]

Nevertheless, in the midst of this growing wave of murder, manslaughter,
and lynching, South Carolinians could lay almost exclusive claim to one type
of crime, which they perfected to a high degree: the specter of a well-educated,
even office-holding white—a man who had taken an oath to uphold the law—
shooting an unarmed adversary and then going straight to the sheriff with a
seemingly contrived claim of self-defense. We have already encountered a doctor,
a lieutenant governor, and a policeman who did so with great success, as well as
a sturdy farmer who almost pulled it off. As will be seen, others sought to invoke
this same strange code of "personal justice."

8

ONE-ON-ONE

Nearly all of these fatal confrontations, fifteen of them, were two-man affairs in which the loser rarely was armed. Admittedly, a handful may have had knives or guns—or at least the winner, his attorney, and his friends usually tried to convince the public and judge and jury such was the case. But whatever the truth may have been, no victim was able to use a weapon (if he indeed had one) with much effect. Few who prevailed sustained more than a blow or two, if that, and no winner suffered a wound that caused blood to flow. Of these fifteen murderers, only five ended up in prison. It took three trials to put one member of this select group behind bars, and another was immediately pardoned by a new governor under questionable circumstances.

Eight of these encounters were relatively simple matters. Two men had differences of some sort, so A shot and killed B. Only one black was involved, Stephney Riley of Charleston, who was slain in 1885 by county physician Armour M. Bellinger. About nine o'clock on the evening of 1 October, Dr. Bellinger was returning home after visiting a patient who lived on Bull Street. His way was blocked by a carriage, the driver of which, he later claimed, was cursing and whipping his horses. Unable to see the individual, Bellinger remonstrated with the man, who turned out to be Riley, a livery stable operator known to the doctor and most residents of Charleston, black and white, largely because of his successful business and prominence as a Democrat during Reconstruction. This tall, stylish former slave from John's Island, called "Dimocrack" Riley by many, frequently was introduced to prominent visitors as a "good Negro." However, one such person, Sir George Campbell, author of *White and Black* (New York, 1879), thought Riley's story too pat, too rehearsed. His tale of slave days, being taught to read by his mistress, and how he cared for his poverty-stricken master and mistress after the war and eventually buried them seemed a bit contrived. Riley was shunned and even hated by fellow blacks, and white Democrats once gave him five thousand dollars to repair his stable after it was attacked and vandalized. Significantly, Riley—fifty-eight years old and a major in the National Guard—had only white customers.

Whatever disagreement erupted between Riley and Bellinger was rekindled the following morning. Bellinger, who had just left the bedside of Sarah Morgan Dawson, one of his patients and wife of editor Francis Warrington Dawson, either stopped by Riley's stable or was hailed by him as he passed. The exchange between the two men became heated, and according to Bellinger, Riley advanced toward him with a knife and he defended himself. Several individuals were in the area, but their stories differed greatly—whites supporting the doctor, blacks claiming Riley had no knife and was not acting aggressively when gunned down.

That Stephney Riley in death became a hero to blacks seems to have puzzled the *News and Courier;* nor could the paper comprehend why they were so bitter. This mood was, various reporters concluded, the work of troublesome "firebrands." Not surprisingly, the tragedy was the talk of the city for several days. On 4 October editor Dawson had these words of praise for Riley: "no other colored man in the State endured as much as he for the sake of political principle." That same day a reporter joined hundreds as they trooped through Riley's home. He wrote, "The room in which the corpse was laid out was neatly fitted up, the furniture consisting of a mohair parlor set. In the adjoining room was a similar set of furniture and a number of pictures. The body was dressed in a black broad cloth suit, but only the face and a portion of the chest could be seen through the plate-glass panel in the casket. The casket is of the new pattern of refrigerator coffins. The body is placed in a satin-lined zinc chest, on the outside of which the ice is placed. A polished black walnut casket encloses the refrigerator, shutting air out from the body within."[1]

The funeral procession on Sunday, 5 October, an eye-catching extravaganza, had mounted police, a major general and his staff, several military units, twelve pallbearers, Riley's favorite horse led by a groom dressed in black, one hundred close associates marching arm in arm, and eighteen carriages filled with friends and relatives. As this entourage slowly made its way to Centenary Methodist Church, a reporter remarked that less than ten years ago these same people were trying to kill the man they now were honoring. Among the mourners was a delegation of prominent whites that included Mayor William A. Courtenay and historian Edward McCrady.

At an inquest held the next day, the sharp differences between white and black witnesses became even more apparent and continued throughout two trials that followed. In November 1885 one juror held out for manslaughter, leading to a mistrial, but eight months later Bellinger was acquitted.

Two other clashes of the 1880s fit into the uncomplicated category. The first would have attracted little attention except for the name of one of the participants. About noon on 28 June 1886 mill owner Leroy Springs shot and killed John R. Bell near the Lancaster offices of Heath, Springs & Company. Reminiscent of the Bellinger-Riley fracas, the previous evening Bell ("a large, powerful young man somewhat inclined to drink") accosted Springs near the Catawba House, a local hotel. Springs eventually left the scene to avoid trouble, but the next day Bell renewed his verbal assault and blows were exchanged. As the latter allegedly tried to draw a pistol, Springs reacted. Bell died almost instantly. Springs promptly announced he would pay all funeral expenses and then surrendered himself to the sheriff.[2]

Slightly over a year later a shooting in Laurens and what the *News and Courier* said about it stirred up a real brouhaha. According to the original report, at about 8:30 A.M. on Monday, 4 July 1887, dry goods merchant John D. Sheahan met Rufus L. Bishop, owner of a local barroom, near the courthouse steps and fired several shots into his body as he tried to take refuge in the county clerk's office. Bishop died a short time later. Two days earlier the two men had an intense disagreement over money Bishop owed Sheahan. Trial testimony indicates Sheahan was applying pressure because he had to meet a fifteen-dollar draft. Bishop, who had been drinking, responded with verbal abuse that landed him in the town calaboose for a few hours on Saturday evening. From there he continued to berate Sheahan as a thief, "even imputing a lack of chastity to his mother and sister, all of which was communicated to Sheahan." The first account of this affair, written by a local correspondent, concluded with these words: "The defense claims that the shooting was justified and so speaks public sentiment."[3]

Some who appeared at the trial on 21 July vowed the deceased was, by general reputation, a rowdy, boisterous, dangerous man. Others said he was not. Testimony disclosed that Sheahan's brother, summoned from Greenville, also was at the courthouse that morning and, flourishing a gun, kept the town marshal at bay while Sheahan finished off Bishop by shooting through the windows of the clerk's office from the outside. Why had he contacted his brother? Because, said Sheahan, he thought he should be on hand to take care of their mother and sister if Bishop killed him, as he claimed the deceased had threatened to do. John Sheahan had these interesting comments concerning what happened that morning: "I was going to George Pool's to get a drink. I got down 10 or 15 feet in the ally. I soliloquised that it would be better for me not to drink as I might be killed before night, so I turned around and went toward Patton's store. As I got about ten feet from the south east corner of the Court House, Mr. Bishop came down the street." When Bishop appeared to reach for his gun, Sheahan responded. However, under cross-examination, the defendant alleged he actually thought Bishop was trying to get a gun he knew was in the clerk's office and feared "an ambush." "I shot Bishop for a combination of reasons," he said bluntly. "A sufficient reason was that I was defending my life."

Judge B. C. Pressley was less than happy with such testimony, and his charge to the jury posed several disturbing questions. If the two brothers, both armed, were at the courthouse that morning, how could the meeting with Bishop be called "accidental"? Why did the defendant continue pursuit and shoot repeatedly and yet claim he feared his adversary *might get a gun* and create "an ambush"? Did the brother actually prevent the marshal from intervening and thus permit Sheahan to shoot three more times? And, most important of all, if Sheahan resented Bishop's slurs, why not simply sue for slander? But the jury apparently heard only one small part of the proceedings. The deceased had questioned repeatedly and in a loud voice the chastity of Sheahan's mother and sister, and those words were sufficient grounds for a quick acquittal.[4]

Three days after the trial ended, irate citizens held a public meeting at which they attacked the original account of the murder (written, it turned out, by Sheahan's attorney), condemned the verdict, vowed to uphold the law, and directed especially harsh words at the defendant. The good people of Laurens, they said, regarded John D. Sheahan as "devoid of any respect for the laws of our country, having been charged at nearly every Court since he has been among us for violations of the law."[5] The following day the *News and Courier* (27 July) had this to say concerning the Laurens "manifesto": "Laurens, by the action of a body of its citizens, gives high and patriotic example to all of South Carolina. Human life has been held too cheap. Love of family—the willingness of the father, or brother, or son to sacrifice life in upholding the good name of those near him— is traded upon by the murderer and his advocates. Foul advantage is taken of a sacred sentiment. Better is it—according to the ruling practice—that ten murderers escape than that one woman shall be supposed to have been lightly spoken of with impunity. To such excess has the evil run that it promises to work its own cure."

For good measure, to atone for its own recent sins, on page one of the same issue this daily published a glowing description of "Laurens on the Hills" by reporter Matthew F. Tighe. Yet this revolt against capricious justice and ridiculous verdicts was not without significance, for some three decades later Laurens was, as we have seen, one of the first communities in South Carolina to take a resolute stand against lynching.

A couple of deaths in 1897 and another in 1904 can be added to this list of rather simple, straightforward killings, two of which feature well-known names. On 24 March 1897, in the public square in Edgefield, Tillmanite John William Thurmond, father of twentieth-century governor and senator Strom Thurmond, shot and mortally wounded a Columbia drug company salesman named Willie Harris. At about 5:00 P.M. that afternoon Harris, who had been drinking, berated Thurmond in a local drugstore for his subservience to Ben Tillman and the fact that his father, W. G. Harris, an Edgefield County resident, failed to win reappointment as a magistrate. To avoid an ugly scene, Thurmond, a former member of the legislature and now solicitor of the Eleventh Judicial District, left and went to his nearby office. About an hour later, as Harris and a friend walked by Thurmond's open door, Harris resumed the argument. As voice volume mounted, Harris told Thurmond he had acted the part of "a G-d damn dog and scoundrel," whereupon the latter opened fire, claiming, of course, that Harris had reached for his pocket. Friends helped Harris to a local hotel, where he soon expired.

The *State* (25 March) was appalled since all of Columbia "knew and esteemed" the murdered man. One must await the evidence, N. G. Gonzales said editorially, but then issued this sharp comment:

> Did Solicitor Thurmond shoot Mr. Harris because Mr. Harris, as alleged, cursed him? If so, what justification in law or morals was there for the deed? Did he, instead, shoot him to save his own life? If Mr. Harris drew a pistol, the fact is not stated. If he had a pistol on his person, the fact is not stated. Is a man's putting his hand on his pocket justification for killing him? In the name of God and humanity, ought not any man—the State's attorney above all others—to make sure that his opponent has a weapon and means to use it against him before he shoots him down? What has become of the courage of Edgefield and of South Carolina that a man cannot wait until he sees the color of his adversary's pistol before killing him? And, from a solicitor, a man whose duty it is to prosecute crime, to ensure justice, to preserve the peace, what an example to the public!

However, Thurmond's affidavit filed twenty-four hours after the murder stated that, in the drugstore, Harris boasted of "having a d— good knife and a Colt's pistol in my pocket." He said that when the confrontation resumed, Harris not only swore at him but also lunged toward him with a knife. When kicked backward out of the doorway, Harris reached for his hip pocket (a deft acrobatic feat unless the knife was dropped), and Thurmond fired to protect himself. In August it took twelve men only thirty-five minutes to acquit Solicitor Thurmond and restore him to the full powers of his office.[6]

During these same weeks, on 22 June T. Heber Wannamaker killed Charles F. Jones in Bamberg under equally puzzling circumstances. Wannamaker, "an exceedingly popular young man of brilliant attainments" and a member of the New York Cotton Exchange, was visiting his brother when, at about noon, the two men walked by a livery stable operated by Jones. Since most people were at dinner, there were no witnesses to what happened next. Two years earlier the veracity of testimony given by Jones had been challenged by T. H. Wannamaker in an Orangeburg courtroom. On 22 June, according to the brothers, Jones hailed them, became increasingly agitated as he revived the controversy, and reached for his gun. Fearing for his life, Wannamaker shot, he testified, to protect himself and his brother. Friends of Jones claimed, however, that he had a wounded leg, was in ill health, and was half-asleep or at least sitting peacefully at his place of business when willfully murdered. They insisted he had no gun, and none ever was found.

From the outset the Orangeburg community was four-square behind Wanna-maker, member of a prominent local family. As the *Orangeburg Times and Democrat* stated on 30 June, "Almost any one put in Mr. Wannamaker's place would have acted as he did, as much as they might regret the necessity that compelled them to take a fellow being's life." When both the *News and Courier* and the *State* covered the July trial in a manner Wannamaker partisans thought improper, resentment soared. Even though their hero was easily acquitted, they issued a formal demand that the two dailies publish a full stenographic report of the proceedings. Each defended what it had said and expressed muted regret but declined to do so.

The 1904 incident, on the other hand, was overflowing with witnesses. In fact, sixty-one of them stood in a steamy Manning courtroom in July of that year, individually put their hands on a Bible, and swore to tell the truth about a very public killing that had taken place two months earlier. Shortly after midday on 2 May, at a time when the seat of Clarendon County was thronged with visitors, the twenty-eight-year-old magistrate of that community shot and killed a Sumter attorney with a somewhat unsavory reputation. The following is how the *Manning Times* (4 May) described this "shocking tragedy":

> Shortly after court had reconvened last Monday afternoon, after the county convention had finished its work, and while a large number of people were loitering about the square, and many standing on the balcony of the court house, five pistol shots rang out upon the air, the first three very rapid, an intermission of a second or two, then another shot, a slight intermission, and a shot, and on the ground lay [*sic*] dead was the body of John R. Keels slain by Magistrate S. M. Youmans.[7] All this took place under the court house balcony at the front door to the entrance to the offices, and in the presence of a number of people who were so close that one, Israel Jones, colored, was hit by a ball that passed through the body of the dead man; notwithstanding the fact there were several eyewitnesses, the stories told of the killing vary considerably.[8] All five shots took effect and the man was killed instantly. Sheriff Davis reached the scene of the tragedy in a very short time, and as Mr. Youmans was emptying the shells from his pistol, the sheriff arrested, and disarmed him, and then [he was] taken to the county jail where he will stay until the court grants him bail.

The cause of this affair was a mule. Keels paid Youmans for a mule sold to a black man but then said the animal was worthless and demanded his money back. Youmans replied the transaction was with the black man, not Keels, whereupon the latter sued, threatened bodily harm, and even suggested pistols at ten paces. Youmans claimed Keels struck at him on the day of the shooting and at his trial vowed that up to the fifth and last shot he fully expected his opponent to draw a dirk and stab him. Youmans also seemed to blame a third party for stirring up the trouble that led to the death of Keels.

The initial court proceedings held in July ended in a mistrial, but three months later it took a jury only six minutes to acquit Youmans. No one saw Keels wield a pistol during the struggle, although several witnesses stated he was a violent individual. Soon after the murder the *State* (3 May) called him "a desperate man," conceding, "Youmans was equally as dangerous when aroused." Those who thought Keels violent had basis for such belief. Nearly two decades earlier the Keels and Bowman families, who then lived near Bishopville, were involved in a heated feud. When two members of each clan (including John Keels) appeared armed on the streets of Sumter, local authorities took them to the office of trial justice George E. Haynesworth to sign peace bonds. Once inside, the Keels and Bowmans started shooting, wounding virtually everyone in the room and killing Haynesworth. All of them eventually were acquitted, largely because so many bullets were flying about that no one could say who shot whom. According to rumor, at least one Bowman, fearing for his life, immediately departed for Alabama.[9]

During the World War I era there were two more simple, one-on-one killings, although—a sign of the times perhaps—those indicted ended up in prison. In May 1914 a Gray Court jury, meeting in the local railroad depot, was listening to testimony concerning a suit brought by a schoolteacher against a wayward student. Hubert Sullivan, age eighteen, was charged with "common assault, using profane language in a public place, and committing divers depredation on the property of the school house." In fact, this Tumbling Shoals youth wreaked such havoc that the school had to be shut down before the term ended. Among those taking the stand was Sullivan's sister, although when Laurens attorney John M. Cannon, who was representing the schoolteacher, realized the relationship, he asked her to step down. Sullivan's lawyer then put the young lady back on the stand and asked if blood ties would induce her to deviate from the truth. She, of course, said no. Cannon then disavowed any intention of reflecting upon her integrity, and the incident seemed to be closed.

A short time later, as the jury was debating the case, the crowd surged outdoors. During this interval several supporters of Sullivan, among them the youth's older brother Joseph G. Sullivan, took Cannon to task for his harsh line of questioning. One word led to another, and Cannon (who was using a cane because of a leg injury) struck Sullivan, who then fired five shots into Cannon's body. Cannon—who was thirty-four years old, a Wofford College graduate who had served a term in the state legislature, and chairman of the county Democratic Party—died a short time later, but not before learning that he had won the case.[10]

At a trial held the following month, Sullivan claimed self-defense and exhibited a scar on his head where Cannon had struck him. However, the state introduced evidence that indicated Cannon was not Sullivan's first victim and got the defendant to admit his suits were fitted with a special inside pocket to accommodate a pistol. These proceedings ended in deadlock, but three months later Sullivan was convicted of manslaughter and given a six-year sentence.

The second affair was a brother-in-law shooting that took place near Red Oak Grove Church in Edgefield County in February 1915. W. E. Bush presumably was mistreating his wife, the sister of Eugene Thurmond. The latter wrote Bush asking him to desist. Two weeks later, at about 9:00 A.M. on 16 February, the two men met as Thurmond was driving his fourteen-year-old daughter and two of her friends to school. Bush summarily shot Thurmond in the face and four more times after he fell to the ground from his wagon. He immediately went to the sheriff, claimed self-defense, and produced the guns he said were used in the shooting. However, the young girls testified that Thurmond had no gun, and the state was able to prove Bush acquired the second pistol on his way to town.

It took a jury less than an hour to convict Bush of murder, with mercy, meaning life imprisonment. His attorney moved for a new trial, but the judge ruled that motion out of order, emphasizing this was the first homicide case he ever had tried in which the accused offered "no real excuse." This session of Edgefield County court was memorable for other reasons as well. As the *State* remarked on 6 March 1915, "This has been an unusual term of court. There has not been an acquittal or a mistrial, and not a case has been continued, the docket has been cleared." Perhaps a new day was dawning, even in old Edgefield.

Seven other one-on-one shootings that took place during these decades (1880–1920) merit attention but tend to have been somewhat more complicated. At least two of them grew into intense legal tangles, one almost spawned a lynching, another led to a controversial pardon, and four of them had strong sexual components. Among those acquitted were a sitting member of the lower House of the General Assembly and a state senator who subsequently became chief justice of the South Carolina Supreme Court.

The first of these affairs took place in a crowded Abbeville store early on the afternoon of 24 December 1884. John C. Ferguson, about twenty-four, son of a well-to-do farmer and married to the daughter of a wealthy local resident, walked calmly into Charlie Auerbach's emporium, "the New York Store," and shot an Austrian-born clerk with a "bull-dog," 38-caliber pistol. Town marshal William Riley, who was just outside, rushed past horrified holiday shoppers to find Ferguson, gun in hand, standing over the dying man, Arthur M. Benedict. The cause of the trouble was a load of wood worth seventy-five cents that Ferguson had sold to Benedict. The latter said his boss charged him for the wood.

Auerbach claimed the bill had been paid, but Ferguson disagreed. When reporters queried local residents about Ferguson, they said this young farmer had every prospect for success (money, land, a fine wife, and a good home given to the couple as a wedding present by her father), his only drawback being a love of whiskey.

During the first of four trials the *Charleston News and Courier* (9 February 1885) told how whites sat on one side of the courtroom, blacks on the other. The defendant, who quietly chewed tobacco, was said to be young looking with dark, luxuriant hair—"he would be handsome except for a chin which retreats somewhat abruptly." As for the jury, which included three blacks, a correspondent wrote, "It cannot be said that they fully represent the intelligence of their county, but few juries do that." Ferguson, as usual, claimed self-defense, although the marshal swore Benedict was not armed. Ongoing testimony soon revealed Ferguson indeed did have a fondness for liquor. According to one witness, a few minutes before the shooting he had staggered out of Reub Haddon's barroom and called to a friend, "Come on and see me kill a damned Jew!" Another said he was drunk when he arrived at the bar some hours earlier.

The principal argument of the defense, buttressed by Ferguson's childhood nurse and numerous relatives, was that he suffered from occasional "spells." So, throughout three mistrials amid rumors of "fixed" juries, the litany of drinking bouts and mental aberrations continued. David Haddon, brother of the bar owner, testified at the second trial, "I knew Ferguson as one of our customers. He was a regular customer who took big drinks. His drinks were always big and he took a good many. He took bigger drinks than other men usually do. He general[ly] took two bar glasses at a time."[11]

Interest in Ferguson's fate was keen at the outset, and the *Abbeville Press and Banner* printed column after column of testimony and closely reasoned argument. By the time the third mistrial ended a year later, the editor said most people no longer cared what happened. When Ferguson became a free man in June 1886, reporters said at least one juror did not know which attorneys were speaking for the defendant, and the *Press and Banner* (23 June 1886) concluded, as it well might, that the jury system was in need of repair. Twelve men had declared, in effect, that it was all right to kill "a damned Jew," and no one really believed this represented local sentiment. Juries, the editor added, protect property and convict robbers, but not people who kill people: "Is a peck of corn in a neglected field of more consideration than the life of a human being? Is the price of [a] pig more sacred in the eyes of the law than the life of a citizen? With this State of affairs how long will it be before we will be compelled to resort to lynch law?" This attitude was not by any means limited to Abbeville, nor was the impression, now reinforced, that money could buy justice.[12]

A decade later it was T. C. Aughtry's turn to go through three trials, but there similarities end. Unlike most South Carolinians involved in late nineteenth-century murders, he (a) denied any knowledge of the crime and (b) eventually was found guilty on largely circumstantial evidence. Shortly after midnight on 6 March 1895 the body of a Columbia railroad man named Conway B. Oliver was found in the woods near Shandon Pavilion in Columbia's eastern suburbs. This thirty-two-year-old family man had been shot and possibly robbed. His dinner pail and a string of fish lay near the body, which was guarded by a faithful bull-dog. As mentioned earlier, bullets had pierced a plug of chewing tobacco and a copy of the *State* the victim had in his right breast pocket. A preliminary inquiry revealed that Oliver was en route to his father-in-law's home east of the city, where his wife was waiting for him. It also disclosed that Mrs. Oliver was "pretty intimate" with one T. C. Aughtry, a former mail carrier who recently had been fired for "abstracting" letters addressed to that same lady. Aughtry was detained within twenty-four hours and at length charged with the murder of her husband.

Among those who did not help Aughtry's cause was his estranged wife, who had left him several months earlier because of physical abuse. In her opinion, he planned to run away with Mrs. Oliver. She told the coroner's jury, "I saw enough through a window of Mrs. Oliver's house to convince me that things were not right and that Mr. Aughtry was unfaithful to me."[13] As for Anna Oliver, she knew nothing about the murder. She testified that she expected her husband to come to her father's home after work and bring some fish and a bottle of whiskey if the dispensary was open. Aughtry, she insisted, was merely a good friend.

As the first trial unfolded in early April, the defense strategy became obvious. It was calculated to show that Aughtry carried a shotgun on frequent hunting trips (thus being seen with one on the day of the murder proved nothing) and that he could not have been at the scene of the crime at the time when authori-ties said it took place. Nevertheless, Aughtry was found guilty. However, one juror responded incorrectly when being polled concerning mercy, and the defendant won a new trial.

Shortly before the second round in October, Mrs. Oliver ("an attractive blond") was jailed as an accessory, but nothing came of this charge. That trial ended in a hung jury. Then in April 1896, after deliberating for more than twenty hours, a third panel found Aughtry guilty and recommended mercy. But the jurors erupted in protest when he received a life sentence, claiming they had been misled by the judge. In February 1897 the state supreme court affirmed that verdict; and several months later, following more unsuccessful legal maneu-vers, Aughtry was transferred to the penitentiary. Said to have been a model pris-oner, he worked in the hosiery mill until he succumbed to tuberculosis in April 1909.

This case, as noted, possessed qualities unique for those decades. The crime apparently was a calculated homicide, not the result of sudden anger, and the perpetrator did not go running to the sheriff crying self-defense. Instead, he maintained his innocence and was convicted, for the most part, on circumstantial evidence. And, for once, jurors seem to have weighed the testimony with some care, even if they did not fully understand the meaning of "guilty, with mercy."

Long before the Oliver-Aughtry saga came to a close, Columbia-area residents were savoring an even juicier tale from the nearby village of Lexington. It featured young, star-crossed lovers; well-known family names; a male friendship gone bad; and lots of sex. When the trial opened in September 1896, reporters called it "the most sensational murder case in the state's history." Perhaps this is true, but it would have been even more so if details found in the General Session rolls of Lexington County (Box 24, Case #202) had been revealed.

Sometime in the early 1890s Florrie Harman (born 1871), daughter of the publisher of the *Lexington Dispatch,* launched an intimate relationship with Cal Caughman (born 1876), son of F. C. Caughman. The elder Caughman not only played a leading role in the lynching of Willie Leaphart in May 1890, he also was a political maverick willing to embrace any group, including Republicans. These factors alone might have been enough to ruffle the Harmans, although it is unclear whether young Caughman was pursuer or pursued. Despite efforts to thwart this romance, Florrie and Cal continued their secret trysts, wrote passionate notes to each other (especially after Cal began working as a carpenter in New Brookland a few miles to the east near Columbia), and once even tried to run away together. When Cal reportedly insulted Mrs. Harman, Florrie's brother Mike (Albert M.) tangled with him; but for the most part, the two boys—Mike was two years older than Cal—remained close friends.

Nevertheless, late on a Friday afternoon, 19 June 1896, Mike put a pistol to Cal's head and pulled the trigger. According to the *State* (21 June), Mike had forbidden the couple to meet and became incensed when he saw them talking near the Collegiate Institute. The *Lexington Dispatch* deplored the shooting and expressed hope that Caughman would recover, but he died on 7 July.

At an inquest held on 16 September, Florrie Harman, witness for the state, talked much more freely than necessary about her personal life, especially concerning what happened the day Cal was shot. One can merely conjecture as to why. Perhaps this young lady (a) enjoyed being the center of attention, (b) represented a free spirit fed up with the hypocrisy of small-town life, or (c) was eager to even the score with her brother and put him behind bars. A Baptist minister later testified that Florrie, who took great interest in religious affairs, was decorating the church on the day of the shooting, Cal called for her, and they left together. Florrie, on the other hand, said they met by plan at her home, went for a walk, and had been in the school only ten or fifteen minutes when Mike appeared. In any case it quickly became apparent she and Cal had been doing much more than talking. They were, in fact, making love on the floor of the school vestibule when her brother entered and, without saying a word, shot Caughman. "Callie took advantage of me," she said. "He took all the advantage of me he wanted I reckon."

In answer to questions, Florrie replied she did not give her consent nor did she scream or "holler" for help. Cal simply "caught me in a helpless position . . . threw me down and accomplished his purpose . . . when he was shot he was accomplishing his purpose a second time." She vowed this never had happened before and yet admitted they had been caught in the woods two years earlier "in a compromising position." Florrie also conceded Cal was younger that she was, giving her age as twenty-four and adding that during the past five years he had not been "accomplishing his purpose with me whenever he wanted to." Their meeting that afternoon had been arranged by letter, as had others, including several "in the steeble [sic] of the Lutheran Church by appointment." (Cal was Lutheran, Florrie Baptist).

At the trial (23–26 September) some, but by no means all, of these torrid tidbits were aired. Scores of lovesick letters were introduced into evidence, including one that said, "Many sweet kisses I send you and to get many more, my precious" and was signed "Y. O. D. [Your Own Darling] Wife." For his part Harman claimed he had heard Cal boast only a few days before the shooting that he "never went with a girl unless he got paid for it" and he (Harman) only wanted to protect his sister. Crazed by the scene in the schoolhouse, "I was so mad after I fired I can't say what I did. . . . I thought my sister was a pure woman. . . . I never knew anything was wrong with her."

Despite such riveting testimony, Judge Andrew Crawford, one of Harman's attorneys, nearly stole the show as he summed up for the defense:

> An outrage has been committed, flagrant, unpardonable, and most reprehensible. There is no man facing me, no brave, true Lexingtonian, who will not say that if a crime has been perpetrated—here the living is innocent and the dead guilty. Here was the young man (the deceased) stripping this young girl of her virtue, mocking her as she cries to him, the man of her choice, the man whom she placed her arms around and upon whose lips she had showered kisses of love and devotion; when she protests, pleads, cries and struggles, shall she, gentlemen of the jury, be held up as the scapegoat of this prosecution[,] and this defendant, who strikes under those circumstances, be made to forfeit his life for performing his duty and protecting his sister, or will you husbands, brothers, Lexingtonians, my fellow countrymen, brave men, who are resolved to do your duty, will you sacrifice this boy's life for

having done that which your manhood impels you now to say you would have done—struck, struck home, until the last spark of life was left in the quivering body of the libertine that had ruined your home?

Is there a man on this jury who would not have done other than the prisoner?[14]

Solicitor P. H. Nelson, who closed for the state, scoffed at this emotion-charged appeal to a "higher law." The only law recognized in the courts of South Carolina, he warned, is "the written law." Harman, he contended, had perjured himself and concocted his story merely to mask a grudge. The defense, in his opinion, failed to prove either rape or seduction took place that day. As for the deceased, he actually had been seduced by "this vile, depraved, and wretched young woman" when only twelve years of age. The reaction of Judge Crawford to this statement was not recorded.

The jury, after only two hours, found Mike Harman guilty, with recommendation for mercy. A motion for a new trial was overruled, whereupon his lawyers said they would appeal to the state supreme court. The *State* thought the verdict (life in prison) enjoyed general approval, although there was no demonstration in the courtroom. The *Columbia Register* (29 September), on the other hand, said an acquittal had been expected and expressed hope this did not set a precedent: "The law should not punish the men of South Carolina for protecting their women."

In March 1897, only six months later, Mike Harman was a free man, pardoned by a new governor who had declared publicly he would not consider pardon appeals filed with his predecessor (as Harman's had been). The result was a flurry of angry statements in local papers (23–27 March) and a few red faces. According to those who prosecuted Harman, the campaign to overturn the verdict had been handled in a deceitful manner. They alleged that both parties, by mutual agreement, pledged on 5 January to continue the supreme court appeal over to the next term. Yet Harman's attorneys met secretly with Governor William H. Ellerbe on 19 March; withdrew their appeal to the supreme court on Saturday, 20 March, without informing the prosecution; and forty-eight hours later had a pardon in hand. "I had petitions," wrote former solicitor Nelson, "from ministers of the Gospel, from the most intelligent and best conducted citizens of the county, who actually represent the public opinion of the county. I do not hesitate in saying that the public opinion of Lexington County is that the verdict was just and proper and should be sustained."[15]

This blast, one-and-one-half columns long, was answered in kind. Harman's lawyers emphasized that two appeals were being made: one to the governor for a pardon, the other to the supreme court for review of the case. While silent on any agreement relative to the latter, they vowed none was made concerning a pardon. As for Ellerbe, he now claimed he had begun studying the Harman case *before* stating he would not consider pardons filed with former governor John Gary Evans and had been swayed by the many petitions presented on Harman's behalf. On 26 March, in an attempt to quiet the uproar, Ellerbe's secretary issued a letter declaring that the governor "does not consider that he was imposed upon by Harman's counsel, that he made up his mind after reading the petitions, the printed record, and testimony taken at the trial." It is unlikely that these words satisfied Nelson and his associates, who still were smarting because of what they considered an affront to "professional courtesy."

In a compendium of brawls, shootings, and mob violence, it is risky to single out one killing as the most gruesome, and yet the death of Abram Surasky certainly is a contender for such honors. This tragedy occurred in Aiken County near a rural crossroads known as Hawthorne, ten miles south of the county seat. On Tuesday, 28 July 1903, thirty-year-old Surasky, one of five brothers operating a general store in Aiken, set out with a horse and wagon to peddle goods to country folk. At about 2:00 P.M. the following day he stopped by the home of Lee Green, a husky six-foot youth with an unsavory reputation. Green, who owed Surasky fifteen dollars, arrived simultaneously from the mill with a bag of meal slung across the back of the horse he was riding. The peddler offered to carry the meal into the house; and as he did, Green shot him in the back. The motive apparently was twofold: robbery and cancellation of the debt. Surasky, who was not seriously injured at that point, begged for his life; instead, Green shot him four more times and then finished him off with a couple of ax blows to the head. The murder netted, according to one witness, $3.05.

Within an hour or so Green cleaned up the mess in a halfhearted fashion, threw the body into Surasky's wagon, and hid it in nearby woods. He also tried to enlist the aid of two black neighbors, Mary and Henry Drayton, who refused to get involved and subsequently appeared as witnesses for the prosecution.[16] In the days that followed, Surasky's horse appeared at a nearby farm seeking food and water, and circling buzzards drew attention to his mutilated body. On 2 August various newspapers reported that the Aiken County sheriff had arrested one George Toole and was looking for Green. In time it became apparent that Toole's only crime was failure to tell authorities when he found Surasky's body, something he said he was afraid to do. Governor Heyward immediately offered a reward for the capture of Green, but three weeks elapsed before a posse cornered him in a loft of his father's barn. Green assured the sheriff he had planned to give himself up as soon as he arranged bail.[17]

When Lee Green took the stand in June 1904, his story changed dramatically. He hid out, he now said, to avoid a lynch mob and killed Surasky because the Jew assaulted his wife. Family and friends corroborated this tale with enthusiasm and heaped scorn upon Surasky. At least two witnesses told of hearing him make lewd remarks concerning young Mrs. Green; however, when asked to identify a picture of the Aiken peddler, they failed the test. Despite the testimony of the Draytons and substantial evidence that the defendant had committed a ghastly crime (the sheriff found blood stains in Green's yard, the ax he used, and wagon-wheel marks leading from his home to Surasky's battered body), after deliberating twelve hours the jury found Green "not guilty."

The *State* (27 June 1904), still painfully aware of what the Jim Tillman jury had done only nine months earlier, exploded angrily: "It is damnable that justice, righteousness, and decency in South Carolina should be impotent to defend themselves and the honor of the State against such outrages. The blood of that butchered Isrealite [*sic*], who in humbleness and peace was bearing the burden of his race, cried out for justice, the manhood and womanhood of South Carolina rebels—rebels against the disgraceful failure of the law, rebels against the ignominy brought upon the commonwealth, rebels against the accursed ascendancy of vice over virtue in the jury box."

Other editors throughout South Carolina and in nearby states joined this chorus of protest, which grew louder when word spread concerning a member of the jury. A resident of Orangeburg County, not Aiken, he served with the knowledge of at least one court official, an obvious attempt to create grounds for a mistrial, if need be. How could this happen? The *State* (2 July) called upon Green's lawyers to disprove the charge or explain how this man became a juror. Who is responsible, the *State* asked, for "this conspiracy against the commonwealth?" There was no reply.

In contrast to the brutal slaying of Surasky, the Blease-Coleman shooting that occurred in the streets of Saluda in September 1905 was spawned by more mundane matters such as marital infidelity, cuckoldry, drug dependence, and friendship gone sour. Although interest in this case was intense, it would have been even greater if South Carolinians could have known that a quarter of a century later state senator Eugene S. Blease, the winner and brother of Cole, would be chief justice of their realm. This was, in its simplest terms, yet another brother-in-law scrap. Blease, a rising young lawyer, and businessman Joe Ben Coleman married sisters, respectively Saluda and Maude Herbert. Maude died in November 1903, following which Mrs. Blease, who was separated from her husband by the time of the shooting, developed a romantic attachment with Coleman. This relationship was complicated by the fact that the latter was supplying Saluda Blease with drugs, either morphine or ergot. Yet the two men, both popular and highly respected, remained good friends and continued to associate socially. The *Saluda Standard* (7 June 1905) reported, for example, that "J. B. Coleman and E. S. Blease and Mrs. Blease" had gone to Leesville to hear a lecture by John Temple Graves.

On the afternoon of the fatal incident (8 September) H. L. Crouch, another brother-in-law and confidant of both men, was driving toward Saluda when he was overtaken by Blease. The latter—distraught, confused, and perhaps with a drink or two under his belt—poured out his story. He had been to his father-in-law's home, where his wife was staying. While there, the whole business with Coleman was thrashed out; and, in the presence of her father, Saluda said it was true. Nevertheless, Blease begged her to end the relationship for the sake of their daughter and return home. She refused. He also told Crouch that his wife was pregnant "and I doubt if by myself, maybe Joe Ben's, and I thought maybe he wanted to destroy it."[18]

Both Crouch and Saluda's father cautioned Blease not to do anything rash, but about sundown he walked into Coleman's store and in the presence of several customers ordered him out of town at once. Although the two men chatted quietly at first, this was no idle threat: Joe Ben was to leave Saluda within thirty minutes and never come back. Coleman, turning to Crouch, who also had entered the store, protested he had a business to run and children to think of and stated, "You know I can't just up and leave tonight." At length he agreed to do so, adding that he might return someday. Still distraught, Blease shouted, "Then you refuse?" This outburst was followed by yet another query, "Joe Ben, are you armed?" When Coleman replied he was not, Blease placed a small derringer on the counter, ordered Coleman to pick it up, and reached for his pistol. At that moment Crouch threw his arms around Blease and told Coleman to run. Coleman rushed out into the street and literally ran for his life. But Blease struggled free and shot him down in the presence of numerous witnesses. As the *State* (10 September) observed, some fifty people were in the immediate area, "but Providence seemed to direct all of the shots at the figure which excited Blease's wrath." Coleman died in agony nine hours later.

In a bail application dated 16 September, Blease provided his version of what happened. He told of his relations with Joe Ben, how he loved him like a brother and yet came to suspect he was intimate with his wife. As noted, he then told Coleman of her confession and ordered him out of Saluda forever. Coleman, he stated, refused to leave, "whereupon the said Joe Ben Coleman sneered in deponent's face and said, 'What if she has confessed, God-damn you, what are you going to do about it?' Deponent crazed with grief and trouble, and from this gross insult, together with the awful realization that he had been betrayed, that his wife had been led astray by that man, his name, and that of his little daughter, disgraced, and, the sanctity of his home invaded, deponent could not restrain himself and shot Joe Ben Coleman."[19]

The entire Saluda County bar immediately agreed to defend Blease, despite the widespread popularity of Coleman, once a serious contender for the office of sheriff. The deceased—thirty-two years old, survived by three small children, and insured by Woodmen of the World—was conducted to his final resting place by members of the Masonic order. Yet neither the inquest nor the trial that followed provided answers to two vital questions: was the derringer Blease offered Coleman actually loaded, and did the latter have a pistol in his hand as he ran down the street? Some witnesses answered both queries in the affirmative; others did not. True, two weapons were found beside the dying man—one perhaps placed there by friends of Blease and the other thrown down by the murderer as he shouted for all to hear, "I shot him about my wife!"

In the weeks that ensued there was an effort to move the trial to another county, but this campaign eventually faltered. The proceedings, held on Tuesday, 10 April 1906, before a jury composed entirely of married men, lasted only five hours. As at the inquest, Mrs. Blease's father, Crouch, and Blease were the key witnesses. The climax came when Blease, his face encased in tears, told of his love and affection for Joe Ben Coleman, how he and his family had lived with the Bleases after his wife's death (she died in their home), the struggle he had getting them to leave, efforts to find Joe Ben a position, and the ruin, shame, and disgrace that followed. "At the conclusion of this dramatic scene the situation was rendered even more dramatic when the defendant swooned as he was leaving the stand and became limp as death. He had to be carried to the jury room, where he remained during the entire time of the arguments attended by his physician."[20] The jury, which retired after eight o'clock, then ordered supper; after finishing their meal, the jurors returned the verdict: not guilty.

Blease, who died in 1963, subsequently moved to Newberry, where he and his daughter (also named Saluda) were living with his mother in 1910. He eventually remarried but abjured politics until 1922, when he won a House seat. Elected to the state supreme court four years later, Blease served as chief justice from 1931 to 1934. Although he quit the court for health reasons, eight years later he made an unsuccessful bid for a seat in the United States Senate.

While the town of Saluda was coming to grips with Joe Ben's death, a double murder occurred in Gaffney. This case failed to fit the familiar pattern of those years and may actually have been a "two-on-one" confrontation. In December 1905 a traveling theater company performing the musical comedy *Nothing but Money* came to town and took rooms at the Piedmont Inn. Soon after the group arrived, the twenty-one-year-old brother of those operating the establishment made suggestive overtures to a female member of the cast and then tried to get into the room of another. Whether pasty-faced George Hasty was a true Lothario or just a kid with a heavy load of hormones is unclear, but at breakfast on 15 December the two women pointed him out to their associates. Musical director Milan Bennett, who was planning to marry one of the young ladies, accosted

Hasty and demanded he apologize for his behavior. Young Hasty denied any wrongdoing, a scuffle ensued, comedian Abbot Davison (fiancé of the other woman) joined in, and Hasty fired two shots. Bennett died almost instantly. Davison, who was able to summon the police, then collapsed and expired eighteen hours later.

The community was shocked, for the death of "outsiders" at the hands of a local resident was highly embarrassing. Gaffney churches took up a special collection to aid the thespians, the Masons and Pythians contributed a huge floral display ("a thing of beauty"), more than five hundred people thronged the railroad depot to bid the group good-bye, and the editor of the *Gaffney Ledger* accompanied the bodies north. The *State* (18 December) said both the shock and indignation expressed by Gaffney should surprise no one. "What a spectacle do we present to the world! And what do the men and women of South Carolina think about it[?] In this State, where the boast is so often shouted that 'our women shall be protected,' in this State where a woman, however humble, is supposed to command a degree of respect from the men who call themselves chivalric, two women are grossly insulted in their hotel by one of the proprietors,[21] and their natural protectors, who protect, are shot to death. 'Our women must be protected!' But are their protectors to be murdered for playing the man?"

The four-day trial, held early in March 1906 for the murder of Bennett, not Davison, attracted considerable attention. Hasty, of course, claimed he was merely defending himself from Bennett, who, he said, had a knife. On 2 March, in a summary of the first day's testimony, the *State* reported "hundreds of ladies" were part of the largest crowd ever seen in Gaffney under one roof. Even the judge's stand had to be cleared of spectators before proceedings could begin. On that same day the *Gaffney Ledger* suggested that women should not attend "as the attorneys for the defense are liable to break down the character of some of the witnesses and in so doing will very probably ask some direct questions which ladies might not desire to hear."

As predicted, lawyers tried to portray the two women involved in the case as lewd showgirls who reportedly did the "hootchy-coochy" in a Gastonia livery stable for a group of delighted males. They also asserted that George Hasty actually was searching for cause to evict the cast on moral grounds, a statement that brought smiles to the faces of those familiar with the Piedmont Inn. Despite repeated warnings, ladies continued to show up in great numbers each day; and even if they had not, both the *State* and the *Ledger* thoughtfully reproduced word-for-word every highly suggestive query that was overruled by the judge. After the jury was out for twenty hours, many thought this would be another mistrial; but instead, Hasty was found guilty and given a life sentence, a decision widely applauded as a triumph of law, order, and decency.

In another case, the fury that almost led to a lynching and tore a town apart was fueled, plain and simple, by political warfare at the grassroots level. The battleground was the little community of Wagener in eastern Aiken County, and the protagonists were an individual unaccustomed to having his views questioned and a dynamic newcomer who not only became mayor but also won a seat in the state House of Representatives. Hugh C. Long, a Wake Forest graduate, moved from Bennettsville to Wagener in September 1911 and established a new weekly, the *Edisto News*. Within a few months he became head of local government, initiated a movement for a new county with Wagener as its "capital," and plunged into a bruising campaign for higher office that challenged the reign of Pickens Gunter—bank president, son of the man who founded the town, and a powerful figure with substantial landholdings and various community interests.

During the summer of 1912 Gunter and his cronies traveled from one "speaking" to another to "howl down" Long, only to discover Long had emerged victorious in the second primary.[22] Furious, they warned his life was in danger if he came back to Wagener. However, a couple of weeks later, when a Gunter stalwart prevailed in the runoff for yet another House seat, Long thought it safe to leave his temporary refuge in Aiken, and on Saturday, 28 September, he returned to Wagener. There he found his newspaper office and home had been vandalized in his absence. At about 6:00 P.M., while Long was standing near the center of town scanning mail he had picked up at the post office, Gunter (who was a somewhat larger man) struck him from behind and wrestled him to the ground. Hayes Gunter, a relative but a Long partisan, tried to separate the pair; but as the three men struggled, Long fired two shots, one of which hit Pickens Gunter in the stomach, a wound that proved fatal forty-eight hours later.[23]

As darkness fell, the community mood turned ugly. Long, unable to get to his home, took refuge in a nearby house, where he had ready access to still more weaponry. Summoned to the scene, Sheriff T. P. Raborn and his deputies found local authorities uncooperative and soon were facing an angry mob bent on vengeance. As one youth later told a reporter, that evening "everybody had 'em er gun."[24] The sheriff asked Governor Cole Blease for troops but then withdrew the request. Meanwhile, unruly citizens knocked down telephone lines, barricaded roads leading out of Wagener, and set up pickets. During the night, as those intent on a lynching kept an eye on the sheriff's auto, Long and two deputies crept out a back door and made their way to Aiken on foot.

Despite the tense situation, several factors tended to restrain mob action. When the sheriff asked leaders what they wanted, they said they intended to keep Long in Wagener until daylight, presumably to see if Gunter was still alive. He replied he had no intention of carrying Long away by auto before that time, causing those watching the house to relax their guard somewhat. Also, Mrs. Gardiner, whose home had been taken over by Long and the sheriff, was an invalid, and many thought storming it might endanger her, her family, and Long's wife and children as well. But, most important of all, so long as Gunter was alive, excessive violence seemed unwarranted. However, a few members of the group vented their frustrations on the offices of the *Edisto News*, breaking windows and wrecking whatever had not already been damaged.

In contrast to other cases described herein, the trial, postponed until June so Long could attend the annual session of the state legislature, was virtually a tea party. The defense called fifty-two witnesses, most of whom attested to the sterling qualities of Hugh C. Long, a gentleman who had three brothers who were ministers and a father who had served gallantly in the Civil War. The jurors were so impressed that, to the distress of the judge and some of the attorneys, they refused to hear the traditional closing arguments. Their minds, they said, were made up. Nevertheless, at the insistence of his honor, they retired for ninety seconds before returning to declare Long "not guilty."[25]

Taken as a whole, these fifteen cases present a disturbing picture. Nearly half of them occurred in communities within forty-five miles of the Savannah River, the same region where lynching long held sway, and substantiate forcefully what Spartanburg's police captain said in 1904: many South Carolinians believed in the taking of human life. Of the victims, only one (John Bell, the man gunned down by industrialist Leroy Springs) probably was armed, although he was unable to use his weapon. The lone survivor who clearly did not initiate what became a fatal encounter was Hugh Long, and only Eugene Blease made any effort to arm his opponent. Even that perhaps was an empty gesture since the pistol proffered to Joe Ben Coleman may not have been loaded. It may be folly to look for fair play in the midst of murder (a conflict in terms?), and yet the phrase "self-defense" uttered so casually by those who killed implies an equality that we know did not exist. Perhaps it can be found in shoot-outs in which both sides, not just one, had guns and bullets.

9

SHOOT-OUTS, WESTERN STYLE

Anyone old enough to have spent Saturday afternoons in a noisy movie theater filled with kids and popcorn or able to recall *Gunsmoke* and *Rawhide*—those golden years before all of our heroes donned space suits—needs no introduction to shoot-outs. In simplest terms, two or more individuals decide to settle random differences of opinion by trying to kill those holding dissimilar views. Presumably this is a winner-take-all proposition, although there sometimes are no survivors and thus it is unclear who won and whose opinion prevailed. One usually places such activity somewhere beyond the Mississippi, even "west of the Pecos" in "Judge" Roy Bean country; but in fact the realm of Calhoun, Hampton, and Tillman was right up there with the best of them when it came to turn-of-the-century gunfights.

The majority of these altercations, much like one-on-ones, were caused by personal disputes, family matters, excessive drinking, or perhaps downright cussedness. Politics and liquor laws also could stir men to action. This was especially true during the reign of Ben Tillman as his dispensary constables tried to work their magic or when federal revenue agents sought to bust up family stills in isolated mountain coves.[1]

In 1880, 1892, and 1915 blood was shed during political disagreements in Edgefield, rural Anderson County, and downtown Charleston, respectively, and it spilled ever so slightly into Anderson's public square in 1885. The Edgefield affair occurred at the polls during a 12 April 1880 municipal election that pitted "Straight-Out" Democrats against a splinter group willing to cooperate with leading blacks. The latter favored reducing the cost of an annual liquor license from $200 to $150; Straight-Outs did not. When Lawrence Cain, a black former senator, tried to vote, he was challenged by Dr. Wallace E. Bland, a Straight-Out. A. A. Clisby, a candidate for warden, spoke up for Cain, the discussion escalated, Bland struck Clisby, and the shooting started.

Bland, shot in the bowels, died the following day, but not before casting his ballot. Arthur A. Glover, Clisby's father-in-law, and St. Julien Bland, the doctor's younger brother, also joined in, the latter shooting Clisby in the bowels and Glover in the thigh. The death of Bland, only thirty years of age and a physician trained in Paris, was a distinct loss to the community. As an Augusta correspondent of the *News and Courier* wrote on 14 April, "The whole affair is greatly regretted," adding it was sad "that another dark and bloody day should roll over the records of Edgefield." That same daily observed editorially, "Had no pistols been worn in the Town of Edgefield on Monday, Bland, Clisby, and Glover would be hale and hearty today." The following year it took a jury only twenty-five minutes to clear Clisby, and the court decided to drop assault and battery charges filed against Glover and young Bland.

Although ten shots were fired in Anderson's public square on the afternoon of 15 September 1885, no one was seriously injured. At issue was Prohibition and what Senator John B. Moore, who favored it, had said in a speech at Flat Rock Church. E. B. Murray, anti-Prohibitionist editor of the *Anderson Intelligencer,* claimed in his columns that Moore had not told the whole truth and hinted he was a coward. In fact, he called Moore's statement concerning the matter "a wilful, malicious, and depraved lie!" Friends tried to reconcile these differences but were unable to do so.

At about 4:30 P.M. Murray, who had been out of town for a few days, left his office and walked down Depot Street. Moore, eager to confront him, ran toward him. Both men drew their weapons and began to fire—Murray flourishing "a thirty-two calibre, self-cocking Smith & Wesson improved pistol," and the senator using a similar revolver but not "improved." For a few moments the editor took refuge behind a boxed tree; then, after expending all of his ammunition, he ran back to his office with Moore only fifteen feet behind him and still firing.

Chief of Police J. R. Fant, it turned out, was present during the entire fusillade and at one point advanced toward Murray, "but as Mr. Murray had presented his pistol he did not make the effort [to arrest him]."[2] Moore was slightly injured, hit once in the right thigh. Murray emerged unscathed. Both were required to post peace bonds and subsequently were fined in mayor's court.

The 1892 shoot-out, also in Anderson County, took place during the Cleveland-Harrison election. A disagreement erupted between Republicans and Democrats on 8 November at polls located at Holland's Store on the Savannah River about fifteen miles southwest of the county seat. Election supervisor J. R. "Bob" Carter, characterized by the *Anderson Intelligencer* (9 November) as "the notorious white Republican of that section," fell to arguing with Democrat James W. Earle on the piazza of the store. Carter drew his pistol, but his arm was jerked as he fired and Columbus Glenn, who had come to the door to investigate the disturbance, was killed instantly. Following a slight pause, both men resumed the encounter, Carter shooting Earle in the stomach. According to the *State* (10 November), the bullet "glanced around and did not go through." During this exchange a black bystander, Henry Holland, was nicked by a stray bullet.

What happened next is unclear. The *State* reported that after both men ran out of ammunition Carter went behind the store to reload and Earle ran through a nearby house, picked up a shotgun, and "poured the contents into Carter." Carter, "terribly shot up," died that evening. It was noted he was from Georgia, had killed other men, and was "a dangerous fellow, especially when in liquor." The *Anderson Intelligencer* reported, on the other hand, that Hampton Earle (brother of James) fortuitously returned from a hunting trip in the midst of this affray and shot Carter in the breast, and "the ball went through him." Carter's friends, according to this local weekly, came and took him home. "People were horrified at the awful tragedy and lament it," the editor wrote. "The enormity of the deed can scarcely be grasped by the mind. That so deadly a fight could take place in our County startles us. That two souls should be sent unwarned to judgment shocks us."

With the death of Earle a few days later, a third "unwarned" soul was sent on its way. The inquest into Carter's death (none was held concerning that of Earle) revealed that the two men were arguing over a speech Carter had made, Earle pushed or shoved Carter off the piazza, and bullets started flying.[3]

The Charleston shooting of 1915 is perhaps more shocking because it took place in the heart of the city and was caused by a spat among Democrats, not a face-off between rival political parties. For over a decade beginning in 1911, John P. Grace—now memorialized by giant bridges spanning the Cooper River—was a major force in local politics. As mayor he was something of a Blease man and critic of the business community, the *News and Courier,* and an entrenched party machine run by the sheriff. In the rough-and-tumble municipal election of October 1915 Grace seemingly lost by nineteen votes to real estate man Tristram P. Hyde, the colorless darling of the "Broad Street crowd." It was up to the local Democratic executive committee, however, to canvass the results and make a final decision.

At noon on 15 October that body, with Hyde men holding a shaky majority, convened in a large room on the second floor of a building at the corner of King and George streets. The chairman had barely gaveled the session to order when scuffling erupted in a hallway outside the meeting room. Shots were fired, and the police, partisans of Mayor Grace, joined in with both pistols and clubs. Sidney J. Cohen, a young reporter for the *Charleston Evening Post,* was killed almost instantly, and four Grace men were wounded, two of them seriously.[4] Apparently Grace men, with the aid of the police, created a disturbance, during which several ballot boxes and various party club books were thrown out a window into the street, where they subsequently were recovered. Cohen and others also tried to get out windows, one man being beaten on the head by police as he slid down a telephone pole. Eight individuals were charged with carrying "concealed weapons" but then released, and the confusion was so great that no one ever was indicted for Cohen's death.

The *Evening Post* declined to call the affair a riot, but the *News and Courier* (16 October) had no such reservations as it hastened to fix blame on Grace and the police, who probably were at fault since it was in their interest to overturn the election results. The governor closed all liquor dispensaries and put various military and naval units on alert but did not declare martial law. Two days later the committee met again under tight security in the German Artillery Armory and, as expected, declared Hyde the winner. In 1919 Hyde and Grace did battle once more. In another knock-down, gutter-level campaign, Hyde prevailed by a single vote only to have the Grace forces, who now controlled the executive committee, honor enough challenges to put their man back in city hall.

As fitting as this turnabout may have been, it lacked the ironic backdrop of the 1915 campaign. In that year, despite bloodshed and bullets, Charleston, with its defeated mayor leading the way, was about to celebrate "Victories of Peace" on 13–17 December. This dual-purpose extravaganza was designed to mark the semicentennial of peace among the American states (the end of the Civil War, that is) and play host to the seventh annual convention of the Southern Commercial Congress.

In the 1880s and 1890s there were at least four sensational shoot-outs inspired by federal liquor laws and Tillman's dispensary, to which one might add the Prohibition tangle of Messrs. Murray and Moore in Anderson's public square in 1885. The first took place near Central on 20 July 1881 when a United States deputy collector of internal revenue, one Thomas L. Brayton, decided to arrest John McDow. The latter, the *Charleston News and Courier* reported on 22 July, was "a well-to-do farmer, possessing a rudimentary education, and is well spoken of." Brayton and five men left Greenville at midnight by train to conduct a raid on McDow's illicit distillery, and before daybreak several of them were doing just that, while Brayton and a companion laid siege to McDow.

McDow, about thirty-five years of age and a heavily built man of average height, accepted a warrant for his arrest but balked at going to jail before breakfast. As he put it, "I'll have to get my fixins." Brayton and the other man, George Butler, agreed to wait, with Brayton guarding the rear of the house and Butler the front. Then, following more stirring within, McDow stuck "a Spencer gun" out of an upstairs window, fired, and struck Brayton in the chest, killing him instantly. At an inquest two days later, Butler told how he had straightened out the body, pushed back Brayton's hair, and retrieved his hat. However, since McDow, his son, and his son-in-law had continued to fire from the house, this seems unlikely. Not only did this vigorous gunplay continue, but also a short time later McDow and several relatives appeared in Central vowing to kill any member of the posse they could find. Butler, it was reported, left for Liberty "with all possible dispatch" and there caught a train back to Greenville.[5]

In succeeding weeks McDow became something of a local hero as the *Pickens Sentinel* railed against despotic federal power, naming at least three citizens of Anderson and Pickens counties who had been "murdered" by revenue agents. If they were brought to justice, then it might be proper to arrest McDow and bring him to trial too. "We are not a crouching spaniel, to lick the rod that smites us," cried the *Sentinel* editor. Pickens had been badly treated by these "freebooters," he wrote. They had arrested innocent citizens, insulted women, and threatened to burn and pillage. One agent, according to this gentleman, even "carried a portable United States commissioner with him who, it is said, would issue a warrant against a citizen they might chance to meet in the road as soon as they ascertained his name, whether they had heard of him or not. They would terrify, curse and abuse women, ransack chests, bureau drawers and other private places in houses." No wonder the local citizenry resisted such people, he added. If Washington sent men of "character and discretion" it would be different. "Revenue agents had invariably exaggerated every difficulty in the county, in order to cover up their own outrages, and to give them an excuse for committing others. . . . All we demand is justice."[6]

There may be some truth to these charges, but two points not mentioned are that these federal employees invariably belonged to the hated Republican Party and usually were "outsiders." The unfortunate Brayton, for example, although living in Greenville with his family, was a native of Fall River, Massachusetts. As for John McDow, the *News and Courier* reported on 4 August that he had "gone west."

A dozen years later a public sale in the mountains near the Greenville-Spartanburg line produced another fatal clash when those importing "blockade" liquor from North Carolina tangled with men thought to have been dispensary officials. The *State* (22 November 1893) reported that "whiskey flowed freely, and there was more or less fighting all day." The *Carolina Spartan* conceded on 29 November, "The fact is, the crowd was in a fighting humor. Before the sale pistols were drawn and threats were made. After the sale the jower[i]ng continued until about night when the shooting took place." (As one witness commented at the trial, "It was getting right smartly dusky.")

Several days earlier Henry Fisher was thwarted when, according to rumor, he tried to arrest W. B. Parris, a North Carolina bootlegger. When Fisher, Parris, and their associates met at a sale held on the farm of Tom Burns near Campobello, trouble was inevitable. As the *Carolina Spartan* put it on 22 November, "There was plenty of whiskey on the ground and when they got pretty full they began to shoot." Both Parris and Fisher were killed almost instantly, but by whom was not immediately clear. "Several others were wounded, three seriously," said the *State*, "and nearly everybody had a slash from a knife or a blow from a revolver as a souvenir of the occasion."

The following week the *Carolina Spartan* reported that Tom Calmes, who had disappeared, had shot Parris, George W. Howard had been jailed for killing Fisher, and R. H. Wofford was being detained as an accessory in connection with Fisher's death. But Mr. Fisher, it turned out, was not really a state constable after all, although he may have been deputized temporarily or perhaps was only the sort of individual who enjoyed a good brawl. Whatever his true role, this affair points up a problem that bedeviled South Carolina life during these decades. Tillman, Grace, and various other political leaders were quick to grant police power much too freely to ordinary citizens. These men usually wore no uniforms and might or might not have badges to flash, and one could accept or reject with a pistol or a blow to the head their claim to represent authority. During these same weeks, by the way, North Carolina bootleggers retrieved at gunpoint a team of horses that dispensary officials had seized sometime earlier and put in a Greenville livery stable.

There are, admittedly, extraneous aspects of confrontations of this sort to be considered. J. Dean Crain, a respected Baptist theologian born in the northern-most reaches of Greenville County in 1881, said feuding families were "their own law" when he was a boy. They meted out justice according to local needs and in keeping with regional ideas concerning such matters. The only signs of organized law enforcement ever seen in his valley were raids by "revenuers" or perhaps a sheriff's posse that came prowling around after a murder was reported. His birthplace was, Crain noted with some pride, a land of stills, and he added he once saw twenty of them in a two-mile area. As a youngster he excelled in breaking up mash with his feet, for moonshining was a way of life in those hills. It was fun, injected a bit of excitement into an often monotonous daily grind, and was a way to make money. A bushel of corn that one sold on the open market in the 1890s might bring sixty cents; converted into three gallons of first-rate whiskey it could fetch as much as six dollars, or roughly ten times as much. Also, Crain's neighbors, like many mountain folk, could see no reason why the federal government should monopolize the liquor trade or interfere with their traditional customs. "If the government had a right to operate distilleries," they argued, "then the mountaineer had the same right."[7]

Nine months after the Parris-Fisher affair, a smoldering, merchant-constable feud left two dead in the little town of Blackville, enabling the *State* to proclaim in exultant tones on 29 August 1894 that it was "Tillman's Doing," a natural outcome of his much-despised dispensary law. The principals in this tragedy were the powerful Brown family (Simon and sons Solomon, Herman, and Isadore) and Irish-born John Gribben. The latter, about forty years of age, served in both the British and American armed forces before settling down in Black-ville, where he became town marshal. However, as a Tillmanite he alienated local conservatives, especially the Browns, who engineered his dismissal, whereupon

Gribben vented his spleen by posting an anti-Jewish letter and subsequently gained a position as a dispensary constable.

In this capacity he frequently opened boxes of merchandise consigned to the Browns, claiming, of course, that he was looking for liquor. At about 1:30 P.M. on 28 August 1894 the Browns decided enough was enough. The three sons and their father challenged Gribben, and he, in turn, offered to fight any one of them. Isadore, the youngest, a stalwart lad of twenty, accepted the offer; Gribben removed his coat and badge; and the two went at it. But as soon as Isadore sent Gribben crashing into the wall of George Still's store, bullets started flying and at least eleven shots were exchanged. Gribben, wounded three times, staggered backward into the store, firing as he retreated, and Solomon Brown fell to the ground. Solomon, hit in the right side, right arm, back, heart, chest, and brain, died almost instantly. Meanwhile, Gribben walked through the store to the back-yard, where he stumbled, collapsed, and died within a few minutes.

Three hours later county coroner H. P. Dyches convened an inquest, only to have the solicitor stop the proceedings because Dyches, he claimed, had been involved in the shooting. Backed up by the sheriff, Dyches hotly denied the charge but was overruled by the trial justice, who promptly put him behind bars. Simon Brown and his two sons, as well as Dyches, eventually were charged with murder; the Browns allegedly shot Gribben, and Dyches, who was inside the store, was said to have killed Solomon Brown. All four men were acquitted, but not before Gribben's daughter, Maggie, wrote Governor Tillman to assure him that neither his policies nor his dispensary were to blame for what happened. Brown, she stated, ousted her father as marshal with the aid of black votes, which he bought, and at the time of his death John Gribben was hot on the trail of an illicit liquor ring. "When my father opened the box at the freight depot," she declared, "there was not one word said to him, but Brown went home and armed the family to be ready to butcher my father when he made his appearance on the streets again; and they succeeded, but it took four of them to do it. . . . The open-ing of the box was only the match to the magazine of their infernal hatred of long standing."[8]

For some reason liquor-related shoot-outs do not seem to have garnered major headlines during the next quarter century, although this does not mean they ceased. It may be that, as the Prohibition movement gained steam, liquor fans went out of their way to suppress such tales. Or, as when revenue agent Robert Moore and moonshiner R. T. Thrift killed each other near Walhalla in January 1895, simultaneous deaths of all concerned left nothing much to write about. Nevertheless the *State* (12 January) noted in passing that this was Oconee County's sixth murder in seven months. Another possibility is that, after 1900, those interested in South Carolina's public image sought to bury incidents of this sort, which, to put it mildly, might discourage outside investment and tourism.

Yet, as a reminder that such things could happen, even in a growing commercial center such as Greenville, early in July 1919 revenue officer Jake Gosnell shot and killed a popular young sheriff named Hendrix Rector in Briscoe's Garage on West Court Street. However, since Rector was unable to draw his gun, this was more properly a one-on-one encounter.[9]

When one turns to shoot-outs inspired by personal concerns (1880–1920), one notices a similar lull in the action during the first decade or so of this century—at least no truly sensational clashes seem to have occurred within the state from the close of 1900 to 1915. However, this drought ended in the spring of 1915 with a truly spectacular gun battle (and the word *battle* is not too strong) in the little community of Pageland and a dramatic hail of bullets at Winnsboro's historic Robert Mills courthouse that left four dead. But first to the final years of the nineteenth century, when nearly a dozen such confrontations took place.

One of these affairs seems to have had no real conclusion, and yet it highlights gnawing fear present throughout the South and much of the nation during those years: all-out race war. The first hint of trouble appeared in the *Charleston News and Courier* on 16 July 1890:

> At about half-past 8 o'clock this morning [the fifteenth] the quiet hamlet of Bamberg was startled by the sudden appearance of a dashing courier, his horse all covered with foam. The messenger came for help, immediate help. The white people of Kearse's settlement feared serious trouble and called on their neighbors for the aid which they knew if they asked would be cheerfully given.
>
> The news of the trouble at Kearse spread like wildfire. Soon twenty-five of Bamberg's brave and noble men were on the way to the assistance of their neighbors.

Telegrams to Graham and Barnwell brought more volunteers to the scene.

This dispute began at a fish fry three weeks earlier. While whites were eating their catch, blacks took their boats and went fishing, despite orders to the contrary. This disobedience led to harsh words, and one young black, Pink Priester Jr., became offensive and used abusive language. Struck with a buggy whip by Robert Kearse, Priester struck back and then fled with his companions. When a small posse went to Priester's home to arrest him, the group was attacked from ambush and six men slightly wounded. The injured included two Chittys and four Kearses, among them Robert.

For a day or so blacks did not appear for work, but then they gradually straggled back. When another posse tried to make what authorities said were legitimate arrests, a more serious gunfight erupted, and in this one Henry Gantt (black) was killed and two white men badly wounded. It was this exchange that led to the cry for help. However, there does not seem to have been any resolution to the matter. The blacks being sought simply vanished, and the *News and Courier* and local weeklies were quite willing to forget that anything had disrupted the daily routine.

The remainder of these pre-1901 shootings involved personal differences or legal matters, sometimes a bit of both flavored with liquor. One incident, truly sensational, occurred in the Newberry office of trial justice Henry Blease, father of Cole and Eugene Blease, on 26 March 1887. Two rising young attorneys, John B. Jones and George Johnstone, were representing opposing parties from North Carolina in a lawsuit involving ownership of tobacco brought into this state to be sold. This hotly contested matter had already led Jones to suggest he and Johnstone meet on the field of honor. Tempers were near the boiling point, and both men were heavily armed.

As Jones tried to address the court, Johnstone, despite the admonition of Justice Blease, repeatedly interrupted him. A welter of words ensued, during which Johnstone, who was slightly older, called his twenty-seven-year-old adversary "an insolent young puppy." In less than a minute, with the two men only a few feet apart, nine shots rang out. Caught between them was Johnstone's partner, George B. Cromer, who either tried to stem the violence or perhaps sought to assist Johnstone. Both men emptied their pistols, and Johnstone drew a second one that he did not use. Miraculously, Cromer was not hurt, although several bullets tore through his clothing. Johnstone suffered three minor wounds, and Jones died a week later.

The *News and Courier* (28 March) called this outburst of gunfire "A Reproach to the State." "The principals in the duel were not cowboys," it said, "but prominent lawyers, men of fine education and large political influence, who, whatever their real or fanciful grievances, should have had some consideration for the public welfare. . . . What hope is there for the State when lawyers, who, of all men, should be shining examples of the dignity and supremacy of the law, convert a crowded Court-room into a shooting gallery and try to fill each other's bodies with bullets!"

A few days later, on 31 March, the *Newberry Herald and News* echoed these sentiments:

If these gentlemen had not been in violation of the law against carrying deadly weapons concealed, in all probability it would not have resulted so seriously. It was wrong in them to go into a court of Justice with deadly pistols in their pockets. And so long as men of high standing in the community go armed, in violation of the law, and public sentiment stands as it does, we may expect such things to happen. And how can we expect men in the lower walks of life to be law-abiding when men of influence thus disregard the law.

We sometimes think that the law against carrying deadly weapons is a dead letter anyway, and it will remain such, until public sentiment condemns its violation in terms unmistakable.

At the trial in November, Johnstone, who declared he was merely defending himself, furnished a full account of what happened. He had, he said, a large pistol in his right pants pocket and a smaller one in his right-hand, inside, coat pocket.[10] Jones, he insisted, fired first when only eighteen inches away, and there was a glare in his gaze—"it was the light of the assassin's eye." Johnstone told how, a few seconds later, as Jones "threw himself" against Cromer, Johnstone pulled the trigger of his large pistol:

> I know that was the shot that killed him, for he winced on both sides. His eyes rolled and I knew he was mortally wounded, for I knew he was shot entirely through. He staggered back, then rushed behind Mr. Cromar [sic], and from that time forward he used him as a breastwork from which to shoot at me as he got the opportunity. While attempting to fire again he exposed his right side, and I took deliberate aim and fired, but I think I missed my aim on account of the dislocation of vision caused by the effect of the powder on my face. The ball struck near the window sill. Trying to shoot again he exposed his left side. I then fired again and that was my third shot. He was then standing with his hand over Mr. Cromar's shoulder. If I fired again I would kill Mr. Cromar, if he fired he would kill me. I fired to the left of him to startle him with the crack of the pistol and with the object of covering myself with smoke. I did so, and pulled out my other pistol with my left hand and grasped it.[11]

The fifth and last shot by Jones did little damage. Then Johnstone recalled he heard Jones say something like "out" and snap his pistol. Friends grabbed Johnstone's arm and urged him to leave. He protested he had done nothing "legally or morally wrong" and, in his words, refused "to budge a peg" until told he had "done for" Jones.

It took the jury only four minutes to acquit Johnstone, although the testimony raised yet another sticky issue that had to be resolved. Was Justice Blease under his bench during the shoot-out? This assertion was put to rest by young Cole Blease, who vowed it was one of the litigants, not his father, who sought refuge there.

During the late 1880s and early 1890s the intersection of Main and Washington streets in downtown Columbia was the setting for several shootings. Shortly after 6:00 P.M. on 19 June 1890, two first cousins from the lower part of Richland County, both prominent young men, emptied their pistols in the presence of a crowd of startled onlookers, including the chief of police. On that occasion

Frank H. Weston flourished a "38-calibre, self-cocking, hammerless Smith & Wesson," and Dr. W. W. Ray used "a 32-calibre, double-action Smith & Wesson." In this instance "double-action" won out over "self-cocking, hammerless," although both men were injured. Weston, only twenty-three and recently named trial justice, came off second best, his shirt front blackened by powder fired at close range.[12]

Ray, about ten years older than Weston and a member of the General Assembly (1884–85), practiced medicine at Congaree near Eastover. According to friends, he had come to town by train earlier that same day with no hint of what would ensue. They said a court case of some sort was the source of the trouble, but this strained relationship was complicated by the fact that young Weston was making his home at the Columbia residence of his aunt, Dr. Ray's mother.

Ten months earlier, on 3 August 1889, also a few minutes after 6:00 P.M., W. B. Meetze shot and killed James I. Clark at the same intersection. This was, said the *News and Courier,* Columbia's first fatal shooting in a decade. Meetze, a short, stocky native of Lexington County, had been a trial justice in New Brookland before moving across the Congaree River to set up a shooting gallery, livery stable, and saloon. Meetze became convinced that Clark, something of a Lothario, was sending "offensive" notes to his wife and, at one point, threatened to kill the messenger, his uncle "Dug" Meetze. The police apprehended W. B. Meetze, who said both Dug and Clark had left town and assured them he was "done" with the matter. A short time later, however, he encountered Clark walking down Main Street with a young lady (said to have been a friend of his daughter) and fired several shots. Two of them hit Clark near each ear, which caused "blood and brainy matter [to ooze] from both."[13] Meetze emptied four barrels of his "five shooter, Smith & Wesson, self-cocker of 38 calibre." Clark, who fired only once, died at about 8:30 P.M.

When asked about his promise to the police, Meetze replied it would have made no difference if they had arrested him at that point; if he had been put in jail, then he would have done the job when he got out: Clark had to die. Following a complicated, five-day mistrial in 1891, Meetze was acquitted in April 1892. He emerged victorious the following year in a verbal skirmish with Ben Tillman (no mean feat) but fared less well in yet another gun battle in February 1894.

The run-in with the governor occurred at the state fair on 9 November 1893. Meetze had permission to sell rice beer at a booth; however, Tillman appeared with dispensary constables and attempted to halt the sale and arrest Meetze. Defiant, the latter claimed Tillman must first get a warrant and "used language to the Governor that was most emphatic, and is not usually found in books."[14] Angered by this resistance, Tillman sought the help of the Richland County sheriff and a local trial justice, neither of whom proved cooperative, and he even considered calling out the Richland Volunteers. Meanwhile, Meetze sold out and closed his booth.

Meetze's second shoot-out near Main and Washington streets took place on 2 February 1894 during a break in a trial concerning sale of illicit liquor by one William Seal. As a crowd of spectators came out of the courthouse, J. D. Miller, who testified that Seal ran a blind tiger, and Burt Fry, who denied buying liquor from Seal, fell to arguing. Meetze, scornful of anyone thought to be prodispensary, jumped into the fray. After calling Miller "a liar," he challenged him to shoot: "Pull your pistol and shoot, you —!"[15]

Miller, who had lived in Texas for several years and learned a bit while there, pulled out not one but *two* handsome 38-caliber Smith & Wessons, one with a beautiful pearl handle, which he fired "with lightning like rapidity." People scattered behind trees and posts as bullets flew. When the smoke cleared, Meetze was on the ground, shot in the side; his wound, though serious, was not fatal. Following the first shoot-out, the *News and Courier* (4 August 1889) hailed Meetze as "one of the best shots" in Columbia, but in Miller he had obviously met a superior, two-gun-toting marksman.

Five years later it was young Willie Meetze's turn. On 28 February 1899 the twenty-one-year-old son of W. B. Meetze shot and killed Alex Cartledge near Tom Lane's restaurant for blacks at 929 Gervais Street. The pair, ostensibly good friends and members of the same military company, became embroiled in an argument when Meetze twitted Cartledge about his alleged association with the dispensary. Fists and then bullets flew, although Cartledge was not armed. Like his dad, Willie had to sit through a mistrial before being set free in July 1899.[16]

As the freewheeling activities of the Meetze family indicate, the 1890s were a lively time in South Carolina. Late on the afternoon of 11 October 1890, Joe David Chandler shot and killed his brother-in-law, James B. Hurst, near a group of law offices in Sumter. Each man fired four shots, although Chandler emerged unscathed. A few days earlier C. M. Hurst, father of Mrs. Chandler, had Chandler arrested for assault and battery after his daughter, bruised and shaken, fled to the Sumter home of her sister. Trial justice Mark Reynolds forced Chandler to post a peace bond, and there matters stood until Saturday afternoon (the eleventh), when James Hurst appeared in the office of Reynolds to find out what had been done.[17]

According to testimony at a trial held in March 1891, Hurst then left and, amid threats to kill Chandler, tried to borrow a pistol. Unable to do so, he bought a weapon and returned to the law offices. A few moments later Chandler, who lived five miles outside of town, rode up to the same spot to inquire, he said, about the terms of his peace bond. He had barely hitched his horse when shots rang out, forcing him backward off the porch and around the corner of a building. Hurst obviously fired first, but his new pistol jammed after three shots. As he tried frantically to turn the chamber by hand, Chandler continued to blaze away. The jury needed only ten minutes to find him "not guilty." Moral of the story: know your weapon, and never go into battle with new, untried equipment.

A year later a similar ruckus erupted in nearby Florence when machinist Thomas W. Talbot cowhided Charlie Barringer, barkeeper at the Central Hotel, for making "scurrilous remarks" and writing "unbecoming poetry" about his eldest daughter. This happened on Saturday, 5 March 1892, and two days later Will Barringer, day clerk at the same establishment, walked up to Talbot as he was chatting with friends in front of John Stackley's store and accused him of taking advantage of his brother. Hot words ensued, "the lie was passed," and pistols were drawn by both men. Friends intervened momentarily and tried to convert the disagreement into a fistfight. However, Charlie Barringer suddenly shot Talbot, whereupon his brother joined in. Talbot, no match for two guns, ran into Stackley's store, but not before he was shot in the kidney. According to the *State* (8 March), the wounded man sat down without realizing he was hurt and died a short time later. "Everybody was terribly excited over the tragedy," a local correspondent reported. "The Florence Rifles have been ordered out to guard the jail tonight."

Talbot, who left a widow and seven children, clearly was an individual of some importance in that emerging rail center, and his death at the hands of two gun-wielding brothers aroused considerable resentment. He was both founder of the Machinists Union and past grand mechanic of that order and also a member in good standing of Florence Lodge No. 1300, Knights of Honor, insured for two thousand dollars. The Barringers, convicted of manslaughter, appealed and won a new trial, which ended on 2 February 1893. The judge's charge to the jury took forty-five minutes; the jurors needed only forty to set the Barringers free.

In 1895 another brother-in-law feud made headlines when guns blazed at the Hammond & Company store in Edgefield. John C. Swearingen, the victim, was married to a sister of Ben Tillman, and Swearingen's sister was the wife of Benjamin L. Jones, the handsome, distinguished-looking Texan who did the killing. The two families lived about a mile apart some eight miles from Edgefield. The difficulty, which had originated years before when Swearingen objected to his sister's marriage, was complicated by a recent fight over fence rails that blocked a public road. Jones sued Swearingen and won, even though the latter insisted the rails had been placed on his own land in a safe manner. In any case, the rails subsequently were burned, whereupon Swearingen blamed young Luther Jones, while the Joneses retorted that Swearingen himself did the burning. A few days before the shooting, Swearingen had been instrumental in the arrest of a black man named Jim Davis, an individual he said could prove his claims against

Luther Jones. The elder Jones (acquitted some years earlier of killing a local black) paid Davis's bail and got him released.

On the morning of 24 April 1895 Swearingen and young Jones met in Hammond's store. Not surprisingly, an argument erupted. The father then appeared on the porch and said any disagreement should be aired with him, not his son, and the shooting started. Neither of the Joneses was hit; Swearingen died within twenty minutes. An inquest revealed that several individuals were in the store at the time, although at least one man (B. W. Sheppard) fled to the basement when he realized what was about to happen. The coroner reported Swearingen had six gunshot wounds, several of them in the back. These apparently were inflicted by Luther Jones from inside the store and his father, who was outside, although the gun used by the latter never was found.[18] However, such things were not needed at an Edgefield trial. In August a jury easily acquitted both father and son.

The little community of Brunson in Hampton County probably never has again seen a Saturday night quite like that of 8 April 1899, when a pitched battle left at least two dead, several others seriously wounded, and a populace badly shaken. The Preachers, a family related by marriage to the largest landowners in the region, hired a black farmhand employed by George Reid. Early that evening the Reids went to the Preacher home and told them in unmistakable language what they thought of such an underhanded maneuver and of the Preachers themselves. An hour or so later three Preachers, three Reids, and Joseph Connelly (a friend of the Reids) exchanged some forty shots on a village street crowded with farmers and their families.

George Reid, hit nine times, died almost instantly, and Mack Reid, James Preacher, and Connelly were badly shot up. In addition Ulmer Newton, a respected black man, died in a freak accident. Alarmed by the gunfire and thinking a policeman had been killed, Newton had grabbed his rifle and run into the street. His son, fearing his father might get into trouble, tried to disarm him. As they grappled for control of the weapon, the elder Newton was accidentally shot. The three Preacher brothers—James, Arron [sic], and Charlie—ultimately were charged with the murder of George Reid. In June a jury weighed their fate for two hours before voting to acquit them.[19]

Those hoping a new century might bring relief from such mayhem quickly were disappointed. In January 1900 the *State* told readers of murders in Anderson ("HOT SUPPER AND COFFINS . . . Another negro hot supper and another negro killing"), North (well-to-do farmer and son kill another son in land dispute), and Columbia, where, following fisticuffs, barber Sylvester Brown shot mulatto athlete John Taylor "dead in his tracks." On 6 January two murderers were hanged in Charleston, and two days later the attorney general's report for 1899 cited 227 homicides, 103 convictions, and 83 acquittals. During the same week F. W.

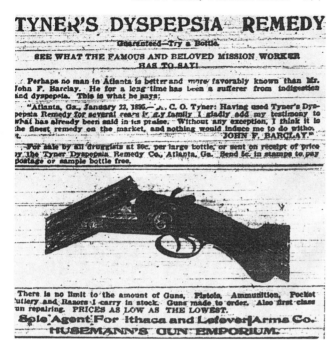
Ad for Husemann's Gun Emporium of Columbia in the *State* (4 January 1900). Courtesy of South Caroliniana Library, University of South Carolina, Columbia

Husemann of Husemann's Gun Emporium (1510 Main Street, Columbia) published his usual ad in the *State* (4 January): "There is no limit to the amount of Guns, Pistols, Ammunition, Pocket Cutlery, and Razors I carry in stock. Guns made to order. Also first class gun repairing. PRICES AS LOW AS THE LOWEST."

On 1 March 1900 seven white men from the Dutch Fork area of Lexington County were cleared of killing farmer W. Patrick Bowers from ambush the previous summer. Bowers, a prosperous but contentious fellow white, may have twice burned down a local sawmill; hence the shooting. To prevent further disorder, the judge closed the Lexington dispensary during the trial. According to the *State* (2 March), "After the jury rendered the verdict[,] the happy defendants repaired to their distant homes, after visiting the reopened dispensary, where the 'chemically pure' flowed freely. Thus ends another mysterious and sensational murder case."

Although some may have thought this ambush affair "sensational," that word should have been saved for what soon followed in Bamberg and Abbeville. At about 10:00 A.M. on the morning of 4 May, the Reverend W. E. Johnson, pastor of Bamberg's Baptist church—momentarily forgetting ancient admonitions such as "Love Thy Neighbor" and "Thou Shalt Not Kill"—rushed out of the parsonage carrying a double-barreled shotgun. Storming across the street, he stopped by a telephone pole, steadied his weapon, and took careful aim at the son of his next-door neighbor, attorney John R. Bellinger. Young Willie Bellinger, a slight youth of about twenty-five years, who was returning from the post office with a newspaper in hand, drew his pistol and fired once or twice, but not before Johnson's only blast inflicted fatal wounds.

This rather remarkable confrontation, which took place in front of the Carlisle Fitting School, was witnessed by several students as well as Joe Brown, Bellinger's brother-in-law. (The fact that Reverend Johnson had performed the ceremony uniting Brown and Bellinger's sister in holy matrimony the previous June was one cause of this feud.) Brown apparently drove up just as Johnson emerged, passively watched the shooting from his carriage, rode over to inspect the body of his dying brother-in-law, and then continued on his way. According to the *State* (5 May 1900), the victim, court stenographer of the Second Judicial District, was "struck by twelve buck and eight small shot, which penetrated his lungs and liver, causing almost instant death." Reverend Johnson immediately returned to his home, where, he later testified, he spent several hours quieting his wife, "who was very much excited." At about one o'clock, in the company of merchant S. H. Sanders, he went to the county jail and surrendered to the sheriff.

Trial testimony also revealed that the day before the shooting Sanders had presented Johnson with the gun he used, loaded and ready to fire. Why? Because Johnson was his pastor and was in danger. Sanders said Johnson's home was being invaded, he had a wife and three small children, and "I thought it the duty of any patriotic citizen to offer him protection." He would, he vowed, have done the same for his friend Bellinger.[20]

The immediate cause of this tragedy was a property-line fence being erected by the Bellingers, proof that fences may not make good neighbors after all. Twenty-four hours earlier Johnson and the Bellingers had shouted conflicting orders to a black man hired by the latter to paint part of this yet-to-be-completed barrier—the pastor telling him to get off his land and the Bellingers directing the poor man to ignore such demands. Reverend Johnson, who was six feet tall and weighed 140 pounds, suggested he and Willie settle the matter "out in the road," meaning a simple exercise with bare knuckles. But when Willie (one foot shorter and thirty pounds lighter) emerged with a pistol, the pastor withdrew his offer. It was this turn of events that Sanders interpreted as an "invasion" of the Johnson home and imminent danger to its occupants.

The trial, with young James F. Byrnes as court stenographer, opened on 6 December 1900 and continued for three days. The courtroom, said the *State*, was "packed to suffocation. The best people of Bamberg were in attendance, many of them ladies." It was standing room only during final arguments on Saturday, the eighth, and at 6:30 P.M. the jury retired. Eleven hours later, as many were betting on a mistrial, they emerged and pronounced the Reverend Johnson not guilty. He "quietly and pleasantly" shook the hand of each juror and then went home to prepare for the regular eleven o'clock service. Reporters failed to disclose what text he chose for his sermon.

Two days later the *State* commented editorially that the outcome was no surprise. Since the secular usually were acquitted of murder in South Carolina, one would expect holy men to receive equal consideration at the hands of jurors. There was, of course, no reason to challenge the verdict. "We only wish to suggest to congregations of all denominations in this State that they institute some inquiry before engaging a spiritual pastor and make sure that he is not addicted to the pistol or shotgun habit. Timely precaution in this matter may mean the saving of much bad blood in our churches, and perhaps the saving of some good blood as well. . . . We do not know quite what to say about the members of Mr. Johnson's congregation who incited him to shed the blood of his neighbor— of course in self-defense—loaned him a pistol [*sic*] and loaded the gun with slugs. On the whole, however, we are inclined to believe they are worthy to receive communion from his hands."

The *State* characterized the Abbeville shoot-out that took place a few weeks later, on 29 December 1900, as something that might have occurred in "a western border town." It was, in fact, much like a scene from a grade B cowboy movie: a bunch of the boys gather for a few hands of poker, the town bully enters, an argument ensues, guns blaze, and three men die. In this instance contractor William Kyle, having completed work on an addition to a local cotton mill, was planning to leave the following morning for his home in Massachusetts. During his last night in town, he and several companions met for a social evening of cards in the office of the Carolina Hotel. Just how they were passing the time is unclear. Both local weeklies, much concerned with propriety in the midst of murder, went to great lengths to assure readers that nothing unseemly was taking place. The *Abbeville Medium* (3 January) reported the men were engaged in a few rounds of "harmless" poker, each one keeping score with goobers—inferring that no money was changing hands. The *Abbeville Press and Banner* (2 January 1901) stated flatly there was no gambling going on: "There never has been any betting at the Carolina Hotel."

Earlier that same day Kyle, a slender man in his late forties, had warm words with John Dansby, a rather unsavory local character some ten years younger, who once had been a deputy U.S. marshal. At about nine o'clock Dansby, who had been drinking, entered the hotel office and asked to join in the fun.[21] He also urged Kyle to shake hands and forget their little spat. Kyle refused, whereupon Dansby called him "a damned son of a bitch." This led to more words, and as Dansby reached for his 45-caliber Colt, one of the men grabbed his arm. However, Dansby skillfully passed the weapon behind his back and shot with the other hand, hitting Kyle in the stomach. Still flourishing his gun, he then backed out of the room, declaring he would kill anyone who made a move to stop him. He then fled to his father-in-law's home in the mill village. Within a short time town police and Sheriff R. L. Kennedy (who had assumed office only nineteen days earlier) surrounded the building and called for Dansby to give himself up. Eventually he emerged, carefully closed the door behind him, and challenged Kennedy with these words: "Well, we'll go to hell together!"[22]

Both men emptied their barrels. Kennedy fell, but Dansby staggered some fifty feet before he was seized by police and taken to jail. By 2:00 A.M., only five hours after the first shot was fired, three men lay dead: Kyle, Kennedy, and Dansby. The *State* (31 December) heaped scorn upon the latter as a reckless man, a notorious gambler, and an individual who often terrorized the community where he lived. According to rumor, he had killed other men and, it was said, associated principally with blacks. The *Abbeville Press and Banner* (2 January 1901) agreed John Dansby led a "stormy" life, but the paper then chose to probe deeper. Why did such things happen? In the opinion of this editor, too many "red-handed" slayers were going unpunished and juries seemed especially reluctant to convict white men charged with murder. Even if sent to prison, an influential white usually could get a pardon, for any solicitor or judge seeking reelection was obliged to sign his appeal.

As noted, shoot-outs apparently went out of style for a time (1901–14), or at least no truly memorable encounters seem to have occurred in this state for a decade or so. Then in the spring of 1915 trouble flared in Pageland and Winnsboro, followed four years later by still more personal fireworks in Denmark and St. Stephen. The St. Stephen slaughter was a simple, in-house, family affair that left all participants dead. Dr. J. H. Pratt, a prominent local physician who was living with relatives, returned from "preaching" on a Sunday evening (14 December 1919) to find a young Charlestonian of whom he did not approve, one Royall Cotton, visiting at the home of his mother-in-law, Mrs. J. T. Bell. Having warned Cotton to stay away, Pratt shot at the caller (but evidently missed him) and went up to his room.[23]

John Bell, Pratt's brother-in-law and a friend of Cotton, hearing the noise, rushed downstairs. As he opened the parlor door, Cotton, thinking the doctor was returning, fired, killing Bell. A few moments later Pratt reappeared, and both men died in the gunfire that ensued. Mrs. Bell and a daughter, the object of Cotton's fatal visit, were slightly injured during the shoot-out. As was true in Abbeville in 1900, there were no survivors; hence no trial.

What actually happened in Denmark a few months earlier is still a bit hazy since most accounts fail to agree on who was involved. What is known is that three men died and one later was found guilty of murder. It had all began several months before when George Stevens, a black telephone company employee, stole some watermelons from a patch near where he was working. Agent Brown, the owner of the watermelons, chased Stevens, who was shielded by his associates. The case came to trial late on the afternoon of 18 July 1919, and when court adjourned for the day, the matter still was unresolved. However, Brown and his brother-in-law Ozelle Anderson clearly were not happy with the drift of the testimony, and once outside they began shooting.

In the cross fire Brown, Stevens, and an innocent bystander (Henry Murray Ray, the twenty-two-year-old son of Sheriff S. G. Ray) were killed. Two more whites were seriously injured: Carroll Mobley, a key witness in the case being heard; and J. Ralph Thompson, who suffered a shattered arm. The *State* and the *Barnwell People* agreed only three men died, but both papers cited a fourth victim, Elmer Luper, a black from Marietta, Georgia. "Luper," it appears, may have been an alias used by Stevens, or vice versa. Three months later Mobley (white) was cleared of all wrongdoing; Anderson (black) was convicted of murder.

Perhaps the most interesting aspect of this watermelon story is the reaction of a local weekly. The *Barnwell People* (24 July) featured a banner headline— DENMARK RACE RIOT COSTS LIVES OF THREE—that was augmented by yet another tale of racial turmoil in Washington, D.C. The cause in both instances, this editor said, might be "insidious literature" being circulated from Baltimore that advised blacks to lynch lynchers, arm themselves with Winchesters, and prepare for any eventuality. His editorial—entitled "Is Poison at Work?"—is reminiscent of those published throughout South Carolina in the 1840s and 1850s. As then, no one had actually *seen* this incendiary material but merely had heard rumors about it.

Yet this courtroom-inspired fracas in Denmark was child's play compared to the shootings in Pageland and Winnsboro, both of which had loose ties to the judicial process. The immediate cause of the Pageland tragedy was much the same as that of the 1899 Preacher-Reid row in Brunson. One of the West boys allegedly broke a labor contract with a Mrs. Treat, sister of an Arant, to go to work for Dock Wallace. (All of those involved were members of white families living in the northwest section of Chesterfield County, a collection of individuals who had been at odds over one thing or another for years.) The Arants sought damages, but on 12 March 1915 a Pageland magistrate ruled the case lacked merit and threw it out of court. A short time later the main street of that little town rang with some fifty to one hundred shots in what was probably the largest shoot-out ever staged in South Carolina.

At least ten Arants, Wallaces, and Wests, plus several friends, were involved, and this awesome sight was witnessed by over one hundred spectators. Two men were killed (Dock Wallace and J. Wesley Arant), four others seriously injured, and several more slightly wounded. Press reports indicate the toll was about equal on both sides; fortunately, for once, no bystanders were hit.

The trial, held in March 1916, lasted five days, attracted widespread attention, and required the services of eight attorneys. The *Pageland Journal* (8 March) noted that much of the first day "was consumed by the lawyers in an attempt to agree as to how the case should be tried. The final agreement seems to have been that they should first try to find out who killed J. D. Wallace; next who killed J. W. Arant; and finally how many were guilty of the charge of riot." There was, said the *Journal,* "a whole army of witnesses" to be heard, and the paper quoted a lawyer as saying that by the time they finished, "a reasonable doubt might be left in the minds of the jurors as to whether any shooting at all was done or not." Testimony indicated, the *State* remarked on 11 March, that those involved came to town "armed with pistols and rifles and extra ammunition, and . . . engaged in a free-for-all-fight, shooting and killing each other."

In the end, the lawyer who foresaw confusion was right. Unable to make sense of the case after listening to fifty-nine witnesses, the jurors merely convicted five Wests (John E., Baxter, Arthur, Sheppard, and Luther) of rioting, a crime that carried a fine of $150 or a year on the county chain gang. Ten other defendants— the Wallaces, the Arants, and their friends—were acquitted. The *Pageland Journal* thought the jury had done what "seemed best," noting that the trial would "cost well above the seven hundred mark, and the county was the looser [*sic*]."

In April 1915 a black farmhand named Jules Smith allegedly assaulted the wife of a well-known Fairfield County farmer, Clyde Isenhower. After eluding a posse for three days, Smith finally was captured near Blythewood on 22 April and taken to the state penitentiary. Two months later—closely guarded by Sheriff Adam D. Hood, eight deputies, and twenty special deputies—he was brought back to Winnsboro for trial. As the group (Smith in the center) walked up the courthouse stairs, Clyde Isenhower opened fire. Two minutes and fifty bullets later, three men were dead or dying and a fourth, fatally wounded, lingered until early July. Hood, according to the *State* (15 June), was "literally shot to pieces," although this daily conceded many bullets went wild, "striking a bystander here and there." It appears that Clyde Isenhower had taken a position on the second-story porch and was shooting through the banisters at Smith. Before Isenhower died as a result of thirteen slugs in his body, he reportedly said, "I did not want to shoot the sheriff. I had nothing against him. God told me to shoot the negro. Sheriff Hood shot me in the arm and then I shot him." When asked if he was prepared to die, Isenhower again stated he only did what the Almighty directed him to do, adding, "I am satisfied."[24]

This is how the "Battle of Winnsboro" unfolded: Clyde Isenhower was determined to kill Jules Smith. Hood, serving his eleventh year as sheriff, was equally firm in his resolve to deliver his prisoner to the bar of justice—which he did, but just barely. Clyde's brother Ernest, a tall, muscular, thirty-year-old schoolteacher, was on the first-floor porch of the courthouse talking to the solicitor when the firing commenced. He and several friends quickly came to the defense of his brother, and the deputies, in turn, began shooting at them to protect the sheriff, themselves, and the prisoner.[25] Hood was able to stagger into the courtroom and drop Smith's nearly lifeless body before the judge. Court officials eased the dying sheriff into a chair and then did the same for rural policeman J. R. Boulware, the special deputy who died a few weeks later. Meanwhile, three other deputies found Clyde Isenhower, badly shot up, stretched out on the floor of the sheriff's office unbreeching his gun and, in the words of a *State* reporter, "drilled him clean." There were, the reporter said, blood stains and puddles of blood "everywhere."

In the wake of this spectacular shoot-out, Ernest Isenhower, Jesse Morrison, and James Rawls were charged with several counts of murder and hustled off to Columbia to avert further bloodshed. Within hours a movement developed to honor Hood, and a large plaque placed in the county courtroom keeps his memory alive. However, some, including Mrs. A. J. Gross of Bascomville in nearby Chester County, disagreed as to who deserved to be honored after the incident. Clyde Isenhower was, as Mrs. Gross wrote in a letter published in the *State* (30 June), "our hero . . . the bravest of the brave." Those who followed the dictates of Sheriff Hood, according to Mrs. Gross, were wrong; they were sinners:

God told Moses that all such as Jule [*sic*] Smith should be stoned to death. That is God's law and it stands everywhere. I do not think Lee or Jackson did a braver deed than Clyde. I hope all the ladies of our land will contribute to build a monument to his memory. If our governor or any other great man's home had been treated as Clyde's, how different things would have been. Jule would not have fared any better than a mad dog. I think Morrison, Rawls or Isenhower . . . would make a safe sheriff for our women. I hope our governor and all men in power will send the three men they have in prison to their homes. They are needed there to protect women. I am a mother, one that was reared and lived through the war, 60 to 65, and remember '76. The negroes are no better now than they were then. We need brave men at home to protect us and work. I have sons. If they would not protect women, not Jule Smiths, I would not own them as my boys. I have written the sentiments of my mind, also of a great many more.

Despite such eloquence, in December 1915 the three men were brought to trial in York, not Winnsboro, for the murder of rural policeman Boulware. Former governor Cole Blease, chief defense counsel, quickly transformed the proceedings into a referendum on Jules Smith and black rapists in general. For example, his cross-examination of one deputy went like this:

Blease: "You were ready to shoot a white man to protect a negro who raped
   a white woman?"

Deputy: "Yes."

Blease: "We haven't got many men in this country like you."[26]

At every opportunity Blease reminded jurors that the whole state was watching
them to see if twelve men "would uphold the virtue of the women of South
Carolina." He also told them in summation, "Every negro in South Carolina is
eagerly awaiting your verdict today. If you find Ernest Isenhower guilty[,] every
negro will say, 'I can ravish a white woman and the law will vindicate me.'" Blease
vowed he respected written law but then—like Mrs. Gross—pointed to the dictates of Moses. Almost as an afterthought, he noted that of course Ernest Isenhower did nothing but what he himself and any other man would do: he came
to the aid of his brother.

Both the solicitor and the judge cautioned jurors to base their verdict on the
evidence presented and state statutes, not some unwritten, "higher" law; but this
was to no avail. It took the jury only ninety minutes to clear the three men of
killing Boulware. Eleven months later this story was repeated in the same courtroom with virtually the same cast (and the same ending) when the trio were tried
for the murder of Adam Hood. Apparently no one ever was prosecuted for the
death of Jules Smith.

As H. V. Redfield observed in the late 1870s, shoot-outs occurred all too frequently in South Carolina—so often that it reminded one of the rough-and-
ready, outlaw West. Four decades later the *State*, the *News and Courier*, and other
newspapers were saying much the same thing. What is most striking is the minor
role blacks played in the two dozen or so altercations described in this chapter.[27]
Except as spectators or innocent victims, they took part in only four of these
shoot-outs (about 16 percent), and on only two occasions—Bamberg in 1890
and Denmark in 1919—did they have weapons. There is but one logical conclusion: white South Carolinians, using the argument they needed guns to protect
themselves from former slaves, acquired arms and then slipped easily into the
habit of killing each other.

10

THE WEIRD, BIZARRE, AND INSANE

The incidents that follow are so varied that classification of them is a bit difficult. They reveal that, during these years, bad food, bad moods, baseball games, mistreatment of dogs, treading on toes, even disputes over who would preach the sermon or attend a social event could lead to murder. Yet one general category does emerge: child murder, meaning murder *by* children, not of them. According to common law, a child under the age of seven was presumed incapable of criminal intent. A similar presumption applied to those between seven and fourteen unless there was proof the youngster was intelligent enough to understand the nature of the act involved. Those fourteen and older were considered adults.

This interpretation was upheld by the South Carolina Supreme Court in an 1881 decision (*State v. Toney*), which said that "the capacity of an infant under fourteen years of age to commit the crime of malicious trespass is a question to be determined by the facts; independent evidence of such capacity is not essential."[1] Thus juveniles, children under the age of fourteen, existed in a sort of legal limbo in late nineteenth-century South Carolina, and what should be done with them if they broke the law was unclear. They might or might not be held accountable. At the same time, they were "infants" when it came to civil matters such as contracts and inheriting property.

The constitutions of 1868 and 1895 talked of facilities for juvenile offenders, but none appeared until 1900, when a state farm for young white and black males (to be segregated, of course) was created in Lexington County, followed by an industrial school for white boys (eight to sixteen years of age) in 1906 and a similar institution for white girls (eight to twenty) in 1918. Meanwhile, in 1917 Columbia's Recorder's Court was given authority to care for neglected and incorrigible children, the beginnings of juvenile courts in this state.

In the absence of both established guidelines and juvenile detention centers, during the final decades of the nineteenth century some youngsters were locked up with older, hardened criminals. Between 1880 and 1900, of 11,281 individuals admitted to the state penitentiary, 156 were less than fourteen years of age. Virtually all of them were black, which is not surprising since the racial ratio at that institution in the mid-1890s was ten to one black.[2] Most had stolen something; several were guilty of rape, arson, assault and battery, or endangering railway traffic; and a dozen between the ages of nine and thirteen had killed someone, often a playmate. (Seven others convicted on similar charges of murder or manslaughter appear to have been fourteen years of age.) These youngsters usually served two or three years and then were released, although a few fared less well and received much stiffer sentences.

Several of these homicide cases (all of them black) are especially revealing. Richard Davis, not quite fourteen and scheduled to be hanged in Marion County in 1885, had his sentence commuted to life. Governor Hugh S. Thompson observed that Davis "had very little, if any, mental and moral training" and "the ends of public justice would not be met by the execution of a boy so young and [so] lacking in intelligence that he fails to understand the crime committed."[3] In January of that year, authorities found the battered body of Perry B. Richardson, a widower who lived in rural Marion County, his head split by an ax blow. Within a few days young Davis was behind bars and duly convicted.

Two years later Axy Cherry of Barnwell County, age eleven, was about to be hanged for murder. Axy had administered a potion of concentrated lye to a white infant under her care. The *Barnwell People* (14 July 1887) reported that when she appeared in court, the accused exhibited no fear and "pleaded not guilty in unfaltering voice." When asked about sparing her life, the judge who passed sentence on her had this comment: "I have nothing to say now except to remark that one so young ought not be hanged; she is a little wretch of a villain, and should be punished, but not by death."[4] In August 1887 Axy's sentence was commuted to five years in prison.

The following year Charles Du Pre—age nine, four feet and three inches tall, a precocious Marlboro County lad—was granted a similar reprieve when his death sentence was reduced to thirty years. Clearly a well-developed bully, Charles scuffled with a seven-year-old playmate and his five-year-old brother because they called him "Peter." When the two younger boys barricaded themselves in their home (the parents were working in the fields), Charles broke down the door and hacked both of them with an ax, wounds that proved fatal to the older child. According to Governor John P. Richardson, "The boy did not seem to understand the nature of his crime, or to think he had done anything particularly wrong. After pleading guilty to the charge of murder, he said, 'and now I want to go home.'"[5] All three died behind bars—Richard Davis on 2 May 1905, Axy Cherry on 18 January 1892 (about seven months before she was to be released), and Charles Du Pre on 21 June 1893.

During these same years (the 1880s and 1890s), at least two other black juveniles were acquitted of murder. On 7 April 1888 Laney Walker of Union, who was about eight, stabbed and killed a little black girl named Sibbie Thomas near a spring where washing was done. Laney was jailed for a time, released on bond, and acquitted on 8 October 1888.[6] A few years later Kelly Backstraw of Chester, age eight, killed a small white playmate. Following a mistrial, he eventually was set free in October 1891.[7]

Reports and Resolutions after 1900 present a more complete accounting of those charged with murder and their ages. Of about fifty young people fourteen and under so indicted during the next two decades, seventeen were convicted. Nearly all of those found guilty were thirteen or fourteen years of age. In 1906 a Chester County jury spent an entire morning deliberating the fate of Stephen Neal, age eight, who allegedly killed a playmate during a rock fight. Stephen, a black youngster, was found innocent.[8] Three years later six-year-old Fred Bell (black) was lodged in the Union County jail for shooting a three-year-old black girl and hiding her body behind an outhouse. Although Ethel Thomas was alive when found, she succumbed to her wounds. Local authorities eventually decided the affair was "accidental," and Fred was released.[9]

Two years after that, Rosa Ficklin of Barnwell County, also black and only eight, was charged with assault and intent to kill. At length, she was convicted of simple assault and fined five dollars or five days in jail; but, on condition of good behavior, even that sentence was suspended.[10] That same year an eight-year-old black youngster named George Bynard, who shot and killed one playmate and wounded another on a Beaufort plantation, was "released on his own recognizance."[11]

To some degree, days and nights in jail and the ordeal of a trial probably were designed "to teach the kid a lesson." But as years passed, and especially after the establishment of reform facilities for delinquent boys, fewer and fewer small children were being formally arraigned. A Georgetown solicitor ruled in 1912 that murderer Willie Godwin (black, age eight) was not accountable for his acts under the laws of the state of South Carolina.[12] In 1919 a Spartanburg County grand jury declined to indict a Woodruff eight-year-old named Buster Cooker (white). Buster, furious when his brother Fred, age five, dashed a glass of water on him while he was sleeping, crawled into an attic, got his uncle's shotgun, and "almost completely blew his little brother's head off."[13] And in 1920 an Orangeburg judge directed a verdict of not guilty in the case of Booker T. Perry, age nine. Two years earlier Perry (black) killed a playmate and then tried to hide his body, which would seem to indicate some awareness of the nature of the deed.[14]

On at least three occasions between 1880 and 1920 bad food, a foul mood, or a combination of both resulted in homicides. The first such incident occurred in Walterboro on Saturday, 19 July 1884. (Few will be surprised to learn that weekends were a prime time for violence, especially Saturdays.) Dr. W. H. Miller, who worked in the Colleton County clerk's office, went home, had a drink or two, and, according to various sources, was "considerably excited" by the time dinner was served. "Dr. Miller immediately commenced finding fault with everything at the table, and worked himself into a very irritable humor, got up from the table, went to his room apparently and got his pistol, a Colt's navy revolver, loaded it with powder and ball, not with cartridges. Mrs. Miller [his stepmother] got up and went to the door [of his room] to coax him back to the table, saying to him, according to her account and that of Col. Miller, 'William, come in to dinner, it mightn't suit you exactly, but come and eat it anyhow.'"[15] The reply was a shot, following which Mrs. Miller went to her husband, loosened her dress, and said, "William shot me here." At first it was thought the lady would survive, but twenty-four hours later she took "a bad turn" and died on Monday evening.

As for William, at first he claimed he only meant to scare his stepmother by shooting over her head. Then, amid much profane language and more drinking, he shouted, "Somebody had to do it, and I did it!" The doctor later became even more irrational and jumped out of a window before being charged with murder and jailed. This tragedy, a Walterboro correspondent wrote, caused much sorrow since the deceased was related to more than half of the residents in the community.

Sixteen years later, again in Colleton County, spoiled food almost led to a lynching. In mid-July 1900 W. P. Felder bought a string of fish from a man named Ferrel. When the fish proved to be tainted, the two quarreled in a country store owned by a Captain Shaffer. Clayburn Herndon, a popular young clerk who tried to mediate, was shot and killed.[16] The county sheriff, fearing mob action, appealed to the governor, and Felder was whisked away to Columbia. He subsequently was acquitted of the crime.

In 1920 Bennett Clary, a mute with a wife and six children, was found innocent following a breakfast brawl during which he shot and killed his brother-in-law, Will Holt. All of these people (white) lived with Mrs. Clary's parents, Mr. and Mrs. Sumter Holt, in the Newberry County community of Helena. Will, the last to arise, came to the table in "a bad humor" at about 5:30 A.M. He fell to arguing with his sister, Mrs. Clary, and, according to the *State* (20 July), "was attempting to use a chair on some members of the family" when he was shot. Holt died three hours later.

Baseball played some role in homicides occurring in 1889, 1891, and 1900. The latter two incidents clearly involved the game itself. In September 1891 a black youth named Charlie Young "brained" Jim Walls with a bat during a contest being waged in a settlement called "Twin Pines," located three miles from Winnsboro. The *State* (7 September) reported that Young, who fled, hit Walls, dropping him to the ground, and then "pounded him several good licks." Two days later the *Fairfield News and Herald* noted this time it was not the umpire who was killed. During the summer of 1900 a baseball game played by blacks at Cypress Plantation in Colleton County came to a quick end when Joe Huger (age eighteen) threw a fast ball that hit Robert Jiveur (age fifteen) on the foot. A fight ensued, and Jiveur shot Huger in the head.[17]

The first baseball death is somewhat more complicated. On Saturday, 15 June 1889, the Aiken and Graniteville teams met. That evening Richard Hobbs, a young night watchman at Gunther's store in Madison, shot and killed Willis Curry. Hobbs, then behind bars, described what happened: "The drum and fife corps, of which I am a member and in which I play the bass drum, furnished the music while the game was being played. Aiken was winning, and during the game Curry accused me of taking sides with the visiting club. I told him if he was not satisfied to quit playing, which he did. At night Curry came to Mr. Gunter's [sic] store, where I am employed as night watchman, and he called me outside the store, and after cursing me he pulled his knife out and threatened to cut my throat. I backed out of his way, but he continued advancing, and when I thought my life was in jeopardy, I pulled my pistol and fired two shots, but only one ball took effect, which lodged in his breast and produced immediate death."[18] Although Hobbs was acquitted, trial testimony indicates Curry's friends claimed he had no knife and furnished evidence that Hobbs was at fault. However, it is true a knife was found in the dead man's hand and Hobbs surrendered voluntarily to authorities the following morning.

During these turn-of-the-century years, dogs were the cause of several homicides involving whites. Late in the evening of 16 July 1896, Tench Styles was walking past the home of his neighbor Abner Pearson in the Sandy Flat community, twelve miles north of Greenville. When Pearson's dog lunged at him, Styles shot the animal. Pearson, who was asleep, heard the noise, jumped up, got on his horse, and pursued Styles, who offered to pay for the dog. Pearson refused this gesture and opened fire. But Styles was armed too; as the encounter intensified, Styles shot Pearson in the chest, knocking him from his horse, and then fired twice more as his onetime friend lay dying on the ground.[19] Four months later a jury cleared Styles of all charges stemming from this incident.

In mid-January of the following year, Capers Stephens, "a dissipated, roving character," shot and killed his brother-in-law James Bell near Bell's Cross Roads in Colleton County. The first account in the *State* (19 January 1897) said the pair were arguing, a pointer belonging to Stephens came between them, and Bell kicked the dog. Stephens became enraged, and his sister (Bell's wife) tried to separate the two men, but Stephens inserted his gun under her arm and killed her husband. Another version (24 January) told how Bell, fed up with his brother-in-law's aimless ways, objected to the dog sleeping in his bed and this led to the fatal encounter. During an inquest the jury concluded Stephens was insane and shipped him off to the Walterboro jail. "He has not been considered in his right mind for some time past," a local correspondent added.[20]

Under the headline "HUMAN LIFE IS CHEAP IN SOUTH CAROLINA," the *State* told on 3 February 1903 of a Florence County shooting that occurred when Samuel

Rogers asked William King to pay for feeding and sheltering his dog. Rogers apparently found the animal and did not know to whom it belonged. Then, after several weeks, he met King in town and discovered he was the owner, and the latter agreed to some form of compensation. However, when the two men got to the Rogers home, King started shooting, killing Rogers almost instantly, mortally wounding his father, and snapping his empty gun at Rogers's mother after he ran out of bullets. In a somewhat unusual twist, King (age fifty-three) was found guilty of murder at the June term of court.

In these same decades stepping on toes cost the lives of blacks living in Bamberg and Hartsville. On 5 July 1895, as a revival meeting was getting under way in a Bamberg school, Alex Brabham, "a bright young mulatto," was pushing through the crowd when he "incautiously tread[ed]" on the toe of one Adam Hannibal. Despite religious surroundings, the latter, "to vent his wounded spirit," drew a shining Smith & Wesson and shot Brabham through the heart. The *State* reported two days later that "the pandemonium that followed amounted to a stampede. Hannibal held the exit with his revolver, while the excited crowd poured through the windows, regardless of shutters or sash." Hannibal, the paper said, soon disappeared and had not been seen since the shooting.

The second affair was more typical. It was Saturday night (8 October 1904), the streets of Florence were crowded, and Henry Bradshaw, a husky, thirty-five-year-old black from Hartsville, stepped on the toes of Edward Kelly, a white youth half his age. Words followed, and Bradshaw, said to have been "an impudent fellow," tried to pull a pistol, but Kelly shot first. He was immediately arrested but evidently never was indicted for the killing. Concerning the deceased, the *State* had this to say on 9 October: "He had a number of scars on his person, which were convincing evidence of the fact that his past reputation was bad."

Sunday school at Hunter's Chapel in Midway on 4 July 1886 was much more exciting than the faithful had anticipated. A month earlier the *Charleston News and Courier* (7 June) reported that John Studley had been cowhided near Bamberg by W. W. Connelly and A. L. Ott for circulating "false and damaging" tales concerning Connelly's sister. A correspondent said Connelly bought a $2.50 whalebone whip, which he wore out as he administered thirty lashes. Two weeks later Studley published a letter in the same daily denying his part in the story and alleging that charges of slander on his part were false. He conceded he told something in confidence that later was divulged; however, he continued, no one was contemplating legal action. He added that Miss Connelly's mother had been supplied with an accurate account of what happened.

What Studley said in rebuttal may have been true, but Emma Connelly, once his fiancée, saw things in a quite different light. During Sunday school on 4 July "she walked into the church with her arms folded and a pistol in one hand, cocked. She passed into the seat in the rear of Studley, and when just behind him shot him. He arose, looked around, tried to get out his pistol, and at the same time made for the door. Miss Connelly snapped her pistol again, but it failed to go off. If it had gone off [,] the chances are that some one else would have been hurt, as the church was crowded."[21] Studley fell at the church door and was dead three minutes later.

The following day Miss Connelly, said to be "in good spirits," consulted her attorneys in Barnwell but was not detained by authorities. Ten days later this tall, good-looking brunette, a lady in her early twenties, appeared in court and told of her lifelong affection for the deceased. Supported by family members, Miss Connelly testified she had seen the letters in question, but her lawyers refused to let her say more. The jury needed only twenty-five minutes to return a "not guilty" verdict.

A row in the black church at Mount Prospect in Chester County left two dead in April 1915. Apparently Eli Sullivan, whom the *State* (2 May) described as a man who "talks very fine . . . [and] tries to speak very properly and use big words," became angry when not permitted to assume the pulpit occupied by Pastor John Colvin. The result was a shoot-out between opposing factions in which Colvin and his friend Samuel L. Sanders came off second best. It was, a coroner told the governor, "the most atrocious murder" he had investigated in years. Sullivan—the *State* conceded he was "a little cranky on religion"—immediately vanished, but two of his associates, William Mobley Jr. and Sr., were convicted of manslaughter a few months later.

Yet another preacher, a white man named H. D. Granger, was shot and killed from ambush a decade earlier under strange circumstances. Granger, a Baptist, lived in what was known as Horry County's "dead stretch," an expanse of land lying between Bayboro and Loris where blacks were not welcome. Contrary to local custom, Granger hired two blacks to work on his farm, protected them, and even permitted them to sleep on the premises. Hence the mysterious shooting.[22]

Social gatherings big and small also could lead to sudden death. Late on a Saturday evening in February 1903, Henderson Garrett arrived unannounced and uninvited at the Cedar Grove home of Perry Cooper in Laurens County and "proceeded to give a little musical concert."[23] These young blacks knew each other well; and when Garrett failed to explain the reason for this impromptu entertainment, Cooper shot him dead. Six months later he was convicted of murder.

According to the initial report, three died in a general fusillade at a black dance being held near Varennes Church in Anderson County in January 1911; however, one of the "deceased" showed up at the inquest a few days later. In any case it appears two were killed and eight seriously hurt, some by bullets and others by running into a barbed wire fence in their eagerness to flee the scene. The cause of all this activity was a lively black female from Atlanta (the same individual who "rose from the dead") whose presence on the dance floor prompted an exchange of one hundred or more shots. Although four men were arrested—some for shooting within the building and others for firing into it—apparently no one ever was tried and convicted.[24]

Six months earlier, in yet another part of Anderson County, a Honea Path man learned much about the fury of social frustration. As S. B. Wright was dressing to go to a funeral, he informed his wife that she could not go. Under a black headline, "DETERMINED TO ATTEND FUNERAL," the *State* (5 June 1910) told how she replied, "If she couldn't, he shouldn't." Wright remained firm, so she shot him as he was bending over to tie his shoelaces. "The woman gives as excuse for the shooting," said the *State*, "that she was mad." The *Anderson Daily Mail* (6 June), providing more details, said "Boot" Wright, about twenty-five years of age, was a well-known, "progressive" farmer whose wife was said to be "mentally unbalanced." Both dailies described the wounds as fatal, but a few days later the Anderson paper reported that Wright might recover.

Less fortunate were three men who died near Greenwood in the fall of 1916. The scene was the county prison farm, and the precipitating factor was a chance to see John Robinson's circus, "the world's oldest and greatest show." On Saturday, 7 October, Charley Luquire, a chain-gang guard, spent the day in town, where he attended the circus, drank a bit too much, and tried to pick a fight in a pool hall, after which he returned to the farm in an ugly mood. When he arrived, Tom McCombs, captain of county chain gangs, rebuked him mildly for being late and perhaps preventing others from getting to the evening performance on time.

Without a word in reply, Luquire shot McCombs in the chest, which prompted elderly Pomp Davis, father-in-law of farm manager Milton Townsend, to exclaim, "Why, Charley, you killed Mr. Tom!" Luquire then turned his gun on Davis. This volley brought Townsend rushing to the scene, where he suffered a similar fate. Still not speaking, Luquire went to his room. When he emerged a few moments later (apparently having reloaded his gun), McCombs looked up at him and said, "Well, Charley, you killed three of us." At last breaking his silence, Luquire said that was precisely what he had planned to do, whereupon he shot himself in the head.

Although wounded in the lungs, McCombs survived; however, the deaths of Davis, Townsend, and Luquire sent shock waves through the community. The editor of the *Greenwood Daily Journal* (9 October) blamed the tragedy on "cheap whiskey" shipped in from Chattanooga that "dethroned" Luquire of his reason. Sermons and mass meetings followed in a concerted effort to suppress blind tigers, part of a general Prohibition surge that soon would triumph throughout the nation.

Not permitting his daughters to attend an ice cream supper in a nearby tobacco barn proved to be a fatal mistake for a respected black farmer who lived near

Muldrow's Mill in Florence County. This murder, described by the *State* (19 July 1919) as "brutality of an almost inconceivable nature," snuffed out the life of one Sylbert Myers, a man neighbors said was "anxious to rear his children correctly." As he ate supper, his daughters Lillian and Rebecca hit him in the head with an ax, dragged his body into the yard, watched him die, and then got dressed in their Sunday best and went off to eat ice cream. Several hours later, as they returned home from the party, two young men accompanying them discovered the bloody scene. Each of these teenage young ladies was convicted and sentenced to two years in prison.[25]

Axes also played a starring role in an especially gruesome duel in Edgefield County in 1896. This clipping sums up what happened:

CUT HIS HEAD OFF

A White Man and a Negro Fight with Axes

Special to The State. Edgefield, May 13.—A few days ago a white man named Gary Dorn and a negro got into an altercation near Donisville [*sic*] in this county. They fought with axes, and Dorn broke the negro's arm with his first blow, cut him on the arm, then knocked him in the head; and after he was down chopped off his head. Trial Justice Abe Gilchrist acted as coroner and decided it was justifiable homicide, and turned the prisoner loose.[26]

Two Christmas Eve tragedies—one in 1895 and the other in 1912—featured fireworks. In the first instance, John Brown, a sixteen-year-old black youth, disrupted a dance in the Hamburg Heights section of Spartanburg by setting off explosives. When he persisted despite pleas to stop, a trio of blacks began beating him and then yet another (Andy Thompson) pulled out a pistol and fired. Brown yelled, "Lordy, I'm shot" and fell flat on his face, dead. "The dancers scattered," said the *State* (27 December), "and five minutes later only two black boys were on the scene." The following November, Thompson and several others involved in this fracas were convicted of murder.

The 1912 fireworks affair, somewhat more spectacular, occurred in the main street of McBee, a little Chesterfield County community. At about three o'clock in the afternoon, several individuals, in the carefree spirit of the holiday season, began shooting off Roman candles. In time this bit of sport degenerated into "a friendly duel" between J. P. Wallace, a local farmer, and druggist Clyde McManus. When Wallace ran out of candles and McManus continued to fire away, Wallace became irritated and complained that the flames were too close to his face. Another version of the story is that Wallace was upset because he seemed to be losing. Whatever the truth, he drew a pistol; and as the two men struggled, McManus suffered flesh wounds to his hands and stomach.

Flying into a rage, the druggist grabbed the gun, threw Wallace to the ground, straddled him, and in the words of one witness, "shot him deliberately [in the head] (as if he were firing at a target). Then McManus got up off him, walked off to the drug store, still holding the pistol in his left hand."[27] A few months later McManus was sentenced to two years in the penitentiary. At that time he planned to appeal to the state supreme court but apparently did not.

Similar fits of pique led to a trunk murder in Columbia in 1916 and an Aiken matricide in 1918. The latter tragedy unfolded when the elderly mother of Govan Stephenson Jr. of Perry continued to use a garden path her son wanted kept closed. As they quarreled on 8 June, he became infuriated and shot the seventy-year-old semi-invalid three times in the head. Stephenson, son of a well-to-do farmer, married, and father of two, also wounded a niece during this outburst. The *Aiken Journal and Review* (12 June) said he appeared unmoved by the crime. But in a new twist Stephenson pled guilty when arraigned and was sentenced to life on the chain gang.

The trunk murder, perhaps Columbia's first, occurred on or about 31 July 1916—at least that was the last day anyone saw Genevieve Williams alive. Her mother discovered her hacked-up remains three days later when neighbors complained of a foul odor. The unfortunate Genevieve was the live-in companion of Jesse Murphey (both black), with whom she shared a house at 1504 Gadsden Street. Murphey, about thirty and employed at a Gervais Street meat-packing house, was nowhere to be found. Three years later, however, he was tracked down in Pittsburgh (evidence of new diligence on the part of local detectives), brought back to Columbia, convicted, and sentenced to death. Jesse admitted killing Genevieve but then told a most ingenious story of how it occurred. According to his testimony, in the midst of a scuffle he "accidentally" choked his girlfriend to death and she happened to fall into an open trunk, which gave him "an idea" of how to hide the crime from the police.[28]

Five other tales scattered throughout these decades are equally bizarre, perhaps even more so. Leaving the gate open to North Carolina almost cost William Killgore his life in April 1891. The gate in question was located on the state boundary at the upper edge of Spartanburg County, and Killgore—to the irritation of Bob Simms, who lived nearby—failed to close it whenever he passed through. Shots were exchanged on several occasions, and this feud was renewed with great vigor when Killgore (now a constable) served legal papers on the brother of Simms. Incensed by this act and recalling the often-left-open gate, Simms tracked down Killgore and shot him. The *State* (14 April) reported he would die, but the following day the *Carolina Spartan* noted only that his wounds were serious. "It was an old quarrel," the *Spartan* commented in a bored, rambling fashion. "Whiskey, no doubt, had much to do with it."

Whiskey most certainly was a factor in a Boer War murder that took place in Charleston on 23 December 1899. Matthew Gleason (Irish) and Alex Logan

(English) got into a bitter argument concerning the fighting in the Transvaal. Discussion became so heated that Logan, very drunk, stormed home to get his "old-fashioned, double-barreled, muzzle-loader shot gun." When he returned to the corner of Blake and Drake streets where he had left Gleason, the latter had departed. So in a drunken stupor, using a weapon loaded with nails, Logan shot and killed another Irishman instead, a man named Mike Hogan.

"Too much John Barleycorn, rather than admiration for either John Bull or Paul Kruger, was at the bottom of the affair," the *State* said on 24 December. However, the *News and Courier* reported that, even though Logan was inebriated, he recognized his friend Hogan and called him by name. In the opinion of this daily, Logan simply was in "a killing humor," adding that for a time he held at bay four policemen sent to arrest him. The *News and Courier* also recalled that during the previous Yuletide season (1898) Logan had tried to kill yet another man; nevertheless this forty-one-year-old English patriot was acquitted of murder at the June court term.

Gunplay that left two dead in a Columbia restaurant in 1911 proves with much force the old adage (if anyone ever doubted it) that the customer is *always* right. Shortly after noon on 6 May, a Saturday, Ernest F. Grimsley, once a guard with a Richland County chain-gang detail, entered the Acme Restaurant and Grocery Store at 1219 Taylor Street and ordered a bowl of soup. A few minutes later the owner, Mrs. Rosa Bessinger, turned down his request for another roll or a slice of bread to go with the remainder of his soup.

Angry, this twenty-three-year-old man departed and went to a nearby shop, where he bought twenty cartridges. At 3:30 P.M. he returned to the restaurant and shot Walter Sandifer (Mrs. Bessinger's nephew) as Sandifer was cutting up onions and chatting with Confederate veteran Frank M. High. After Sandifer fell to the floor, Grimsley walked behind the counter and shot him again. He then, according to High, proceeded into the kitchen, where he shot and killed Mrs. Bessinger.[29] In June, Grimsley and his lawyers put forth an insanity plea, but after three-and-one-half hours a jury found him guilty (with mercy). Sentenced to life in prison, Grimsley, like the McBee druggist who liked Roman candles, talked of an appeal but eventually abandoned such efforts.

During these same years a weird tale was unfolding in Lee County. In September 1910 M. L. "Bob" Garrett was arraigned for incest. Garrett, a white man and a Clarendon County native, pled guilty and was sentenced to two years in the state penitentiary. Gertrude, his fifteen-year-old daughter, was in court, but the solicitor chose not to press charges against her. Garrett was released in July 1912 and, according to Bishopville's *Leader and Vindicator* (22 May 1913), quickly resumed his old habits. Such activity or perhaps other pastimes (the local weekly is vague on this point) earned him a place on the county chain gang, from which he soon escaped. After drifting about a bit, Garrett settled down near Dalzell in adjoining Sumter County, where he worked as a blacksmith.

Meanwhile, without consulting her father, Gertrude decided to marry Aaron Campbell, a twenty-four-year-old youth who lived on Rose Hill Plantation in Lee County, some fifteen miles from Dalzell. The ceremony was performed on Friday, 16 May 1913. Her father learned about it twenty-four hours later, and twenty-four hours after that Gertrude was a widow. At about 1:30 P.M. on a pleasant Sunday afternoon, Garrett quietly approached the Campbell home with a loaded shotgun. John H. Campbell, Gertrude's father-in-law, having had a fine meal, was stretched out on the porch sleeping, his shoes off and his head resting on a pillow. As he snoozed in the springtime sun, Garrett shot him in the bowels. Campbell's son Aaron, hearing the noise, rushed to the door and grabbed his gun, but it was too late. Garrett's second fatal volley took the top of his head off. Garrett then grabbed Gertrude and dragged her into a nearby swamp.

Within hours the Lee County sheriff and a posse were in pursuit; and as darkness fell, Gertrude emerged—having escaped from her father, she said—and was lodged in jail.[30] The next morning, with the aid of "Joe" and "Ben," bloodhounds sent from the penitentiary in Columbia, Garrett was captured. Although well armed, he did not put up much resistance. Ironically, the fugitive had been the keeper of the dogs when in prison, so for them this was a joyous reunion.

The following month Garrett pled "not guilty" to the charge of murder, and his court-appointed counsel (Thomas H. Tatum and C. B. Ruffin) put up a stiff fight as they mounted a "temporary insanity" plea. This did not save their client from being convicted of killing the elder Campbell, but to the surprise of many, it almost won a recommendation for mercy. According to the *Leader and Vindicator* (19 June), Garrett sat through the day-long proceedings "with as much composure as if he were being tried for selling whiskey." It took jurors only ten minutes to reach a decision; and only as they returned did the prisoner display any nervousness. When condemned to die in the electric chair, he buried his face in his hands. Garrett was executed on 14 July 1913, one year after South Carolina's first such death on 6 July 1912, when William Reed, an Anderson black convicted of criminal assault, was electrocuted.

The last of these grisly episodes is also one of the most puzzling. It is an old axiom in many British murder mysteries that the butler is the culprit—"the butler did it." But how often does someone shoot the butler? At about 9:00 A.M. on Saturday, 3 February 1912, William Dobson, trusted employee of Charleston's well-known Hacker family for many years, ever since bookkeeper J. Fred Hacker was a mere boy, was busy preparing breakfast for the household at 33 Pitt Street. Suddenly, without warning, Hacker, seated at the dining room table waiting to be served, shot Dobson in the neck. The man was dead by the time he arrived at Roper Hospital.

According to the *State* (4 February), Dobson was "a sporty sort" of individual, a familiar figure in the black community. The Columbia paper also reported that as Hacker stepped from a police wagon at headquarters, he still had the murder weapon, a magazine pistol, clasped firmly in one hand and an "ordinary" revolver in the other. The *News and Courier* of the same date conceded "the shooting raised a small sensation. . . . No motive for the killing has been suggested and it is the commonly accepted theory that Mr. Hacker was not mentally responsible when he fired the fatal shot." Two weeks later a judge signed an order committing J. Fred Hacker to the state mental hospital for treatment.

Little is to be gained by trying to make sense of tragedies such as these— eight-year-olds who kill their little brothers and adults who, for the flimsiest of reasons (or none at all), shoot servants, family members, friends, ex-lovers, and strangers who step on their toes. However, these tales point once more to the dangerous game brothers-in-law played during these decades and a general tendency to go forth armed. Shootings in country stores, at baseball games, during church and Sunday school, and on the streets of various towns and cities indicate that South Carolinians of all social levels owned and carried with them weapons they were quite willing to use if provoked, which seems to have been incredibly easy to do. Perhaps the only lessons to be learned from these pages are to heed any customer's request, remember that dog is man's best friend, let your wife go to funerals, and shut the gate when going to or coming from North Carolina.

11

CHANGE IN A CHANGELESS SOCIETY

It is easy to view South Carolina as a place where things remain much the same year after year and both native son and visitor have been beguiled by what can be portrayed as a comfortable, slow-paced existence. In recent decades South Carolinians have published delightful personal tales claiming they came out of the eighteenth century (John Andrew Rice) or that time actually had forgotten their state (William Watts Ball). Yet everyone knows such ramblings, charming as they may be, are not true—not even during the forty years encompassed by this book.

South Carolina in 1880 and the state in 1920 were quite different places. Overall population rose from 995,577 to 1,683,724 during those decades, while the percentage of blacks declined from 60.7 to 51.4. The number of urban dwellers swelled from 78,519 to 293,987, with a concomitant drop in farm workers from 294,602 to 192,693. At the same time, the number of people holding manufacturing jobs quadrupled (19,698 to 79,450), with the greatest increase evident among mill folk (2,304 to 48,079).

It is apparent that during the same forty years dueling disappeared, lynching waxed and waned, and—although homicides increased—more and more people were being charged with manslaughter, not murder. Another upward constant on the graph of violence was the number of pistols bought and used with tragic results.

Yet despite failure to control concealed weapons, efforts to do so did not cease. In 1898 Judge Joshua Hilary Hudson of Bennettsville, the state's most ardent advocate of judicial reform during these years, forcefully suggested that authorities simply prohibit the manufacture, sale, and carrying of a pistol, what he called "the greatest of all evils." This could be done, in his opinion, without infringing on any constitutional right to bear arms. "Neither militia in time of peace, nor soldiers in time of war, parade, march, or fight with pistols, dirks, daggers, and razors dangling at their sides or concealed in their pockets. These are not arms for common defence like the shotgun, musket, and rifle."[1] The *State* immediately replied that such a ban was impractical and, in the spirit of the times, fixed blame for the great number of homicides on blacks and the turmoil of Reconstruction, which had passed into history a full generation earlier.

Seven years later John William Thurmond, a man familiar with pistols and their use, tried a different approach. As he rounded out his second term as solicitor of the Fifth Circuit, this Edgefield resident recommended that the concealed-weapons law be amended. He suggested banning the wearing of pistols and stipulating that any weapon carried had to be clearly visible and have a barrel at least twenty inches long.

Thurmond made no secret of the fact that he, like Hudson, thought pistols were the prime cause of homicides. Of much less importance, in his view, were liquor, the end of dueling, and race. "The determination of the white man to maintain his supremacy over the negro and the ambition of the negro to enjoy equal rights with the white man are," he conceded, "responsible for some deaths."[2] Ruminating further on racial matters, Thurmond added that black jurors, even in counties where blacks were numerous, were reluctant "to jump the bars" and, despite evidence submitted to them, continued to favor a white man against a black: "The way to hold the negro down, under any and all circumstances, and yet meet [sic] out justice between the white man and the black man, has not been discovered where the rights of both are adjudicated in the same tribunal, and by the same jurors."

On 4 July 1905 Judge Henry Hammond of Augusta, while addressing Aiken's Law and Order League, also attacked the menace of the concealed pistol head-on:

> My fellow countrymen, look who is to right and left of you? Your friends, and your neighbors, your mother, sister, wife, sweetheart, and men old and young with whom, shoulder to shoulder, you must work out the destiny of this fair land, which the Lord your God has given you. Would you murder them, would you shoot them to their death with that six-chambered, hammerless, four-barrel, self-cocking, 32 calibre, Smith & Wesson pistol that you, at this blessed moment, have in your right-hand hip pocket? Then, in heaven's name why did you bring it here? For protection, did you say? Protection against whom? A highwayman? Nonsense! There hasn't been a "hold-up" in Aiken county in 20 years. The political and social conditions do not warrant, or suggest, your turning yourself into a walking arsenal. Be a "pistol-toter," if you please, but don't be an Annanias [sic] too. Say to yourself what you know to be the truth: "I brought this pistol here to shoot and kill my fellow human beings when, in my judgment, it becomes proper to do so. It is true that my judgment will not be cool; it will be inflamed. Though the wrong done me may be overlooked entirely without compromising my honor, though it may be righted by words or a blow with the hand, I will not rely upon, or be content with any of these mild measures; for my pistol will cry to me from my irresistibly convenient hip-pocket: 'I am here, take me in your right hand, draw me, aim me, pull the trigger, I will do the rest.'"[3]

If a pistol were not at hand, Hammond argued, an individual would continue to talk and perhaps fight. Thus, in his view, the first unlawful act was taking a weapon to a social gathering. He agreed wholeheartedly with Judge Hudson's proposal to ban pistols: "The constitutional right given to bear arms was a right given to resist a despotic ruler; it has come to signify a sanction of the practice of carrying a Colt pistol with which to shoot your neighbor."

Despite such appeals, only one governor of these years addressed the issue of pistols in an annual message to the General Assembly. In 1913 Cole Blease called the concealed-weapons law "a farce" and advocated replacing it with thirty-day licenses and stiff punishment for offenders. Those who failed to get licenses or sold a pistol without proper authority to do so would, if convicted, be sentenced to twelve months of hard labor. In passing, Blease mentioned that "Negroes and some others habitually carry pistols," revealing the racist intent of this proposal. "If you watch your Criminal courts," he emphasized, "you will see that most of the people who meet violent deaths are killed with these little cheap pistols that are carried continuously in the pockets of the crap shooter, the blind tiger, and the loafer."[4]

So in the long run, efforts to control the proliferation of pistols went nowhere, although many conceded the enormity of the problem. Liquor, on the other hand, received much more attention and eventually became the subject of national concern, leading in 1920 to Prohibition. Viewed at the grass roots, as John William Thurmond admitted, the whiskey trade was a "puzzlement." Few doubted its bad effects, but no one knew quite what to do about it. In 1883 a Darlington district court judge, fearing jurors, witnesses, and lawyers might "get warmed up with a drink or two and become unfit for duty at the re-assembling of court," ruled sessions would last, without breaks, from 10:00 A.M. to 4:00 P.M.[5]

In his first annual message as governor (November 1891), Ben Tillman directed attention to liquor, although at the time he grouped it with other matters of "minor importance." Tillman's main target was a licensing process that enabled some municipalities to forgo any other form of revenue, including taxes. Yet, in his opinion, crime fostered by the state's seven or eight hundred barrooms placed a heavy burden on rural residents. This was, Tillman vowed, "unjust and unequal" and should cease. His famous dispensary (state control of liquor sales and distribution of profits to various localities) was his solution to this dilemma.

These campaigns to control pistols and liquor in South Carolina had obvious racial overtones, just as national Prohibition smacked of an anti-immigrant, antiforeign bias. Also, it is quite possible that the antiliquor drive succeeded in South Carolina only because some residents thought its constrictions would not apply to them, and any attempt to limit the use of handguns failed because some of the same individuals feared they indeed might be affected.

Going back to the last decades of the nineteenth century for a moment, it should be noted that South Carolina's dailies and especially its weeklies occasionally went out of their way to condone and even promote violence. When a white Orangeburg jury sentenced a black man who had assaulted a white girl to life in prison, not the gallows, the *News and Courier* (10 October 1881) headlined the story "AN ENCOURAGEMENT TO LYNCHING." A similar decision by the jurors concerning a black who assaulted a black girl was called "squeamish." Within forty-eight hours the first black was duly lynched, eliciting editorial praise from the Charleston daily. Four years later, as he reflected on the restless upcountry, Francis W. Dawson composed this headline: "HANGING NEEDED IN LAURENS."[6] Although a few weeklies would continue to defend local violence as necessary, especially lynching, by 1900 leading dailies such as the *Charleston News and Courier,* the *State,* and the *Greenville Daily News* were singing a different tune, and this chorus increased in volume and intensity as the Progressive movement grew ever more powerful.

Yet even as Dawson was encouraging citizens of Orangeburg to lynch and those of Laurens to hang, he was becoming distressed by peripheral aspects of the crime scene, such as cumbersome court procedures, easy acquittal of whites, and mistrials. Following the first of John Ferguson's three mistrials—he was the young man who shot the Jewish clerk named Benedict on Christmas Eve in 1884—the *News and Courier* (10 February 1885) said forcefully, "Trials for murder will soon become a veritable farce, if there is no conviction where the evidence of guilt is so clear and strong as in the trial for murder at Abbeville last week."

During the ensuing few years Judge Hudson, Greenville solicitor James L. Orr, and other legal luminaries expounded on the theme of court reform. Hudson, the most vocal critic of the way things were being done, published a voluminous, five-part essay in the *News and Courier* (7–14 September 1887) entitled "The Verdict of Acquittal." His principal targets were inept coroners, the many peremptory challenges allowed defendants during jury selection, bail too readily granted, and too many appeals after verdicts were rendered. Harking back to earlier times, Hudson, who graduated with first honors from South Carolina College in 1852, deplored the many advantages granted the accused in post–Civil War courts. A judge no longer could "review" and "sum up" as before, making him, he said, a mere cipher or figurehead. Permitting those who had taken human life to testify in their own behalf was, Hudson added, ridiculous. "The man who will deliberately commit murder will not scruple to save his life by perverting the facts on the witness stand. He values his life above the consequences of perjury. This is human nature—certainly the nature of the wilful murderer, ravisher and incendiary. But jurors must hear and weigh his testimony and in mercy will give heed to it."[7]

Hudson's specific recommendations were:

1. Outside of Charleston (where the coroner was, he thought, able and properly compensated), merge the office of coroner with that of a leading trial justice residing at the county seat. Define his duties, pay him an adequate salary, and see to it that he attends court and assists the solicitor in the prosecution of murderers.
2. Summon a larger panel of jurors and increase the number of peremptory challenges allowed the state in capital cases.
3. Provide comfortable quarters for juries involved in murder trials and keep them together until a verdict is rendered.
4. Restore to the judge his pre–Civil War powers.
5. Repeal an 1884 act allowing bail to those convicted of crimes while they appeal their convictions.

In later years Hudson suggested that county courts might operate as supreme courts do, ruling by majority and not seeking unanimity when making decisions. Nevertheless, when a Greenwood jury on its own did just that, reporting a "unanimous" vote once two-thirds agreed on a verdict, the ruling justice was furious and yet refused to grant a new trial in the manslaughter case being heard.[8]

Throughout the 1890s Hudson continued to make similar pronouncements, most of which enjoyed scattered support, and in January 1898 he bluntly confronted the question of why there were so many homicides in the nation as a whole and in South Carolina in particular. "What is the cause and what is the remedy? The one is more easily answered than the other. The practice of carrying the concealed pistol, and the readiness of juries to acquit, are the chief causes of so many homicides. To this may be added the habit of drink, but our people are no more intemperate than in the past, and to that habit I am not disposed unduly to attribute the alarming increase of homicides. The chief causes are really to be found in the facility furnished by the nimble pistol, and the immunity from punishment."[9] If those contemplating criminal acts knew punishment would be swift, he argued, crime would decrease. But, as the *State* observed nearly a decade later on 27 November 1907, hangings and long sentences were becoming rare and more and more murderers were going unpunished. "As someone has recently remarked," the paper said editorially, "it is safer to be a murderer in South Carolina than a brakeman on one of its railroads."

So perhaps the solution was to change the jury system, and in 1909 the *State* floated several trial balloons. These included drawing juries for capital cases from another county within the circuit (thus isolating the defendant and jurors from relatives and friends), selecting juries only a few days before court opened so they could not be "fixed," or perhaps hearing murder and manslaughter cases before district instead of county courts. None of these proposals stirred much interest; in fact, several readers reacted negatively, one of them suggesting the way to get better jurors was to have better schools.[10]

There were those, however, such as James L. Orr and a few prominent editors, who were beginning to blame the state's soaring murder rate not on guns, judges, juries, or courts, but on the public at large. Confronting the same question that Judge Hudson had tackled thirteen years before, the *State,* shocked by the murder of Rosa Bessinger and her nephew in a Columbia restaurant, on 9 May 1911 asked why so many South Carolinians were being killed and then quickly furnished its own reply:

> The explanation is simple enough. The people of South Carolina will not protect themselves by doing their duty in the jury room and in the legislature. There are too many South Carolinians who, for the sake of carrying their own pistols, prefer to take their chances, depending more on a quick hand and sure eye than on the courts of justice, a part of which courts they are—or should be.
>
> Murder flourishes in South Carolina because some tens of thousands of white men do not and will not try to stamp it out.

This may be the best answer to questions posed by this study. Stripped of excuses, rationalization, and racism, murder in its many forms thrived and prospered from 1880 to 1920 because white men of influence and power chose not to do anything about it. They became aware of the problem in the 1880s, heaped special blame on blacks throughout the 1890s, and after 1900—swept up by both progressivism and the spirit of progress—considered tinkering with the judicial process, shifted responsibility for the rising death toll to others, or simply ignored the violence involved since it did not comport well with the image they wanted to project to the outside world.

This is a sad commentary on the men who led South Carolina during those decades. Yet most other states, for whatever reasons, ended up in much the same fix—hundreds of murders each year, thousands of pistols and shotguns, and few attempts to curb the annual carnage. It would seem, then, that South Carolina's governors, lawyers, bankers, businessmen, and theologians of that era had no more guts or foresight than did their contemporaries in other communities throughout the nation. Sad it may be, but whoever thought a tale of blood, mayhem, and death would end happily?

APPENDIX

Additional Tables

TABLE A.1 — **Verified lynchings in South Carolina, 1880–1947**

This list is compiled from local newspapers, *Chicago Tribune* year-end summaries (1882–89), NAACP data, and University of South Carolina theses by Jack S. Mullins and Susan Page Garris. If the act was tantamount to simple murder, a victim's name appears in italics. If county boundaries have changed, the present site is expressed in brackets. The "potential witnesses" column indicates whether the affair was conducted in such a manner that area residents—people other than law officers (who perhaps relinquished the victim)—may have seen the mob in action. Thus an affirmative evaluation suggests a large, public gathering, and a negative evaluation, a smaller, clandestine operation.

APPROXIMATE DATE	RACE	NAME	COUNTY	ALLEGED CAUSE	POTENTIAL WITNESSES
3/01/80*	B	Lewis Kinder	Orangeburg	sex assault	yes
8/18/80	B	Prue Grier	Newberry	sex assault	no
8/18/80	B	Dorsey Grier	Newberry	sex assault	no
12/08/80	B	Vance Brandt	Clarendon [Florence]	murder	yes
12/08/80	B	Julia Brandt	Clarendon [Florence]	murder	yes
12/08/80	B	Joe Barnes	Clarendon [Florence]	murder	yes
1/19/81	B	Dave Spearman	Newberry	murder	yes
1/19/81	B	Sam Fair	Newberry	murder	yes
4/09/81	B	Judy Metts	Laurens	arson	yes
10/12/81	B	Jack Williams	Orangeburg	sex assault	yes
11/04/81	B	Bob Williams	Greenville	sex assault	yes
6/02/82	B	Caleb Campbell	Fairfield	sex assault	yes
6/12/82	B	John Johnson	York	rape	yes
7/15/82	B	David Cook	Kershaw	sex assault	no
7/25/82	B	Martin Becket	Hampton	sex assault	yes
8/08/82	B	Dan Blakeney	Lancaster	sex assault	yes
9/13/82	B	Nathan Bonnet	Barnwell	sex assault	yes
12/03/82	B	Dave Roberts	Abbeville	theft/assault	yes
4/01/84	B	Frank Elliott	York	sex assault	yes
7/04/85	B	Charles Williams	Laurens	sex assault	no
9/22/85	W	O. T. Culbreath	Edgefield	murder	yes
3/01/86	B	Abe Thompson	Spartanburg	sex assault	yes

*Dates given in tables in the appendix are expressed in month/day/year order.

Table A.1 continued

APPROXIMATE DATE	RACE	NAME	COUNTY	ALLEGED CAUSE	POTENTIAL WITNESSES
3/08/86	B	Charles Gregory	Hampton [Jasper]	assault	no
5/05/86	B	Wesley Williams	Kershaw	sex assault	no
11/30/86	B	Caesar Robinson	Darlington [Florence]	sex assault	no
5/05/87	B	Giles Good	York	murder	yes
5/05/87	B	Bailey Dowdle	York	murder	yes
5/05/87	B	Prindley Thompson	York	murder	yes
5/05/87	B	Moses Lipscomb	York	murder	yes
5/05/87	B	Dan Roberts	York	murder	yes
12/30/87	W	Manse Waldrop	Pickens	rape/murder	yes
9/30/88	B	Sam Cornwell	Chester	argument	no
5/08/89	B	Tut Danford	Abbeville [McCormick]	gave evidence	no
6/21/89	B	Andy Caldwell[1]	Fairfield	assault	yes
6/26/89	B	Andrew McKnight	Union	fighting, slander	no
12/28/89	B	Ripley Johnson	Barnwell	murder	yes
12/28/89	B	Mitchell Adams	Barnwell	murder	yes
12/28/89	B	Peter Bell	Barnwell	murder	yes
12/28/89	B	Ralph Morral	Barnwell	witness	yes
12/28/89	B	Hugh Furz	Barnwell	accessory	yes
12/28/89	B	Harrison Johnson	Barnwell	witness	yes
12/28/89	B	Robert J. Phoenix	Barnwell	witness	yes
12/28/89	B	Judge Jones	Barnwell	witness	yes
1/07/90	B	*William Blake*	Barnwell	burglary	no
2/24/90	W	*Bob Pope*	Hampton	obnoxious	no
2/24/90	W	—— *Pope* (son)	Hampton	witness	no
5/05/90	B	Willie Leaphart	Lexington	sex assault	yes
12/03/90	B	Henry Welsby	Pickens	sex assault	yes
12/07/91	B	Dick Lundy	Edgefield	murder	yes
11/21/92	B	Nathan White	York	arson	yes
4/24/93	B	John Peterson	Barnwell [Bamberg]	sex assault	yes
5/05/93	B	Sam Gilliard	Williamsburg	sex assault	yes
5/10/93	B	Heyward Barksdale	Laurens	sex assault	yes
5/30/93	B	Isaac Lincoln	Oconee	seduction?	?
7/16/93	W	Dub Meetze	Lexington	horse thief, forgery, arson	no
7/30/93	B	Will Thompson	Lexington	rape	yes

APPROXIMATE DATE	RACE	NAME	COUNTY	ALLEGED CAUSE	POTENTIAL WITNESSES
7/30/93	B	Tom Preston	Lexington	rape	yes
7/31/93	B	Handy Kaigler	Lexington	rape	yes
8/21/93	B	Jake Davis	Abbeville [Greenwood]	sex assault	yes
9/27/93	B	Calvin Stewart	Aiken	murder	no
10/02/93	B	George McFadden	Williamsburg	rape	yes
11/07/93	B	Bob Kennedy	Spartanburg	sex assault	no
12/03/93	B	Will Lawton	Abbeville [Greenwood]	assault, robbery	yes
12/10/93	B	——[2]	Aiken	sex assault	?
12/20/93	B	Ike Anderson	Spartanburg	miscegenation	no
6/02/94	B	Jeff Crawford	York	murder	yes
6/03/94	B	Hardy Gill[3]	Lancaster	assault	yes
8/30/94	B	Clem Davis	Laurens	selling whiskey	no
9/25/94	B	John McKenney[4]	Edgefield [Greenwood]	gave evidence	yes
12/13/94	B	Ed Sullivan	Anderson	murder	yes
6/22/95	B	Bill Stokes	Colleton	sex assault	no
6/22/95	B	John Barnwell	Orangeburg	race prejudice	no
7/15/95	B	Ira Johnson	Greenville	murder	yes
10/17/95	B	William Blake, Sr.	Hampton	murder	yes
12/02/95	B	*Isom Kearse*	Colleton	burglary	no
12/02/95	B	*Hannah Kearse*	Colleton	knowledge of burglary	no
2/28/96	B	Calvin Kennedy	Aiken	seduction	yes
4/19/96	B	Tom Price	Kershaw	shot at whites	yes
7/18/96	B	Dick Hickson	Aiken	sex assault	yes
1/06/97	B	Lawrence Brown	Orangeburg	arson	no
1/08/97	B	Simon Cooper	Sumter	murder	yes
7/22/97	B	Henry (Jim) Gray	Laurens	sex assault	yes
12/28/97	B	Sam Turner	Williamsburg	murder	yes
1/04/98	B	David Hunter	Laurens	violated contract	no
1/27/98	B	John A. Belin	Florence	murder	yes
2/22/98	B	F. B. Baker	Williamsburg [Florence]	race prejudice	yes
2/22/98	B	Dora Baker	Williamsburg [Florence]	race prejudice	yes
5/25/98	B	Elbert Harris	Anderson	arson	no
10/25/98	B	Jim Mackey	Edgefield [McCormick]	murder	yes
10/25/98	B	Luther Sullivan	Edgefield [McCormick]	murder	yes

Table A.1 continued

APPROXIMATE DATE	RACE	NAME	COUNTY	ALLEGED CAUSE	POTENTIAL WITNESSES
11/08/98	W	*Bose Ethridge*	Greenwood	political riot	yes
11/09/98	B	*Wade H. McKenney*	Greenwood	political riot	yes
11/09/98	B	*Columbus Jackson*	Greenwood	political riot	yes
11/09/98	B	*Drayton Watts*	Greenwood	political riot	yes
11/09/98	B	*Jesse Williams*	Greenwood	political riot	yes
11/10/98	B	*Essex Harrison*	Greenwood	political riot	yes
11/10/98	B	*Ben Collins*	Greenwood	political riot	yes
11/12/98	B	*Sam Howard*	Florence	adultery	no
11/17/98	B	*George Logan*	Greenwood	political riot	yes
11/18/98	B	*Eliza Goode*	Greenwood	political riot	yes
1/07/00	B	*Rufus Salter*	Union	arson	no
2/17/00	B	Will Burts	Aiken	attempted murder	yes
1/14/01	B	Charles L. Robinson	Barnwell	rape	yes
10/18/01	B	William Sanders	Hampton	burglary	yes
11/24/01	B	John Ladderly	Anderson	assault	yes
11/24/01	W	*Rachel Powell*	Oconee	adultery	no
12/11/01	B	*Ben Gates*	Lexington	?	?
6/04/02	B	Jim Black	Charleston	murder	yes
6/06/02	B	Cain Ford	Colleton	accessory to murder	?
6/28/02	B	—— Coleman	Aiken	race riot	yes
6/28/02	B	Wyatt Holmes	Aiken	race riot	yes
12/26/02	B	Oliver Wideman	Greenwood	murder	no
12/26/02	B	Mrs. Wideman (wife)[5]	Greenwood	murder	no
2/11/03	B	*Jake Haines*	Charleston	theft	no
6/30/03	B	*Reuben Elrod*	Anderson	adultery	no
7/01/03	B	Charles Evans	Orangeburg	assault	yes
7/16/03	B	Dennis Head	Aiken	attempted murder	no
11/21/03	B	Jim Nelson	Chesterfield	sex assault	no
11/29/03	B	John Fogle	Dorchester	sex assault	yes
1/13/04	B	"General" Lee	Dorchester	frightened woman	yes
6/30/04	B	Cairo Williams	Florence	murder	no
7/05/04	B	John Taylor	Chesterfield	sex assault	no
7/11/04	B	*Keitt Bookhard*	Orangeburg	harmless threat	no
9/24/04	B	James Stuart	Greenwood	sex assault	no

APPROXIMATE DATE	RACE	NAME	COUNTY	ALLEGED CAUSE	POTENTIAL WITNESSES
10/01/04	W	John Morrison	Lancaster [Kershaw]	murder	yes
9/17/05	B	Allen Pendleton	Abbeville	justifiable homicide	yes
12/22/05	B	Frank DeLoach	Barnwell [Allendale]	murder	yes
12/22/05	B	John DeLoach	Barnwell [Allendale]	murder	yes
8/16/06	B	Bob Davis	Greenwood	sex assault	yes
8/20/06	B	Dan Etheredge	Lexington	sex assault	yes
8/20/06	B	Willie Spain	Dorchester	house breaking	yes
5/06/07	B	Lamphold Carmichael	Marion	sex assault	no
6/02/07	B	George Hudson[6]	Edgefield	assault	no
11/23/08	B	Ham Gilmore	Hampton	sex assault	yes
1/08/09	B	*Arthur Davis*	Florence	blinded mule	no
6/11/09	B	Frank Samuels	Colleton	murder, robbery	no
6/11/09	B	Quillie Simmons	Colleton	murder, robbery	no
11/25/10	B	Henry (Luke) Clarke	Newberry	murder	yes
10/10/11	B	Willis Jackson	Anderson	sex assault	yes
10/28/11	B	Wade Tyler	Orangeburg	aided escape of rapist	no
3/13/12	B	Alfred Doublin	Bamberg	arson	no
3/13/12	B	Richard Doublin	Bamberg	arson	no
3/13/12	B	Peter Rivers	Bamberg	arson	no
3/29/12	B	Frank Whisonant	Cherokee	assault, robbery	no
3/29/12	B	Joe Brinson	Cherokee	assault, robbery	no
6/29/12	B	Brooks Garden	Pickens	assault	no
11/22/12	B	Will Thomas	Newberry	murder	no
12/21/12	B	Joe Felder	Orangeburg	fight with whites	no
2/23/13	B	Marion Cantri	Clarendon	assault, battery	no
8/10/13	B	Richard Puckett	Laurens	sex assault	yes
7/12/14	B	Rosa Richardson	Orangeburg	murder	yes
11/24/14	B	Dillard Wilson	Sumter	murder	no
12/04/14	B	Willie Green	Florence	frightened woman	no
12/16/14	B	Allen Seymour	Hampton	sex assault	no
12/20/14	B	Tom Spight[7]	Oconee	arson, race prejudice	yes
12/20/14	B	Green Gibson	Oconee	arson, race prejudice	yes

Table A.1 continued

APPROXIMATE DATE	RACE	NAME	COUNTY	ALLEGED CAUSE	POTENTIAL WITNESSES
12/20/14	B	George Gibson	Oconee	arson, race prejudice	yes
7/12/15	B	Will Lozier	Abbeville	murder	no
7/28/15	B	Manson Shuler	Orangeburg	attempted robbery	no
10/21/16	B	Anthony Crawford	Abbeville	dispute with whites	yes
8/23/17	B	W. T. Sims	York	malicious talk	yes
2/23/18	B	Walter Best[8]	Barnwell	murder	yes
6/07/19	B	Mark Smith	Abbeville	shot deputy, acquitted	yes
2/19/20	B	Ed Blakely[9]	Laurens	murder	yes
4/01/20	B	Joe Steward	Laurens	fight with whites	no
6/19/21	B	Herbert Quarles	McCormick	sex assault	yes
8/24/21	B	Will Allen	Lexington	murder	no
9/08/21	B	Charlie Thompson	Aiken	assault, robbery	yes
9/08/21	B	Mansfield Butler	Aiken	assault, robbery	yes
10/24/21	B	Ed Kirkland	Allendale	murder	yes
12/30/21	B	*Bill McAllister*[10]	Florence	seduction	no
4/20/24	B	Luke Adams	Orangeburg	sex assault	yes
10/08/26	B	Bertha Lowman[11]	Aiken	murder	yes
10/08/26	B	Demon Lowman	Aiken	assault, battery	yes
10/08/26	B	Clarence Lowman	Aiken	murder	yes
4/23/30	B	Allen Green[12]	Oconee	sex assault	yes
6/21/30	B	Dan Jenkins	Union	sex assault	yes
11/02/32	B	Henry Campbell	Horry	shot employer	yes
2/19/33	B	*George Jeter*	Aiken	theft	no
7/05/33	B	*Morris Denby*	Laurens	assault	no
10/08/33	B	*Bennie Thompson*	Greenwood	drew gun on whites	no
11/16/33	B	*George Green*	Greenville	crop dispute	no
5/10/34	B	(unknown black)	Laurens	shot deputy	yes
2/10/41	B	*Bruce Tinsdale*[13]	Georgetown	dispute with whites over job	no
12/08/46	B	*James Walker*	Barnwell	dispute with whites	no
2/17/47	B	Willie Earle	Greenville	murder	no

Notes

1. Lunatic.

2. This lynching, which took place near Kitching's Mill, is mentioned briefly in Columbia and Orangeburg papers but not in those published in Charleston and Aiken. No details are given.

3. Lunatic—apparently struck a white woman while having a fit.

4. McKenney evidently was whipped and killed by blacks because he told authorities about illegal liquor operations. Neither McKenney nor Clem Davis (previous victim) is cited in standard lynching summaries. See Benjamin R. Tillman Papers (Box 62), South Carolina Department of Archives and History, Columbia, for details.

5. It is interesting that the South Carolina press referred to the deceased as "Mrs." Wideman, something editors would not have done during her lifetime.

6. Hudson, who tried to kill a fellow black, was pursued and killed by a racially mixed posse.

7. This altercation at Fair Play actually was a biracial shoot-out.

8. In this instance, the sheriff named about a dozen of the lynchers and five witnesses.

9. Published reports say that Blakely, a tenant farmer who killed his landlord, committed suicide while being pursued by a mob.

10. Various dailies reported that McAllister, on intimate terms with a white woman, was chased by whites and shot and killed in Williamsburg County. A male companion presumably was seriously wounded. But the local *County Record* (5 January 1922) vehemently denied this account with a banner headline: "MOB VIOLENCE IN FLORENCE COUNTY." The editor even went to great length to prove that none of the trio actually was associated with Williamsburg County.

11. The Lowmans were in the midst of a trial. Demon was being held only on assault and battery. Testimony concerning Bertha and Clarence would have been concluded the following day.

12. The death of Green (age fifty-two) and its aftermath were well covered by the local *Keowee Courier* (30 April–12 November 1930, 12 October 1932). A large mob assaulted and overpowered the sheriff, who was hospitalized for twelve days. Seventeen of the most prominent participants, including Walhalla's mayor and night policeman, were indicted and eventually acquitted. Two years later Laudy Harris, a mill operative who was among those cleared, "got religion" and apologized to the sheriff; also, in the presence of his minister, Harris returned a pistol he had taken from the sheriff during the encounter. At about the same time, Horace Miller, an operative at the Kenneth Cotton Mill, confessed he was in the mob that night, although stoutly maintaining he took no part in any violence that ensued. With tears streaming down his face, he sought and got forgiveness from the sheriff and his family. Apparently this belated wave of remorse did not extend to the victim's family, and no legal action was taken as a result of these confessions.

13. Some of the cases cited in 1933 and 1941 appear to have been "whitecapping" that led to homicide—in other words, a few individuals sought to teach the victim "a lesson," but he resisted so strenuously that he was killed. For details of the Anthony Crawford, Allen Green, and Morris Denby lynchings, see Martha Gruening, "Reflection on the South," *Nation* (8 May 1935), an essay inspired by Senator "Cotton Ed" Smith's opposition to antilynching legislation. A mob—hooded and masked—shot and killed George Green near Taylors in November 1933, the only fatality recorded during a brief KKK "reign of terror." Seven men subsequently were tried for the crime and easily acquitted. See the *Greenville News* and *Greenville Piedmont* (17 November 1933, 2–4 November 1934).

TABLE A.2 — **Number of lynching victims, 1880–1947**

COUNTY	1880S	1890S	1900S	1910S	1920–47	TOTAL VICTIMS/INCIDENTS	
1. Abbeville	2	2	1	3	0	8	8
2. Aiken	0	4	4	0	6	14	10
3. Allendale	–	–	–	0	1	1	1
4. Anderson	0	2	2	1	0	5	5
5. Bamberg	–	0	0	3	0	3	1
6. Barnwell	9	2	3	1	1	16	8

Table A.2 continued

COUNTY	1880S	1890S	1900S	1910S	1920–47	VICTIMS/INCIDENTS	
7. Beaufort	0	0	0	0	0	0	0
8. Berkeley	0	0	0	0	0	0	0
9. Calhoun	–	–	0	0	0	0	0
10. Charleston	0	0	2	0	0	2	2
11. Cherokee	–	0	0	2	0	2	1
12. Chester	1	0	0	0	0	1	1
13. Chesterfield	0	0	2	0	0	2	2
14. Clarendon	3	0	0	1	0	4	2
15. Colleton	0	3	3	0	0	6	4
16. Darlington	1	0	0	0	0	1	1
17. Dillon	–	–	–	0	0	0	0
18. Dorchester	–	0	3	0	0	3	3
19. Edgefield	1	4	1	0	0	6	5
20. Fairfield	2	0	0	0	0	2	2
21. Florence	0	2	2	1	1	6	6
22. Georgetown	0	0	0	0	1	1	1
23. Greenville	1	1	0	0	2	4	4
24. Greenwood	–	9	4	0	1	14	5
25. Hampton	2	3	2	1	0	8	7
26. Horry	0	0	0	0	1	1	1
27. Jasper	–	–	–	0	0	0	0
28. Kershaw	2	1	0	0	0	3	3
29. Lancaster	1	1	1	0	0	3	3
30. Laurens	2	4	0	1	4	11	11
31. Lee	–	–	0	0	0	0	0
32. Lexington	0	5	2	0	1	8	6
33. McCormick	–	–	–	0	1	1	1
34. Marion	0	0	1	0	0	1	1
35. Marlboro	0	0	0	0	0	0	0
36. Newberry	4	0	0	2	0	6	4
37. Oconee	0	1	1	3	1	6	4
38. Orangeburg	2	2	2	4	1	11	10
39. Pickens	1	1	0	1	0	3	3
40. Richland	0	0	0	0	0	0	0
41. Saluda	–	0	0	0	0	0	0
42. Spartanburg	1	2	0	0	0	3	3
43. Sumter	0	1	0	1	0	2	2
44. Union	1	0	1	0	1	3	3
45. Williamsburg	0	5	0	0	0	5	4
46. York	7	2	0	1	0	10	6
Totals	**43**	**57**	**37**	**26**	**23**	**186**	**144**

TABLE A.3 — **State population by race, 1880–1920**

	TOTAL	WHITE	BLACK	PERCENTAGE WHITE/BLACK	
1880	995,577	391,105	604,332	39.2	60.7
1890	1,151,149	462,008	688,934	40.1	59.8
1900	1,340,316	557,807	782,821	41.6	58.4
1910	1,515,400	679,161	835,843	44.8	55.2
1920	1,683,724	818,538	864,719	48.6	51.4

Source: U.S. Census

TABLE A.4 — **Black percentage of county population, 1880–1920**

	1880	1890	1900	1910	1920
1. Abbeville	67.7	67.6	66.1	64.7	56.9
2. Aiken	53.9	56.6	55.4	54.6	52.6
3. Allendale	–	–	–	–	77.6
4. Anderson	44.2	42.1	42.2	37.9	34.5
5. Bamberg	–	–	67.3	69.4	68.5
6. Barnwell	65.2	68.1	71.6	72.0	67.5
7. Beaufort	91.9	92.0	90.5	86.9	78.4
8. Berkeley	–	86.1	78.7	77.6	72.5
9. Calhoun	–	–	–	76.6	68.6
10. Charleston	69.9	58.5	68.5	63.2	59.2
11. Cherokee	–	–	34.6	32.5	31.2
12. Chester	68.3	68.1	67.7	65.0	57.9
13. Chesterfield	41.8	40.4	39.9	40.1	39.5
14. Clarendon	67.2	69.9	71.5	72.7	72.0
15. Colleton	66.4	65.1	66.6	63.0	58.1
16. Darlington	62.5	59.6	59.6	59.1	56.7
17. Dillon	–	–	–	51.0	51.2
18. Dorchester	–	–	61.9	61.4	58.8
19. Edgefield	65.0	64.7	71.2	71.1	69.6
20. Fairfield	75.2	75.0	76.0	76.0	76.1
21. Florence	–	58.1	58.5	57.0	49.4
22. Georgetown	82.3	80.5	76.6	72.3	66.6
23. Greenville	38.7	37.8	36.4	30.5	26.5
24. Greenwood	–	–	66.7	62.2	52.8
25. Hampton	66.4	66.7	65.3	64.2	60.6
26. Horry	31.7	28.8	27.1	24.7	24.0
27. Jasper	–	–	–	–	72.1
28. Kershaw	63.3	61.7	59.5	60.7	58.0
29. Lancaster	52.9	49.8	49.8	49.2	45.6
30. Laurens	60.0	58.3	59.3	54.8	51.9

Table A.4 continued

	1880	1890	1900	1910	1920
31. Lee	–	–	–	68.1	67.3
32. Lexington	40.2	37.9	37.8	36.3	32.9
33. McCormick	–	–	–	–	68.5
34. Marion	53.4	51.4	51.6	54.4	55.4
35. Marlboro	61.0	61.4	59.4	60.7	59.3
36. Newberry	68.9	66.0	65.7	63.7	58.1
37. Oconee	26.4	26.7	25.8	25.1	21.2
38. Orangeburg	68.7	68.3	69.5	65.8	65.8
39. Pickens	25.8	25.2	24.8	21.4	17.4
40. Richland	67.8	67.5	61.6	53.6	46.7
41. Saluda	–	–	53.5	53.4	52.7
42. Spartanburg	34.7	33.4	32.3	31.6	29.1
43. Sumter	73.0	72.9	74.9	73.0	70.9
44. Union	55.3	65.7	57.1	51.7	46.3
45. Williamsburg	67.8	66.3	62.7	61.7	66.0
46. York	54.1	52.8	52.4	53.0	47.9

Source: U.S. Census

TABLE A.5 — Charleston population by race, 1880–1920

	TOTAL	WHITE	BLACK	PERCENTAGE WHITE/BLACK	
1880	49,984	22,699	27,276	45.4	54.5
1890	54,955	23,919	31,036	43.5	56.4
1900	55,807	24,238	31,522	43.4	56.4
1910	58,833	27,764	31,056	47.1	52.7
1920	67,957	35,585	32,326	52.3	47.5

Source: U.S. Census

TABLE A.6 — Arrests in Charleston by race, 1880–1920[1]

	TOTAL	WHITE	BLACK	DISCHARGED OR DISMISSED	JAIL OR CHAIN GANG
1880	3,897	1,382	2,515	1,454	819
1890	3,285	1,106	2,179	1,128	1,237
1900	3,455	800	2,655	865	1,457
1910	5,021	1,885	3,136	1,631	1,333
1920	5,048	1,970	3,078	1,730	601

Source: *Charleston City Yearbooks*

Note

1. Actually, the term "arrests" is something of a misnomer since it encompasses lost children, those who applied at the jail for lodgings or were held as witnesses, and individuals found sick, insane, and dead, as well as anyone who was thought to have violated a city ordinance. As a result,

many soon were released or charges were dismissed—1,454 in 1880, for example, or 37.3 percent of all those "arrested." Nevertheless, it is obvious that blacks ran afoul of the law more frequently than whites, and *Yearbook* totals indicate that the most common "crimes" of both races were disorderly conduct, drunkenness, and theft of some sort. Annual reports for Columbia, although less complete, paint the same general picture. See the *State,* 8 January 1908, 4 January 1909, 8 January 1910, and 3 January 1921. In 1920 Columbia police reported 6,688 arrests—2,679 white males, 200 white females, 3,049 black males, and 760 black females. But, as in Charleston, nearly a third of the cases (2,123) were quickly dropped. By that date, Charleston's finest were detaining more citizens for traffic violations (793) than for drunkenness (430) or disorderly conduct (338).

NOTES

Introduction

1. For example, Richland County, home of the state's capital city, Columbia, recorded no lynchings during this period; and when "whitecapping" (done by bands of men riding about at night bent on "correcting" the morals of those they saw as "immoral") emerged in the northern part of the county in March 1896, authorities acted quickly and soon put those responsible behind bars. One suspects that similar responses were evident in other urban areas.

2. *Journal of the Senate of the General Assembly of the State of South Carolina* (Columbia, S.C., 1891), 29.

3. For a perceptive analysis of this ongoing debate, see Wendy Kaminer, "Second Thoughts on the Second Amendment," *Atlantic Monthly* (March 1996): 32, 34, 42–45.

4. *Laurensville Herald,* 1 March–21 June 1878.

5. James R. McGovern, *Anatomy of a Lynching: The Killing of Claude Neal* (Baton Rouge and London, 1982), x.

6. Edward L. Ayers, *Vengeance & Justice: Crime and Punishment in the 19th Century American South* (New York and Oxford, 1984), 240. This title is somewhat misleading since this study concentrates largely on a single state, Georgia.

7. Edward L. Ayers, *The Promise of the New South: Life after Appomattox* (New York and Oxford, 1992), 156–57. This work suggests a new approach to research on lynching. See especially Ayers's penetrating analysis of lynching by regions (1889–1909), 495–97.

8. For an account of this incident, see Columbia's *Daily Phoenix* (10 May 1873). It is discussed in more detail in Phineas T. Ellis's *Call Me Phin* (Caribou, Maine, 1977). My grandfather, then a lad of seven years, said Hayden was a popular figure; hence the violent reaction. According to some sources, Connecticut also recorded a lynching at the turn of the century; however, no such incident is cited in the *Index* to the *New York Times.* Apparently no deaths occurred in New Hampshire, Vermont, Rhode Island, or Massachusetts, although in August 1874 a "whitecapper" was killed on Martha's Vineyard by the man he was seeking to reform; and in 1886 the *New York Times Index* credited Springfield, Massachusetts, with a lynching that took place in Springfield, Missouri. Other states throughout the nation have reported one or more lynchings. One of the bloodiest spectacles, really a slaughter, took place near Pickettsville, Tennessee, in August 1874 when a hundred masked whites dragged sixteen blacks from jail and killed them.

9. Thomas D. Russell, "South Carolina's Largest Slave Auctioneering Firm," *Chicago-Kent Law Review* (1993): 1245.

10. That the *Charleston News and Courier* declared war on liquor and pistols in 1880 can be taken as an indication, perhaps proof, that blacks were acquiring both with such ease that whites were truly alarmed.

11. See Raymond D. Gastil, "Homicide and a Regional Culture of Violence," *American Sociological Review* (June 1971): 412–27; and John Shelton Reed, *One South: An Ethnic Approach to Regional Culture* (Baton Rouge and London, 1982), which is a provocative and highly readable inquiry. Dissenting opinion can be found in Colin Lofton and Robert H. Hill, "Regional Subculture and Homicide: An Examination of the Gastil-Hackney Thesis," *American Sociological Review* (October 1974): 714–24.

12. Sheldon Hackney, "Southern Violence," *American Historical Review* (February 1969): 925. This work contains an important analysis of its subject.

13. Ibid., 921.

14. Ben Robertson, *Red Hills and Cotton* (New York, 1942), 82.

15. Ibid., 44. Use of the past tense indicates Robertson may have thought regional violence was declining in the face of world conflict. Acceptance of some aspects of southern violence as a "natural" way of life also is stressed by Reed in *One South* (142).

16. For a much more recent study of South Carolina violence—especially how it can be handed down through generations and transported to an urban setting—see Fox Butterfield's troubling, provocative, and incisive *All God's Children: The Bosket Family and the American Tradition of Violence* (New York, 1995).

One: The Cash-Shannon Duel

1. The Williamson-Calhoun meeting near the Georgia-Alabama line on 10 August 1889 might be considered a true duel, although neither man was injured. The participants, seconds, and doctors spent several hours eluding various sheriffs before shooting at each other in pitch-black darkness and subsequently settling their differences over bourbon. The only casualty was a reporter who, while showing the principals how to use a pistol, shot off one of his fingers. For details, see the *Atlanta Constitution*, 11 August 1889.

2. Information concerning these fatal duels can be found in the *New York Times*, as well as in some local papers.

3. On 8 March 1874 two black men in Augusta, Peter Blair and Moses Sullivan, traded shots with Ralph Knight and William Armstrong as seconds. Blair apparently told Sullivan he was "no gentleman" and refused to apologize; hence the confrontation. Both men emptied Colt five-shooters without incident and then reloaded. According to the *Charleston News and Courier* (9 March), "The words of command were repeated and the firing recommenced, and was continued until Blair fell to the ground, shot through both legs. The parties then returned to the city [Augusta] immediately. Sullivan fought at the same place last year, and Blair fought another negro [*sic*], near Savannah, some time ago."

4. *New York Times*, 13–16 January 1878; *Columbia Daily Register*, 15 January 1878.

5. See John Hammond Moore, "Strange Encounters," *Virginia Cavalcade* (Autumn 1964): 12–24, for a discussion of the McCarty-Mordecai affair and other nineteenth-century Virginia duels.

6. Mrs. Cash's name was Allan and is so inscribed on her tombstone; however, it appears in various accounts as Allen, Alene, Alliene, and Alleine (the spelling preferred by her daughter).

7. A minor expression of Cash's views is found in a book that was once owned by his mother and is now in the South Caroliniana Library, University of South Carolina, Columbia. This volume (*The Saints' Everlasting Rest*, extracts from the works of Richard Baxter edited by the Methodist pioneer John Wesley) bears these words written when Cash was an adult: "This book contains as much damn nonsense as was ever printed in a similar space. E. B. C. Cash."

8. C. Vann Woodward, *Mary Chesnut's Civil War* (New Haven, Conn., and London, 1981), 31. In subsequent years family ties and developments on the local scene tended to make the Boykin-Chesnut kin anti-Shannon.

9. E. B. C. Cash to Andrew Gordon Magrath (31 March 1865), Magrath Papers, Southern Historical Collection, University of North Carolina at Chapel Hill.

10. Woodward, *Mary Chesnut's Civil War*, 411, 724. This "treachery" involved a dispute between Shannon and her nephew S. Miller Williams, who subsequently met Boggan Cash in a bloodless duel in 1878.

11. Case #1026 (Kershaw County, S.C.), filed 24 December 1878.

12. *Camden Journal*, 14 August 1879. Thomas Henry Clarke (1844–1890) married Sallie Boykin.

13. "Revenge her wrongs" are words used by Cash in a pamphlet he published in 1881 defending his course of action. Entitled simply *The Cash-Shannon Duel*, it was issued by the *Greenville News* and reprinted with assorted documents and newspaper clippings c. 1930 by Cash's daughter Bessie Cash Irby. Many details of this embroglio can be found in both editions, which are available in numerous libraries.

14. Boggan's essay and doggerel verse were circulated first as a broadside and then, following the duel, published in various newspapers.

15. William E. Johnson (1827–1897) was a well-known Camden resident and a close friend of Shannon.

16. Both men presumably were excellent marksmen; thus, it is difficult to explain *why* Shannon fired into the ground at a distance of fifteen paces unless he hoped his opponent would do likewise.

17. *Charleston News and Courier*, 8 July 1880. Beginning on 7 July, this daily gave the duel extensive, front-page coverage. In all, between 7 and 10 July nearly ten full columns of news reports, preduel correspondence, and editorials were published. Ironically, on 2 July this same newspaper printed a facetious editorial ("The Fun of Duelling") ridiculing a bloodless Virginia encounter.

18. These letters are part of a collection assembled by B. M. Ellison Jr. of Lancaster known as the Cash-Shannon Duel Papers, now on deposit at the South Caroliniana Library, University of South Carolina, Columbia.

19. An act passed in December 1880 specifically labeled death by dueling as murder and threatened those involved in any way (for example, serving as seconds, delivering challenges) with up to two years in prison and fines ranging from five hundred dollars to one thousand dollars.

20. During these months Cash clearly lost the public relations battle in South Carolina and throughout the nation, which is not surprising since most dispatches emanated from

the *Charleston News and Courier*. The *New York Times*, for example, portrayed Cash as a "ferocious" bully, murderer, and ruffian and, when he was acquitted, called the outcome "lamentable." By that date, Shannon, one year older than Cash, had become an "aged" lawyer. But the true target of many northern editors was not the colonel but southern society, for this whole episode presented a splendid opportunity to highlight the evil effects of slavery and the barbarism and backwardness of the South, a land, the *Times* stressed on 24 June 1881, that was "far behind the age in its development."

21. *Charleston News and Courier*, 4 September 1882.

Two: Boggan Cash, Outlaw

1. Sperry W. Henley, *The Cash Family of South Carolina: A Truthful Account of the Many Crimes Committed by the Carolina Cavalier Outlaws* (Wadesboro, N.C., 1884), 11. This work, which is hardly truthful but highly entertaining, in effect tells Shannon's side of the controversial duel and much more.

2. Ibid., 14.

3. E. B. C. Cash Papers, South Caroliniana Library, University of South Carolina, Columbia.

4. Watts, who became chief justice of South Carolina's highest court in the late 1920s, married Alleine Cash (1860–1895) in November 1881.

5. *Charleston News and Courier*, 26 April 1884.

6. Ibid., 9–10 May 1884. Ironically, this daily referred to this operation as an "exhibition," which is precisely what it turned out to be.

7. Ibid., 16 May 1884. The *Charleston News and Courier* provides both extensive coverage and editorial comment.

8. Ibid., 17 May 1884.

9. Henley, *Cash Family of South Carolina*, 36–37. According to Henley, Cash's mulatto daughter was named "Juliana."

10. William A. Courtenay Papers, South Caroliniana Library, University of South Carolina, Columbia. Chesterfield County records indicate that during these years (1881–1886) Cash divested himself of his substantial landholdings as some eight thousand acres were sold or deeded to his two surviving daughters. When Alleine received one thousand acres on 30 June 1884, a proviso required her to pay Julia Ann Wilson one hundred dollars a year for the remainder of her life. This woman, apparently the mother of "Juliana," also purchased forty-eight acres of land from Colonel Cash for a nominal fee.

11. *Charleston News and Courier*, 11 March 1888.

12. *Anson Times*, 1 October 1885.

13. Henley, *Cash Family of South Carolina*, 31. Henley ridicules tales that Boggan was "cruel and treacherous when a boy," asserting he actually was kind, tender, and "gentle almost to effeminacy." This North Carolina editor writes of a polished and courtly youth who, upon his return from Virginia Military Institute in 1876, was welcome in the best homes of Chesterfield County and "universally regarded as a 'coming man.'" Yet eight years later Boggan was "an outlaw—a fugitive from justice—a crimson-handed murderer —a despised assassin, shrinking from the public sight, and hiding in the swamps to avoid

arrest for his crimes and to escape the gallows." As noted, Henley blames the colonel for his son's descent from gentleman to renegade.

14. *Time* (30 May 1932), 4–5. The 20 June issue contains yet another Cash-Shannon letter, this one from Bernard Baruch. The famed elder statesman again recalls his memories of the duel (somewhat inaccurately), tells how his family decided to move to New York City, and asks where the editor obtained his information concerning the duel. He replied that it came from materials in the possession of "kin of the principals."

Three: Background

1. "Reflections of a Retired Lawyer," *Southern Literary Messenger* (March 1839): 218–21.

2. An 1856 edition contains four versions of the word: lynch, lynched, lynching, and lynch-law. By 1893, reflecting changing realities, the *Webster's* definition read, "to inflict punishment, especially death, without the forms of law, as by a mob."

3. Although undocumented, this figure (three hundred) has found its way into the writing of J. Elbert Cutler, Wilbur Cash, Eugene Genovese, and others. Someone subsequently decided that 10 percent of these victims were black, not white, and J. Elbert Cutler (*Lynch Law: An Investigation into the History of Lynching in the United States* [New York, 1905], 124) surmised that if the figure was reliable, probably even more blacks were killed "in various insurrectionary excitements."

4. *Keowee Courier,* 27 February 1860. "Slick" was a contemporary slang expression for something done quickly or someone subject to vigilante justice. According to the *Anderson Gazette* (quoted in the *Courier*), Tomlin used seditious language, was told to leave town, and failed to do so.

5. Two years earlier a Richland County grand jury, citing troubles in Texas, spoke out strongly against lynch law and recommended that magistrates and freeholders courts convened to hear slave cases be empowered to arrest, try, and punish those involved in such a crime. Any non–South Carolinian convicted of lynching, the jurors stressed, should be treated as a *slave* before the law. See Richland County Grand Jury Presentment, fall 1860, South Carolina Department of Archives and History, Columbia. However, letters of Columbia resident William C. Preston reveal this matter had little, if anything, to do with Texas. It was simply a local affair—an open threat to those within the state suspected of harboring Unionist sympathies. On 6 January 1860 Preston told Waddy Thompson, "Our town has recovered from the lynching panic and I now go into the streets without fear." In a letter dated simply 23 January, Preston described Columbia as "a focus of slave traders, disunionsts, and lynching societies" and talked of moving north to Charlottesville, Virginia (William C. Preston Papers, South Caroliniana Library, University of South Carolina, Columbia).

6. See Petition #28 to the General Assembly (1862) and records of Anderson County's magistrates and freeholders courts (1862), South Carolina Department of Archives and History, Columbia.

7. See Petition #104 to the General Assembly (1862), South Carolina Department of Archives and History, Columbia.

8. For an intriguing, detailed account of this complex affair see Joan E. Cashin, "A Lynching in Warime Carolina: The Death of Saxe Joiner," in W. Fitzhugh Brundage, ed., *Under the Sentence of Death: Lynching in the South* (Chapel Hill: University of North Carolina Press, 1997), 109–31.

9. See James W. Garner, "Lynching and the Criminal Law," *South Atlantic Quarterly* (October 1906): 333–41; and Henry A. Forster, "Why the United States Leads the World in the Relative Proportion of Murders, Lynchings, and Other Felonies . . . ," *Central Law Journal* (26 October 1917): 299–304.

10. Walter Clark, "The True Remedy for Lynch Law," *American Law Review* (November–December 1894): 801–2.

11. Until 1887 anyone charged with serious crime in South Carolina had twenty peremptory challenges during jury selection and the state had two. In that year the ratio was changed to ten to five, with a maximum of twenty whenever more than one defendant was involved. As Clark in "True Remedy for Lynch Law" observes, under such conditions the accused could almost select his own jury.

12. Clark, "True Remedy for Lynch Law," 806–7.

13. See the *Atlantic Monthly* (February 1877): 177–94; (April 1877): 467–77; (June 1877): 670–84; and (January 1878): 1–12. Although Townsend's name does not appear, authorship subsequently was revealed. The first and last essays deal with politics, the other two with morals and society.

14. The *New York Times* recorded this incident much more briefly, noting Moore was killed by Regulators.

15. The *State,* 25 October 1921.

16. See the *Charleston News and Courier,* 25 July–1 August 1885.

17. The *State,* 16, 21, 26 February; 28, 30 October 1896.

18. *Charleston News and Courier,* 16–28 November 1898, 11 February 1899.

19. The *State,* 26–27 November 1901, 16 March 1902.

Four: Lynchings Galore

1. See the National Association for the Advancement of Colored People's *Thirty Years of Lynching in the United States, 1889–1918* (New York, 1919); Cutler, *Lynch Law;* Frank Shay, *Judge Lynch: His First Hundred Years* (New York, c. 1938); Jack Simpson Mullins, "Lynching in South Carolina, 1900–1914" (Master's thesis, University of South Carolina, 1961); Susan Page Garris, "The Decline of Lynching in South Carolina, 1915–1947" (Master's thesis, University of South Carolina, 1973); and Terence Robert Finnegan, "At the Hands of Parties Unknown: Lynching in Mississippi and South Carolina, 1881–1940" (PhD diss., University of Illinois, 1993).

2. George C. Wright (*Racial Violence in Kentucky, 1865–1940* [Baton Rouge, 1990]) found 215 lynchings (1880–1940), plus 138 more during the previous two decades. W. Fitzhugh Brundage's careful study of two other states, *Lynching in the New South: Georgia and Virginia, 1880–1930,* cites 460 lynchings in Georgia and 86 in Virginia. See also Brundage, ed., *Under the Sentence of Death.*

3. At least a dozen South Carolina entries cited by the NAACP in *Thirty Years of Lynching* (1889–99) would appear to be faulty—wrong address, incorrect names,

insufficient information, for example. There is substantial evidence, for instance, that David Shaw of Laurens County actually was not lynched in 1892 but rather merely beaten (see the *State,* 1–17 June 1892). In the following decade the NAACP said one Louis Higgins was lynched in Bancroft, Maine, when in fact the tragedy occurred in Bancroft, Nebraska—confusion apparently caused by the abbreviations "Me." and "Ne." (see the *Chicago Tribune,* 27 August 1907).

4. The account is based on interviews with B. F. Harvey and Claude Crocker of Clinton and files of the *Clinton Courier.* Harvey, then about ten years old, recalls so many bullets were flying through the air near the village schoolhouse that recess was cancelled that morning.

5. This body also reported that during those years 787 of the victims (21.3 percent) were white. See the Southern Commission on the Study of Lynching, *Lynchings and What They Mean* (Atlanta, c. 1933).

6. The *State,* 31 July 1893.

7. See E. J. "Ebbie" Watson's extensive coverage of these proceedings in the *State,* 27–31 July 1893. This is one of the first such reports to specifically name those at the scene of a lynching. To the distress of many, although given several opportunities to pray, Thompson adamantly refused to do so.

8. *Charleston News and Courier,* 23 April 1887.

9. Arp's essays are found in many southern newspapers. These words appeared in the *Laurens Advertiser,* 25 July 1893.

10. *Charleston News and Courier,* 26 October 1898. Republican Church was in a region that later became part of McCormick County.

11. *Charleston News and Courier,* 26 October 1898. After 1900 the *News and Courier* became remarkably adept at ignoring local lynchings, though not those occurring outside of the South.

12. This appeal—signed by C. G. McIlwaine (chairman) and W. R. Douglas (secretary) —can be found in the Benjamin R. Tillman Papers (Box 62) at the South Carolina Department of Archives and History, Columbia.

13. For details of this saga, see the *Charleston News and Courier,* 19–29 September, 9, 20 October, 3, 12, 21 November 1885, 3–4 March 1886, and 4–6 August 1887; the *Edgefield Advertiser* for these same months; and estate papers of O. T. Culbreath, Edgefield County Courthouse, Edgefield, S.C.

14. There are rumors (impossible to verify) that Heyward was almost white; hence the special concern of those appealing for mercy.

15. *Reports and Resolutions of the General Assembly of the State of South Carolina,* 2 vols. (Columbia, S.C., 1880–1920), 1:199.

16. *Charleston News and Courier,* 6 May, 15 June 1890.

17. Tillman first uttered these words at Barnwell on 7 June 1892. Repeated throughout his reelection campaign to loud applause, they usually were prefaced by "I denounce lynch law," a statement frequently omitted by the *State.* Ironically, this outburst at Barnwell was inspired by reports of the lynching of David Shaw, which probably never occurred. In almost the same breath Tillman said, in reference to Shaw, "Look at Laurens!"

18. The *State,* 7 May 1893.

19. Ibid., 19 May 1893.

20. For details of this bloody spree, see ibid., 8–9 January 1897.

21. There would be five more in 1904 and three each in 1905 and 1906, Heyward's second, two-year term.

22. It is interesting that during Heyward's administration the *State* began to label some lynchings as murder, which perhaps was merely a way to limit the number of incidents to be reported. The Gonzales brothers, friends of the governor and publishers of that Columbia daily, stressed that lynching was proving to be neither a deterrent to crime nor a barrier against presumptions of social equality. Some familiarity, they wrote in an editorial published on 26 September 1904, was inevitable as black men and white women worked side by side on hundreds of South Carolina farms. They knew, they said, of four cases in four different counties where presumptuous advances by black men were not rebuked. No, the answer was not lynching, and yet whites certainly should keep blacks in their place and "maintain their own proper position."

23. Accounts of the Holly Hill incident, the death of a drifter who went by various names, are so confusing (see the *State,* 2 March 1904) that it is not included as a lynching in the Appendix.

24. The *State,* 15 October 1904.

25. John D. Watson Papers, South Caroliniana Library, University of South Carolina, Columbia. The papers of Harry L. Watson (1876–1956) are filed in this collection. Heyward subsequently would say, without reference to Watson's role in the proceedings, he thought his presence saved Davis from being burned. The *State* (17 August) said the "usual ghoulish souvenirs were taken: toes, ears, fingers, etc." It also printed a letter from Greenwood blacks approving of this lynching.

26. The *State,* 11–14 January, 15–17 October 1909.

27. Ibid., 11 October 1911. In 1910 Ashley was charged by federal authorities with twenty counts of peonage. Following acquittal he shook the hand of each juror warmly and said, "I hope, brother, to meet you on the other side of Jordan" (quoted in the *State,* 29 April 1910).

28. N. W. Hardin to Cole Blease, 29 March 1912, Cole Blease Papers, South Carolina Department of Archives and History, Columbia. Hardin (1855–1923), a prominent Blacksburg attorney, often served as intendant (mayor) and also was in the S.C. House of Representatives in 1908 and 1913–1914.

29. Ibid.

30. For a thorough account of this affair, see Garris, "Decline of Lynching in South Carolina," 14–25. She quotes extensively from the correspondence of Governor Manning with detective J. G. Egan, hired by the governor to investigate this tragedy. See also Roy Nash, "The Lynching of Anthony Crawford," *Independent* (11 December 1916): 456–62, an exceptional bit of reporting.

31. According to Garris, "Decline of Lynching in South Carolina," the mayor immediately tore up the check.

32. Nash, "Lynching of Anthony Crawford," 460. This newsman, who posed as a New York resident interested in buying local farmland, at first received favorable comment in

the *Abbeville Press and Banner,* especially after he became a subscriber. However, once his article on Crawford appeared, the editor said his work was full of errors and that the writer obviously failed to understand the local situation.

33. The specter of federal intervention may have been raised by yet another arrest of Will Cann, this time for harassing a black youth employed as a special delivery messenger at the local post office.

34. The *State,* 19 August 1913.

35. Stewart E. Tolnay and E. M. Beck, *A Festival of Violence: An Analysis of Southern Lynchings, 1882–1930* (Urbana and Chicago, 1995), 214. Only Georgia recorded a greater out-migration of blacks in the 1920s—260,000.

36. Kohn's speech, "Some of the Lynchings I Have Attended," was published in the *State* on 21 March 1936. Notes in the August Kohn Papers at the South Caroliniana Library, University of South Carolina, Columbia, indicate he had difficulty composing his concluding remarks.

37. Senator Ernest F. Hollings, who, as a member of the General Assembly, led the fight to pass this measure, says that it was acquittal of the men who killed Willie Earle that inspired him to act; at first, he recalls, the KKK actively opposed the bill (Hollings to author, 6 March 1992).

Five: The Charleston Triangle

1. Quoted in the *Charleston News and Courier,* 28 June 1889.

2. The best summary of Dawson's life, including a sound analysis of his career, can be found in E. Culpepper Clark's *Francis Warrington Dawson and the Politics of Restoration: South Carolina, 1874–1889* (University, Ala., 1980).

3. This should have come as no surprise to Dawson. In 1876, as editor of the *Charleston News and Courier,* he heaped praise upon Chamberlain and vowed that it would be "folly" to oppose his renomination, telling fellow Democrats to concentrate their efforts on electing honest men to other state offices and the legislature. Dawson continued to sing this tune until Hampton was nominated in mid-August; the *News and Courier* suddenly greeted this turn of events with an editorial entitled "Hampton and Victory."

4. The *Charleston World* (18 March 1889) reported that B. R. Riordan, who had lived in New York City for some years, said Dawson, while visiting there, mentioned that his governess was being pestered by "some worthless fellows" and he thought "a horsewhip might be brought into play with some advantage." If true, this statement may not relate to McDow since Dawson was in Manhattan from 26 January to 5 February. According to trial testimony, the doctor began his pursuit of Marie on 1 February.

5. Since 1900 the street numbers of these houses have been changed to 101 Rutledge and 99 Bull.

6. In addition to Clark's biography, see Thomas K. Peck, "The Killing of Captain Dawson," in *Charleston Murders,* ed. Beatrice St. Julien Ravenel (New York, 1947); W. Curtis Worthington Jr., "The Man Who Killed Warrington Dawson," *American Journal of Forensic Medicine and Pathology,* vol. 10, no. 1 (1989): 76–82; and Robert Molloy, *An Afternoon in March* (New York, 1958). Although the latter is fiction, Molloy provides insights into what may have happened and highlights some developments overlooked by

historians. The Peck version relies heavily on the columns of the *Charleston News and Courier*, as does this account. In all, that daily printed nearly forty columns on the murder, funeral, and inquest (13–17 March) and another seventy columns on the trial and its aftermath (25 June–2 July).

7. *Charleston News and Courier*, 13 March 1889. This attack, similar to others initiated by Dawson, was typical of editorial behavior in those decades. In June 1868 he and Alfred Rhett Jr. (the man who was trying to revive his father's *Mercury* and five years later killed a judge in a duel) clashed concerning subscription rolls. However, in published correspondence, Dawson wrote, "It is proper for me to say now that, being a member of the Catholic Church, I cannot, under any circumstances, engage in a duel." Two years later, as still more journalistic fur was flying, editor Myron Fox of Charleston's *Daily Republican* noted on 9 August that whenever challeged, Dawson "hid" behind the Catholic Church. As a result, Dawson charged into Fox's office and assaulted him with a cane while he was seated—just as he would his neighbor McDow two decades later. In 1870 Dawson was arrested, bound to keep the peace for a year, and scheduled to answer assault charges, which evidently were dropped. During these weeks Fox referred to yet another clash that Dawson lost. Dawson apparently attacked a gentleman named Seabrook who, according to Fox, "caned him into several days' sickness, stuffing the said editor's mouth full of sand in the bargain."

8. Inquest testimony as reported in the *Charleston News and Courier*, 15 March 1889. Both the cook and the butler were extremely loyal to McDow and said nothing that would reflect on his character. However, since Patrolman Gordon thought he had seen Moses Johnson moving about the premises in a suspicious manner, the butler-coachman was indicted as an accessory.

9. Quoted in the *Charleston News and Courier*, 28 June 1889.

10. *Charleston News and Courier*, 27 June 1889.

11. The Mitchell-Smith Papers at the South Carolina Historical Society in Charleston contain interesting observations by an Alabama friend of H. A. M. Smith. Distressed by press coverage of the ongoing trial, he advised Smith to become more aggressive. "What a sad commentary upon Dawson's life," he added, "that he should be killed with his name tacked to a servant girl when there were so many other and nobler things to kill him for."

12. Quoted in the *Charleston News and Courier*, 2 July 1889.

13. The *Charleston World* (17 March) noted that Reverend Horn, Mrs. McDow's pastor and a former neighbor, arrived at about 6 P.M. and told the cook to close up the house.

14. "Arthur" appears to have been Edgar S. McDow (born 1871). According to the 1900 census, he was a physician living in Heath Springs with his wife and two daughters, ages two and three. A short time later, however, the family moved to nearby Lancaster.

15. Francis Warrington Dawson Papers, Duke University, Durham, N.C. Ethel alludes to the family's "reduced circumstances" in July 1890 and how "horrid" it is to be poor. The Dawson Papers also contain a volume of newspaper clippings bearing this cryptic note: "Scrapbook made by Mrs. Dawson for Hélène Burdayron on the death of Capt. Dawson—which was to help clear name of the maid in the future. It was left in Charleston."

Six: The Assassination of N. G. Gonzales

1. Lewis Pinckney Jones, *Stormy Petrel: N. G. Gonzales and His State* (Columbia, S.C., 1973), 97. This is a thorough study of this fiery editor's career.

2. N. G. Gonzales to James C. Hemphill (23 March 1889), N. G. Gonzales Papers, South Caroliniana Library, University of South Carolina, Columbia.

3. *Charleston News and Courier,* 8 September 1880.

4. Ibid., 20 January 1881.

5. Ibid., 25 July–1 August 1885.

6. Ibid., 3–6 February 1886.

7. Ibid., 28 October 1886.

8. The *State,* 25–29 November 1891.

9. The Tillmans certainly helped Edgefield gain its reputation for violence, but whether it was more so than other South Carolina counties is debatable. In *Strain of Violence: Historical Studies of American Violence and Vigilantism* (New York, 1975), Richard Maxwell Brown discusses at length the "Edgefield Tradition" of backcountry mayhem, noting that Parson Weems in 1816 called it "a very District of Devils." Yet, Orville Vernon Burton, author of *In My Father's House Are Many Mansions* (Chapel Hill, N.C., and London, 1985)—a massive study of that same county—thinks it probably was typical of upcountry South Carolina in the nineteenth century. Perhaps communities, much like people, develop personalities, and Edgefield's political campaigns (ten governors and five U.S. senators) undoubtedly contributed to the shaping of its well-known reputation. For further analysis, see Lacy K. Ford Jr., "Origins of the Edgefield Tradition: The Late Antebellum Experience and the Roots of Political Insurgency," *South Carolina Historical Magazine* (October 1997): 328–48.

10. Numerous sources say Tillman was born one year earlier; however, there are indications 1869 is correct. This is the date he cited under oath in October 1903, and it also is inscribed on his tombstone. Clark's Hill, now in McCormick County, is located about twenty miles west of Edgefield near the Savannah River.

11. This newspaper published triweekly and weekly editions, but only the latter exist for these months; hence some of this correspondence has been lost.

12. The *State,* 12 April 1893. Speaking in Spartanburg during his 1900 campaign for lieutenant governor, Jim Tillman said one of the greatest mistakes of his life had been to oppose efforts of Gonzales to enter the foreign service. Here was a lesson, said the *State,* "never obstruct the migration of your enemy."

13. George Tillman to N. G. Gonzales (6 February 1895), N. G. Gonzales Papers. Evans, the younger brother of Governor John Gary Evans, continued to be enveloped in controversy. In October 1902 he was acquitted of murder following the sensational shooting death of Captain John James Griffin, commercial agent for the Norfolk & Western Railroad. Griffin died on 13 April 1901 during a two-man drinking spree in quarters rented by Evans at the corner of Main and Lady streets in downtown Columbia. In May 1913 Evans was disbarred from law practice because of questionable financial dealings; however, the state supreme court offered reinstatement if Evans provided proof "he has not for two years immediately preceding his application used intoxicating liquors and that he has reformed his character."

14. Among those accompanying Tillman on the Democratic campaign circuit was Barnard B. Evans, an unsuccessful candidate for railroad commissioner.

15. According to reports in numerous papers, while speaking in Kershaw early in September, Jim Tillman bragged of being "a consistent Presbyterian." When the campaign party arrived in Gaffney, a fellow Democrat joked with him concerning this remark. Ben Tillman, overhearing the conversation, turned to his nephew and asked, "What makes you tell such a G-d d–n lie as that, Jim?"

16. If Tillman actually used "nasty" language, no one should have been surprised. This charge often was levied against his father by those who did not admire him, and his uncle's blunt tongue was legend.

17. *Journal of the Senate* (1902), 326.

18. It would be interesting to know if, by any chance, DeCamp acted at the urging of Gonzales or with his knowledge. DeCamp, writing in the Gaffney *Ledger* (25 July 1902), said he regretted the encounter with Tillman and confronted him only because "his consort in Columbia" called the *Ledger* "a guttersnipe sheet." The meaning of "his consort" is not clear but may refer to the Columbia *Daily Record.* In any case, by 12 August the *Ledger* was calling Tillman "a falsifier, gambler, drunkard, blasphemer, and defaulter."

19. This view that the press should act when others fail to do their duty is typical of Gonzales. On 6 August 1888 during the final meeting of the Democratic canvass in Blackville, for much the same reason he twice called Ben Tillman "an infernal liar." Tillman tempered his response, he said, because ladies were present, a fact Gonzales admitted he had failed to appreciate. However, before they left Blackville, Tillman sought out Gonzales, and the pair resolved their immediate differences, parting on relatively good terms.

20. This may refer to Jim Tillman's statement during the campaign that the *State's* attacks on his uncle in the early 1890s sometimes moved Ben Tillman to tears.

21. Testimony during the murder trial that followed revealed the two men met amicably at times in the 1890s, occasionally chatting at the offices of the *State* and drinking with friends.

22. Jones, *Stormy Petrel,* 302.

23. This appointment caused consternation among friends of Gonzales (see the *State,* 16–26 September 1903). Because of the illness of Judge George W. Gage, Chief Justice Young Y. Pope named Judge D. A. Townsend, the man who permitted the change of venue in April, to take Gage's place in Lexington. However, Townsend was scheduled to hold court at the same in Fairfield County, and reassignment under these conditions, it turned out, was illegal; hence the appointment of Gary, which the *State* termed "jugglery," noting he was known as "Cousin Frank" within Senator Tillman's household.

24. *Charleston News and Courier,* 10 October 1903.

25. *New York World,* 11 October 1903.

26. Ibid., 16 October 1903.

Seven: Analyzing Murder

1. These totals and others cited throughout this chapter come largely from *Reports and Resolutions,* which summarize assault/murder/manslaughter cases by judicial district

and/or county. These volumes also provide information on those found guilty or inno-cent and cases continued or dropped. However, lynchings seldom are included since they rarely were considered to be murder, and some murderers, of course, never were indicted. Until 1900 few were charged with manslaughter, although such individuals almost always were found guilty, which may indicate a form of "plea bargaining." Also, until that time *Reports and Resolutions* published no information concerning race.

2. H. V. Redfield, *Homicide, North and South* (Philadelphia, 1880), 96. This work contains classic pioneer research on its subject.

3. Ibid., 109. For details of the Booth-Toney affair, see W. D. Ramey, comp., *Trial of the Booth and Toney Homicide . . .* (Edgefield, S.C.?, 1880).

4. *Acts and Joint Resolutions of the South Carolina General Assembly* (Columbia, S.C., 1881), 448.

5. Redfield, *Homicide,* 108.

6. In 1880 the *Charleston News and Courier* reported that 41 whites killed whites and an equal number of blacks killed blacks. In addition, 7 whites murdered blacks, and 8 blacks killed whites. A decade later the *State* recorded only 22 murders of whites by whites, 20 black-black homicides, 8 whites killed by blacks, and 9 blacks killed by whites. In most instances the latter allegedly were fleeing criminals shot by police. This same pat-tern is reflected in a six-month survey that a Williamston man published in the *State* (6 January 1908). Louis Barstow counted 158 homicides (July–December 1907) with 79 white and 79 black victims, although slightly more blacks were slayers (85 blacks, 70 whites, 3 cases unknown). Of the deceased, he said, 121 had been shot. Eighty-two lived in "dry" counties and 76 in those with dispensaries, indicating the role of liquor in homi-cides may have been somewhat exaggerated by Prohibition forces.

7. See "Testimony in the Inquest into the Death of Thomas Pinckney, Jr., 1899," South Carolina Department of Archives and History, Columbia. A decade later, during Christmas week 1909, Greenville was shaken by the deaths of two white men (Wesley Russell and J. E. Liddell), apparent victims of bungled burglaries. Fearing a lynching, Governor M. F. Ansel secured the services of a Pinkerton agent, who scoured the area for several months. Despite arrests, no one ever was convicted of either crime; nevertheless, the Pinkerton reports present a unique picture of the Greenville underworld as the agent toured sporting houses and blind tigers while talking with madams, prostitutes, and bootleggers. See M. F. Ansel Papers, South Carolina Department of Archives and History, Columbia.

8. See the appendix, tables A.5 and A.6, which show figures relating to Charleston's population by race and arrests in that community by race, 1880–1920.

9. Since a few counties did not hold court because of the flu epidemic, statistics for 1920 are somewhat misleading.

10. As noted, some counties failed to report such information from time to time, and thirteen new counties were created during these decades. Except for Berkeley (1882) and Florence (1888), these boundary changes occurred after 1895, thus complicating, to some degree, any statistical overview. Edgefield, Darlington, and Florence are not included in this lynching-homicide survey because of incomplete data. Edgefield's record for twenty-nine years stood at 7.16 homicides per year, indicating its well-known reputation for

violence may be somewhat exaggerated. Darlington posted a figure of 5.0 for a similar period, and—with five years missing—Florence averaged 5.2 homicides per year.

11. Complete totals can be found in table 20 (pp. 366–401) of Forrest E. Linder and Robert D. Grove, *Vital Statistics Rates in the United States, 1900–1940* (Washington, D.C., 1943), a volume in the 1940 U.S. Census. A study of the years 1936–45 reveals the mean annual homicide rate per 100,000 to be 23.9 in Columbia and 24.6 in Charleston. Comparable figures for nearby cities include Charlotte (26.3), Columbus (29.7), Atlanta (34.7), Savannah (34.7), Nashville (36.2), Chattanooga (39.0) and Macon (49.8). See Austin L. Porterfield, "Indices of Suicide and Homicide by States and Cities: Some Southern–Non-Southern Contrasts with Implications for Research," *American Sociological Review* (August 1949): 481–90. The general thrust of this article is high homicide and low suicide rates in southern cities, the reverse of trends in other parts of the nation.

12. See Charles R. Wilson and William Ferris, eds., *Encyclopedia of Southern Culture* (Chapel Hill, N.C., and London, 1989), 1474.

13. I am told by a friend that as late as the 1940s residents of rural precincts in some parts of South Carolina went armed to the polls.

14. On Tuesday, 13 April 1993, the *State* published the page-one headline "VIOLENCE MARS WEEKEND" and then told how thirteen people had been killed in South Carolina during the Easter holiday, most of them shot as a result of family arguments. The dead included an Orangeburg man who, before committing suicide, killed his ex-wife, her new husband, and another man he accused of breaking up his marriage; and three Rock Hill residents—two men who died in a shoot-out over a woman, and a seventy-year-old blind woman who perished in a fire set by her son.

15. The *State*, 17 June 1894.

16. Ibid., 9 July 1895.

17. Ibid., 25 November 1896.

18. Ibid., 6 March 1895.

19. Ibid., 9 March 1900. The report carried this subhead: "Gun with Buckshot Used at Close Range, Then His Brains Shot Out with Revolver."

20. The *State*, 23 March, 10, 13 April 1900.

21. Ibid., 10 July 1907.

22. Ibid., 29 May 1919.

23. *Charleston News and Courier*, 13 March 1887.

24. Quoted in *McClure's* (December 1904): 167.

25. According to *Time* (6 April 1992), more Texans died from gunshots in 1990 than from traffic accidents, a new "first" in the bloody toll of gun deaths.

26. *Charleston News and Courier*, 7 August 1886.

27. For examples of biracial homicides dealt with in an unexpected manner, see *Charleston News and Courier*, 24 March 1880, 30 March, 19 September, 11 October 1889; and the *State*, 30 December 1892, 5 September 1894, 3 February 1897, 11 March 1899, 8 May 1903, 27 March, 25 November 1904, 11 March 1905, 19 July, 20 October 1913, 24 February 1915, 24 June 1917, 18 September, 2 October 1919. The 1917 item is especially interesting. In April of that year a Chester policeman shot and killed a

black man. Three months later the father of the deceased had the policeman arrested and charged with the crime.

Eight: One-on-One

1. Other accounts say all pictures in the house were covered with white sheeting and Riley was dressed in a military uniform.

2. *Charleston News and Courier,* 29 June 1886.

3. Ibid., 5 July 1887.

4. Ibid., 22 July 1887. N. G. Gonzales wrote that the 1:00 A.M. verdict was followed by "a curious rapping" that turned out to be Sheahan's feet or knuckles rattling against the dock.

5. *Charleston News and Courier,* 26 July 1887. A native of Augusta, Georgia, Sheahan moved to Laurens from Washington, Georgia, in 1884.

6. If Harris had a knife and a gun, no such weapons ever were found. Despite this incident, both tragic and personally embarrassing, Thurmond subsequently would issue an incisive comment on homicide in South Carolina (which will be discussed later) and go on to become a U.S. district attorney and a special circuit and supreme court judge.

7. During the trial the cause of the "intermissions" became obvious. Youmans was chasing Keels around a column behind which he was trying to hide.

8. The *Charleston News and Courier* (3 May) said Youmans was unwilling to make any comment and those who saw the shooting were "too excited to talk rationally."

9. *Charleston News and Courier,* 31 December 1887.

10. The *State,* 13 May 1914.

11. *Abbeville Press and Banner,* 28 October 1885.

12. Other cases that seemed to have no end (in addition to the Robert Jones imbroglio discussed earlier) include those of Jeff David and Willie Bethune. David, a mulatto, was convicted in the late 1870s of killing an elderly Abbeville County couple. His attorney, W. C. Benet, became suspicious when neighbors appeared too eager to claim reward money, and he waged a three-year fight to free David. During these years David was reprieved from the gallows eight times by four governors. (See the *State,* 3 November 1904.) In 1909 Willie Bethune (black) found a runaway horse and carriage near Manning and went joyriding with two girlfriends. When G. H. Mims, owner of the horse and carriage, tried to reassert control under disputed circumstances, shots were exchanged and Mims was killed. During the next decade Bethune was found guilty seven times, the first six convictions reversed by the state supreme court. The *State* (24 June 1919) provides a summary of this case as Willie was about to be tried for the seventh time.

13. The *State,* 9 March 1895.

14. Ibid., 27 September 1896.

15. Ibid., 25 March 1897.

16. By the time of the trial in June 1904, fearing for their lives, they had left Hawthorne and were living in Aiken. There they worked for one of Surasky's brothers, a relationship the defense sought to exploit.

17. At the inquest held shortly after Surasky's death, Green's father told authorities he was eager for his son to be arraigned and would cooperate with them.

18. General Session Rolls, Case 276, Saluda County, S.C. The pregnancy and estrangement were not mentioned by the press, although the *Saluda Standard* (13 September 1905) conceded the shooting was the result of "domestic infidelity in which Coleman and Blease's wife figured." The next week, following the inquest, the editor said because of the nature of the testimony, "we honestly feel it has no place in a family paper."

19. General Session Rolls, Case 176, Saluda County, S.C.

20. The *State*, 11 April 1906.

21. Hasty, as noted earlier, actually was a younger brother of two men who were operating the inn, not a proprietor.

22. Election returns reveal Long got only about one-third of the votes cast in Wagener in a four-man race but did better in the rest of the county.

23. At his trial Long said he was not accustomed to using or carrying firearms but under the circumstances thought it advisable to do so.

24. The *State*, 1 October 1912.

25. Ibid., 6 June 1913.

Nine: Shoot-outs, Western Style

1. Where the "Darlington Riot" (30 March 1894) fits in the scheme of things is far from clear. Tensions aroused by the presence of dispensary agents led to a shooting fracas that left three men dead. Yet trouble erupted at the railroad depot only as state officials were preparing to leave town and may have been sparked by a fistfight between two local residents. See Gerald D. Holley, "The Darlington Riot of 1894," Master's thesis, University of South Carolina, 1970. The dispensary, a controversial factor in turn-of-the-century South Carolina, was a scheme promoted by Ben Tillman to limit liquor sales to state-controlled outlets (dispensaries). In brief, from 1893 to 1915 all *legal* liquor was distributed through such stores, a system that fostered considerable political heat.

2. *Charleston News and Courier*, 16 September 1885.

3. *Anderson Intelligencer*, 16 November 1892.

4. Cohen, a graduate of the College of Charleston and the University of South Carolina (where he served as a history instructor), also attended the University of Pennsylvania. He had been working for the *Charleston Evening Post* for about a year.

5. *Charleston News and Courier*, 23 July 1881.

6. This lengthy editorial was quoted in the *Charleston News and Courier*, 6 August 1881.

7. Lillie B. Westmoreland, *J. Dean Crain: A Biography* (Greenville, S.C., 1959), 8–11. Crain, who received his first formal education at age ten, once remarked that he never saw a newspaper until he was thirteen.

8. The *State*, 2 September 1894.

9. *Greenville Daily News*, 5 July 1919.

10. According to Johnstone, the weapon in his trousers was so large that it deflected the first shot fired by Jones and thus saved his life.

11. *Charleston News and Courier*, 16 November 1887.

12. Ibid., 20 June 1890.

13. *Columbia Daily Register,* 4 August 1889. "Dug" Meetze, subsequently identified as "Dub" by the Columbia press, fell victim to a Lexington County lynch mob in July 1893.

14. The *State,* 10 November 1893.

15. *Columbia Daily Register,* 3 February 1894. A "blind tiger" was an unlicensed liquor outlet.

16. Three days before Cartledge died, Mrs. John Stewart, wife of a salesman at Mimnaugh's department store, was killed by dispensary agents during a raid on her Laurel Street home across from the governor's mansion. Four constables, who appear to have been seeking a blind tiger where none existed, subsequently were arrested. Among them was J. B. Coleman, the man shot and killed by Eugene Blease in Saluda in September 1905.

17. *Charleston News and Courier,* 12 October 1890.

18. According to the *Edgefield Advertiser* (15 May 1895), Swearingen had a two-thousand-dollar policy with the Knights of Honor and another worth twenty-five hundred dollars with the Union Mutual Life Insurance Company.

19. For details of this affair, see the *State,* 10 April, 18 June 1899.

20. The *State,* 8 December 1900.

21. The *Abbeville Press and Banner* said that Dansby put a silver dollar on the table, a strange gesture if the group was playing for peanuts.

22. The *State,* 31 December 1900.

23. That the good doctor was armed en route from church is of some significance. Yet as the *New York Post* observed in an article reprinted in the *Charleston News and Courier* (22 February 1883), it was strange that the South was such a stronghold of both religious sentiment and murder. To prove his point, the writer quoted a Texan: "Wife, give me my pistol. I'm going to prayer-meeting to-night."

24. Court testimony quoted in the *Yorkville Enquirer,* 10 December 1915.

25. The Isenhowers clearly had no plan of coordinated action; but when asked on the witness stand why he had a pistol that day, Ernest replied, "for no special reason."

26. *Yorkville Enquirer,* 10 December 1915. This pro-Blease paper gives a full account of the trial. See also issues of 7 and 14 December for details.

27. One could argue that the press paid more attention to white deaths than black deaths, which is true. Nevertheless, blacks were more numerous throughout these years, and any shooting by blacks that resulted in multiple deaths undoubtedly was reported. By way of comment, the chief of detectives in "a large Southern city" once remarked, "We have three classes of homicide. If a nigger kills a white man, that's murder. If a white man kills a nigger, that's justifiable homicide. If a nigger kills another nigger, that's one less nigger" (quoted in Raymond B. Fosdick, *American Police Systems* [New York, 1920], 45).

Ten: The Weird, Bizarre, and Insane

1. *South Carolina Reports* (Jersey City, 1882), 15:409–13.

2. Of 2,275 convicts listed in a "central register" (January 1893–December 1897), only 245 were white. These volumes, also designated as "Descriptive Roll of Convicts— S.C. Penitentiary," are available at the South Carolina Department of Archives and History, Columbia.

3. *Reports and Resolutions* (1886), 1:13. Some details of this affair can be found in the *Marion Star,* 14, 21 January 1885.

4. *Reports and Resolutions* (1888), 1:225–26.

5. Ibid. (1890), 1:189.

6. The *State,* 10 April 1909. This incident was recalled years later in connection with a similar case.

7. The *State,* 26 October 1891.

8. *Chester Lantern,* 20 March, 2 April 1906.

9. The *State,* 10 April 1909. According to an extensive account, this homicide occurred near Jonesville.

10. *Barnwell People,* 14 December 1911.

11. *Beaufort Gazette,* 8 September 1911.

12. *Georgetown Times,* 20 March 1912.

13. The *State,* 8 August 1919. However, Buster did spend a few days behind bars.

14. *Orangeburg Times and Democrat,* 15 January 1920.

15. *Charleston News and Courier,* 26 July 1884.

16. The *State,* 14 July 1900.

17. Ibid., 25 July 1900. The shot proved fatal, and Jiveur subsequently was arrested; however, he does not appear to have been indicted for the crime.

18. *Charleston News and Courier,* 17 June 1889.

19. The *State,* 17 July 1896. The report from Greenville bore this headline: "All About a Miserable Dog."

20. The *State,* 24 January 1897.

21. *Charleston News and Courier,* 5 July 1886.

22. The *State,* 24 June 1905.

23. Ibid., 3 February 1903.

24. Ibid., 22 January 1911; *Anderson Daily Mail,* 21, 24 January 1911.

25. The previous year a white tenant farmer living near Bennettsville was charged with hanging his daughter. James Jackson and Lily Mae argued, she ran out of the house, and he followed. Her mother later found her body hanging from a trace chain in a stable, her mouth securely bound with her own apron. See the *State,* 27 September 1918. Jackson subsequently was acquitted in July 1919.

26. The *State,* 14 May 1896. The local weekly chose to ignore this incident.

27. File #2447, Court of General Sessions, Chesterfield County, S.C., March 1913.

28. The *State,* 4 August 1916, 18 March and 7 June 1919.

29. Ibid., 7 May 1911.

30. Gertrude was released the following day to attend the double funeral of her husband and her father-in-law. Although the local editor filled his paper with murder stories from all parts of the country, he seemingly was distressed by Lee County's soaring homicide rate and went to great lengths to point out that Garrett was not a native nor did he reside in the community.

Eleven: Change in a Changeless Society

1. The *State,* 8 January 1898. Hudson expressed a personal view that a man was apt to become more aggressive when armed and resent any sharp comment with a shot: "In

other words, he is more overbearing himself, and more inclined to resent the like conduct in others by shooting them."

2. The *State,* 10 January 1905. In this same statement, really a valedictory address since Thurmond was planning to retire as solicitor, he conceded he did not know how to deal with liquor but thought laws protecting women and curbing epithets might reduce the number of homicides. As for lynching, he suggested lectures in black schools stressing the certainty of death for rape and in all schools concerning the dangers of mob action. Thurmond expressed opposition to the law requiring a county to compensate the family of anyone lynched, specifically because the law was unenforceable, juries would not agree to such payments, and it seemed wrong to tax a murdered man's family to pay that of the murderer (the man lynched).

3. The *State,* 5 July 1905.

4. *Journal of the Senate* (1913), 45–46. During his tenure, Blease spoke out against football, whites teaching in black schools, black fraternal orders, and smoking in public places such as restaurants, especially when ladies were present. In addition, his administration was marked by an unprecedented number of pardons and unconditional paroles (a power granted to governors in 1909). In 1912, when he issued 21 pardons and 161 paroles, Blease concluded a verbose introduction to his official report on such matters with this verse:

> But he who marks from day to day,
> In generous acts his radiant way,
> Treads the same path the Savior trod,
> The path to glory and to God.
> (*Reports and Resolutions* [1913], 3:521–27)

5. *Charleston News and Courier,* 30 June 1883.

6. Ibid., 21 July 1885.

7. Ibid., 12 September 1887.

8. The *State,* 7 January 1912.

9. Ibid., 8 January 1898.

10. Ibid., 2, 13, 20 February, 13, 31 October, 19, 22, 23 November 1909.

BIBLIOGRAPHY

This tale of violence is based largely on newspapers published in three South Carolina communities, namely Charleston's *News and Courier, World,* and *Evening Post;* Columbia's *Register* and *State;* and the *Greenville Daily News.* Material found in other dailies and weeklies throughout the state, as well as files of the *New York Times, New York World, Tidewater Index* (Tappahannock, Va.), and *Anson Times* and *Wadesboro Intelligencer* (both published in Wadesboro, N.C.), help flesh out incidents described in these pages. Courthouse records consulted include those found in these South Carolina counties: Anderson, Charleston, Chesterfield, Edgefield, Fairfield, Kershaw, Lexington, Newberry, Saluda, and Spartanburg. Official documents in Anson County, N.C., and Essex County, Va., yielded data relative to the Cash-Shannon saga.

The files of various academic institutions provided background information, among them, Georgetown University, University of South Carolina, Virginia Military Institute, and Washington and Lee University. Much like academic records, census reports furnish bits of biographical data but little on violence and crime since South Carolina was not a "registration" state until 1917.

Unpublished Material

Ansel, M. F. Papers. South Carolina Department of Archives and History, Columbia.

Ascolillo, Victor H. "The South Carolina Court System for Juveniles." Master's thesis, University of South Carolina, 1969.

Blease, Cole. Papers. South Carolina Department of Archives and History, Columbia.

Cash, E. B. C. Papers. South Caroliniana Library, University of South Carolina, Columbia.

Cash-Shannon Duel Papers. South Caroliniana Library, University of South Carolina, Columbia.

Christensen, Frederik Holmes. Diaries. South Caroliniana Library, University of South Carolina, Columbia.

Courtenay, William A. Papers. South Caroliniana Library, University of South Carolina, Columbia.

Dawson, Francis Warrington. Papers. Duke University, Durham, N.C.

Finnegan, Terence Robert. "At the Hands of Parties Unknown: Lynching in Mississippi and South Carolina, 1881–1940." PhD diss., University of Illinois, 1993.

Fitzsimmons, Mabel Trott. "Hot Words and Hair Triggers." Charleston Library Society, Charleston, S.C.

Garris, Susan Page. "The Decline of Lynching in South Carolina, 1915–1947." Master's thesis, University of South Carolina, 1973.

Gonzales, N. G. Papers. South Caroliniana Library, University of South Carolina, Columbia.

Grand Jury Presentments, 1861–1865. South Carolina Department of Archives and History, Columbia.

Hart, Augustus Griffin. "Crime in South Carolina." Master's thesis, University of South Carolina, 1914.

Holley, Gerald D. "The Darlington Riot of 1894." Master's thesis, University of South Carolina, 1970.

Hollings, Ernest F. Letter to author, 6 March 1992.

Hoyt, James A. "The Death of N. G. Gonzales, Editor of the *State*, 1891–1903." South Caroliniana Library, University of South Carolina, Columbia.

Johnson, William E. Papers. South Caroliniana Library, University of South Carolina, Columbia.

Kohn, August. Papers. South Caroliniana Library, University of South Carolina, Columbia.

Macfarlan, Allan. Papers. South Caroliniana Library, University of South Carolina, Columbia.

Magrath, Andrew Gordon. Papers. Southern Historical Collection, University of North Carolina, Chapel Hill; South Caroliniana Library, University of South Carolina, Columbia.

Mims, Julian L. "The Life and Politics of George Dionysius Tillman." Old Edgefield District Archives, Edgefield.

Mitchell-Smith Papers. South Carolina Historical Society, Charleston.

Mullins, Jack Simpson. "Lynching in South Carolina, 1900–1914." Master's thesis, University of South Carolina, 1961.

Petitions to the General Assembly, 1860–1865. South Carolina Department of Archives and History, Columbia.

Preston, William C. Papers. South Caroliniana Library, University of South Carolina, Columbia.

Salley, Alexander Samuel. Papers. South Caroliniana Library, University of South Carolina, Columbia.

Sewell, Michael. "The Gonzales-Tillman Affair: The Public Conflict of a Politician and a Crusading Newspaper Editor." Master's thesis, University of South Carolina, 1967.

"Testimony in the Inquest into the Death of Thomas Pinckney, Jr., 1899." South Carolina Department of Archives and History, Columbia.

Tillman, Benjamin R. Papers. South Carolina Department of Archives and History, Columbia.

Watson, John D. Papers. South Caroliniana Library, University of South Carolina, Columbia.

West, Stephen A. "From Yeoman to Redneck in Upstate South Carolina, 1850–1915." PhD diss., Columbia University, 1998.

Books and Articles

Acts and Joint Resolutions of the South Carolina General Assembly. Columbia, S.C., 1880–1920.

Ayers, Edward L. *The Promise of the New South: Life after Appomattox.* New York and Oxford, 1992.

———. *Vengeance & Justice: Crime and Punishment in the 19th Century American South.* New York and Oxford, 1984.

Baker, Ray Stannard. "What Is a Lynching?" *McClure's* (January 1905): 299–314.

Baruch, Bernard. *My Own Story.* 2 vols. New York, 1957.

Beck, E. M., and Stewart E. Tolnay. "The Killing Fields of the Deep South: The Market for Cotton and the Lynching of Blacks, 1882–1930." *American Sociological Review* (August 1990): 526–39.

Brearley, H. C. *Homicide in the United States.* Chapel Hill, N.C., 1932.

Brown, Richard Maxwell. *Strain of Violence: Historical Studies of American Violence and Vigilantism.* New York, 1975.

Brundage, W. Fitzhugh. *Lynching in the New South: Georgia and Virginia, 1880–1930.* Urbana and Chicago, 1993.

Brundage, W. Fitzhugh, ed. *Under Sentence of Death: Lynching in the New South.* Chapel Hill, N.C., and London, 1997.

Burton, Orville Vernon. *In My Father's House Are Many Mansions.* Chapel Hill, N.C., and London, 1985.

Butterfield, Fox. *All God's Children: The Bosket Family and the American Tradition of Violence.* New York, 1995.

Campbell, Sir George. *White and Black: The Outcome of a Visit to the United States.* London, 1879.

Cash, E. B. C. *The Cash-Shannon Duel.* Greenville, S.C., 1881.

Cash, W. J. *The Mind of the South.* New York, 1941.

Cashin, Joan E. "A Lynching in Wartime Carolina: The Death of Saxe Joiner." In *Under Sentence of Death: Lynching in the New South,* edited by W. Fitzhugh Brundage, 109–31. Chapel Hill, N.C., and London, 1997.

Charleston City Directories, 1880–1920. Charleston, S.C.

Charleston City Yearbooks, 1880–1920. Charleston, S.C.

Clark, E. Culpepper. *Francis Warrington Dawson and the Politics of Restoration: South Carolina, 1874–1889.* University, Ala., 1980.

Clark, Walter. "The True Remedy for Lynch Law." *American Law Review* (November–December 1894): 801–7.

Code of Laws of South Carolina, 1902. 2 vols. Columbia, 1902.

Cutler, J. Elbert. *Lynch Law: An Investigation into the History of Lynching in the United States.* New York, 1905.

Ellis, Phineas T. *Call Me Phin.* Caribou, Maine, 1977.

Finnegan, Terence. "The Equal of Some White Men and the Superior of Others: Racial Hegemony and the 1916 Lynching of Anthony Crawford in Abbeville County, South Carolina." South Carolina Historical Association *Proceedings* (1994): 54–60.

———. "Lynching and Political Power in Mississippi and South Carolina." In *Under Sentence of Death: Lynching in the New South,* edited by W. Fitzhugh Brundage, 189–218. Chapel Hill, N.C., and London, 1997.

Ford, Lacy K., Jr. "Origins of the Edgefield Tradition: The Late Antebellum Experience and the Roots of Political Insurgency." *South Carolina Historical Magazine* (October 1997): 328–48.

Forster, Henry A. "Why the United States Leads the World in the Relative Proportion of Murders, Lynchings, and Other Felonies, and Why the Anglo-Saxon Countries Not under the American Flag Have the Least Proportion of Murder and Felonies and Know No Lynchings." *Central Law Review* (26 October 1917): 299–304.

Fosdick, Raymond B. *American Police Systems.* New York, 1920.

Gamble, Thomas. *Savannah Duels and Duellists, 1733–1877.* Savannah, 1923.

Garner, James W. "Lynching and the Criminal Law." *South Atlantic Quarterly* (October 1906): 333–41.

Gastil, Raymond D. "Homicide and a Regional Culture of Violence." *American Sociological Review* (June 1971): 412–27.

Glasson, William H. "The Statistics of Lynching." *South Atlantic Quarterly* (October 1906): 342–48.

Graham, Hugh Davis, and Ted Robert Gurr. *The History of Violence in America: Historic and Comparative Perspectives.* New York, 1969.

Gruening, Martha. "Reflection on the South." *Nation* (8 May 1935): 539–40.

Hackney, Sheldon. "Southern Violence." *American Historical Review* (February 1969): 906–25.

Henley, Sperry W. *The Cash Family of South Carolina: A Truthful Account of the Many Crimes Committed by the Carolina Cavalier Outlaws.* Wadesboro, N.C., 1884.

Howard, Walter T. *Lynchings: Extralegal Violence in Florida during the 1930s.* Selinsgrove, Pa., and London, 1995.

Hoyt, James A. "The Phoenix Riot." *Greenwood Index-Journal* (27 April 1938).

Hudson, Josuha Hilary. *Sketches and Reminiscences.* Columbia, S.C., 1903.

Irby, Bessie Cash. *The Cash-Shannon Duel.* Boykin, S.C., 1930.

Jones, Lewis Pinckney. *Stormy Petrel: N. G. Gonzales and His State.* Columbia, S.C., 1973.

Jordan, Michael P., and James L. Roark. *Black Masters: A Free Family of Color in the Old South.* New York, 1984.

Journal of the Senate of the General Assembly of the State of South Carolina. Columbia, S.C., 1891–1913.

Kaminer, Wendy. "Second Thoughts on the Second Amendment." *Atlantic Monthly* (March 1996): 32, 34, 42–45.

Kilgo, John Carlisle. "An Inquiry Regarding Lynching." *South Atlantic Quarterly* (January 1902): 4–13.

Kirkland, Thomas J., and Robert M. Kennedy. *Historic Camden.* 2 vols. Columbia, S.C., 1905, 1926.

Linder, Forrest E., and Robert D. Grove. *Vital Statistics Rates in the United States, 1900–1940.* Washington, D.C., 1943.

Lofton, Colin, and Robert H. Hill. "Regional Subculture and Homicide: An Examination of the Gastil-Hackney Thesis." *American Sociological Review* (October 1974): 714–24.

McClure, S. S. "The Increase of Lawlessness in the United States." *McClure's* (December 1904): 163–71.

McGovern, James R. *Anatomy of a Lynching: The Killing of Claude Neal.* Baton Rouge and London, 1982.

Molloy, Robert. *An Afternoon in March.* New York, 1958.

Moore, John Hammond. "Strange Encounters." *Virginia Cavalcade* (Autumn 1964): 12–24.

Mullen, Harris M. *The Cash-Shannon Duel, Also Duels around Camden, the Code of Honor.* Tampa, Fla., 1963.

Nash, Roy. "The Lynching of Anthony Crawford." *Independent* (11 December 1916): 456–62.

National Association for the Advancement of Colored People. *Thirty Years of Lynching in the United States, 1889–1918.* New York, 1919.

Oswald, F. L. "Lynch Epidemics." *North American Review* (July 1897): 119–21.

Page, Walter Hines. "The Last Hold of the Southern Bully." *Forum* (November 1893): 303–14.

Peck, Thomas K. "The Killing of Captain Dawson." In *Charleston Murders,* edited by Beatrice St. Julien Ravenel. New York, 1947.

Pemberton, Caroline H. "The Barbarism of Civilization." *Arena* (January 1900): 5–15.

Pillsbury, Allen E. "A Brief Inquiry into a Remedy for Lynching." *Harvard Law Review* (May 1902): 707–13.

Poe, Clarence H. "Lynching: A Southern View." *Atlantic Monthly* (February 1904): 155–65.

Porterfield, Austin L. "Indices of Suicide and Homicide by States and Cities: Some Southern–Non-Southern Contrasts with Implications for Research." *American Sociological Review* (August 1949): 481–90.

Ramey, W. D., comp. *Trial of the Booth and Toney Homicide. . . .* Edgefield, S.C.?, 1880.

Raper, Arthur F. *The Tragedy of Lynching.* Chapel Hill, N.C., 1933.

Ravenel, Beatrice St. Julien, ed. *Charleston Murders.* New York, 1947.

Redfield, H. V. *Homicide, North and South.* Philadelphia, 1880.

Reed, John Shelton. *One South: An Ethnic Approach to Regional Culture.* Baton Rouge and London, 1982.

"Reflections of a Retired Lawyer." *Southern Literary Messenger* (March 1839): 218–21.

Reports and Resolutions of the General Assembly of the State of South Carolina. Columbia, S.C., 1880–1920.

Robertson, Ben. *Red Hills and Cotton.* New York, 1942.

Rowe, George C. "How to Prevent Lynching." *Independent* (1 February 1894): 3–4.

Russell, Thomas D. "South Carolina's Largest Slave Auctioneering Firm." *Chicago-Kent Law Review* (1993): 1241–82.

Shay, Frank. *Judge Lynch: His First Hundred Years.* New York, c. 1938.

Simkins, Francis Butler. *Pitchfork Ben Tillman: South Carolinian.* Baton Rouge, 1944.

Simon, Bryant. "The Appeal of Cole Blease of South Carolina: Race, Class, and Sex in the New South." *Journal of Southern History* (February 1996): 56–86.

South Carolina Digest, 1783–1886. St. Paul, Minn., 1922.

Southern Commission on the Study of Lynching. *Lynchings and What They Mean.* Atlanta, c. 1933.

Taylor, Rosser H., and Raven I. McDavid. *Memoirs of Richard Cannon Watts, Chief Justice of the Supreme Court of South Carolina, 1927–1930.* Columbia, S.C., 1938.

Tindall, George Brown. *South Carolina Negroes, 1877–1900.* Columbia, S.C., 1952. See especially chapter 12, "The Context of Violence," 233–59.

Tolnay, Stewart E., and E. M. Beck. *A Festival of Violence: An Analysis of Southern Lynchings, 1882–1930.* Urbana and Chicago, 1995.

Townsend, Belton O'Neall. "South Carolina Morals." *Atlantic Monthly* (April 1877): 467–75.

———. "South Carolina Society." *Atlantic Monthly* (June 1877): 670–84.

Waldrep, Christopher. "War of Words: The Controversy over the Definition of Lynching." *Journal of Southern History* (February 2000): 75–100.

Wells-Barnett, Ida B. "Lynch Law in America." *Arena* (January 1900): 15–24.

Westmoreland, Lillie B. *J. Dean Crain: A Biography.* Greenville, S.C., 1959.

Williams, Jack Kenny. "The Code of Honor in the Ante-Bellum South." *South Carolina Historical Magazine* (April 1953): 113–28.

———. *Vogues in Villainy: Crime and Retribution in Ante-Bellum South Carolina.* Columbia, S.C., 1959.

Wilson, Charles R., and William Ferris, eds. *Encyclopedia of Southern Culture.* Chapel Hill, N.C., and London, 1989.

Winterfield, Charles. "Jack Long; or, Lynch Law and Vengeance." *American Review* (February 1845): 121–36.

Woodward, C. Vann. *Mary Chesnut's Civil War.* New Haven, Conn., and London, 1981.

Worthington, W. Curtis, Jr. "The Man Who Killed Warrington Dawson." *American Journal of Forensic Medicine and Pathology,* vol. 10, no. 1 (1989): 76–82.

Wright, George C. *Racial Violence in Kentucky, 1865–1940.* Baton Rouge, 1990.

Wyatt-Brown, Bertram. *Southern Honor: Ethics and Behavior in the Old South.* New York, 1982.

INDEX